ARCHIBALD ROBERTSON SMALL, M. D.

[OBIT: JUNE 21, 1907.]

GENEALOGY

OF THE

ROBERTSON, SMALL AND RELATED FAMILIES

GENEALOGY

OF THE

ROBERTSON, SMALL AND RELATED FAMILIES

HAMILTON	McDOUGALL
LIVINGSTON	BEVERIDGE
McNAUGHTON	LOURIE
McDONALD	STEWART

BY

ARCHIBALD ROBERTSON SMALL, M. D.
CHICAGO

"Every man is a quotation from all his ancestors."

ISBN: 978-93-5128-878-7(PB)

First Published in 1907
Indian Reprint in 2017

Published by

Kalpaz Publications
C-30, Satyawati Nagar,
Delhi – 110052
E-mail: kalpaz@hotmail.com
Website: kalpazpublications.com
Ph.: +91-9212142040

Cataloging in Publication Data—DK
Courtesy: D.K. Agencies (P) Ltd. <docinfo@dkagencies.com>

Small, Archibald Robertson, 1850-1907, **author.**
Genealogy of the Robertson, Small and related families : Hamilton, Livingston, McNaughton, McDonald, McDougall, Beveridge, Lourie, Stewart / by Archibald Robertson Small.
pages cm
Reprint. Originally published: Indianapolis : Albert Garrett Small, 1907.
ISBN 9789351288787

1. Robertson family. 2. Small family. 3. Scotland—Genealogy. 4. United States—Genealogy. I. Title.

CS71.R645S63 2017 DDC 929.20954 23

CONTENTS

PUBLISHER'S NOTE.

In respectfully submitting this work to the consideration of the family, I do not feel that any apology is necessary. The circumstances attending my connection with Dr. Small's great work are known to the subscribers whose interest in these not inconsiderable labors has made possible this publication. I owe much—more, indeed, than words can repay—to the many kindly messages of encouragement which have proved a constant stimulus to me during the time this work has been in my hands, as no doubt previous expressions of a similar character had stimulated Dr. Small to a continuation of the arduous task he had undertaken, and to which he gave the best part of the later years of his life. To those who may not be acquainted with these circumstances, however, a word of explanation is due.

I did not have the honor of a personal acquaintance with Dr. Small, though I had known him very pleasantly through a sometime and most delightful correspondence on matters relating to his great work. What there was in this correspondence that prompted him to leave to me the honorable task of giving fruition to his labors, I do not know. Whatever it was, I shall always cherish most dearly this mark of his confidence. No one could have been more astonished than was I when. following his sudden and—we can not help feeling—untimely death, I received his precious manuscript with formal notice that it was his last will that I should take up the work where he had been compelled to lay it down, and give publication to these pages. That this was no sudden determination on his part, makes all the more binding upon me the obligation his kindly will imposed. In a letter to Miss Jennie M. Patten, of Yuma, Colorado, whose valuable assistance in the work of compiling these memoirs Dr. Small has gratefully acknowledged in his preface, our biographer wrote, March 3, 1905, more than two years before his death:

"I hope during the summer to have this work all written up in form, and if it is not published right away, and I should die, anyone else who might take enough interest in it could have it published as well as myself. Of course, I would like to complete the work myself before I die, but I do believe there is enough interest manifested already in some quarters to insure its publication even though I should be taken away now. Albert G. Small, of Indianapolis, son of the Rev. Gilbert Small, would be a good man to take hold of it, and he, I think, is sufficiently interested in it to undertake the work. He is the Indianapolis editor for the American Press Association, and is, I think, in every way fully competent to finish it up."

With the learned physician's prescience Dr. Small evidently recognized the imminence of death, and was philosophically reconciling himself to the thought that he might not be permitted to see the completion of his task. Alas, how much we all regret that he was not spared! But this was not to be, and the duty of publication fell upon another.

With the exception of a few corrections and additions which have been contributed since these pages have been in my charge, this record is just as it came from the hand of our lamented and scholarly genealogist.

I shall always think that our family has been singularly and most graciously favored in having been given such a chronicler. The pages before you will speak for themselves. Scholarly, comprehensive and complete, what infinite patience, what self-sacrificing devotion are revealed in this compilation! How grateful we must be that Dr. Small recognized as incumbent upon him this monumental family duty, and that there were combined in him those rare qualities of mind and heart which enabled him to give such fitting expression to the unselfish ambition that rose within him as the work unfolded.

This debt of gratitude, I am sure, will not be confined alone to the present generation. In making possible a degree of family unity which, without this record, would be utterly impossible, he has laid upon our posterity an obligation of memory which shall keep imperishable the name and the dear, kindly heart of our lamented kinsman. He has introduced us to our forefathers and to our "folks." After this introduction, shall we let his work go for naught? "Rely upon it," says William E. Gladstone, "that the man who does not worthily estimate his own dead forefathers, will himself do very little to add credit or do honor to his country."

In accepting this legacy of Dr. Small's inestimable labor of love, I have given my best endeavor to this work of publication. Regarding the mere physical aspect of this volume, I crave your most gracious indulgence. A. G. S.

PREFACE.

In May, 1904, I wrote the records of my own immediate family, consisting of my parents and their descendants, for preservation. When this was done I thought I would try and find out something about the ancestry of the family, at least from the time of first coming to America. At that time I did not know the given name of either of my great-grandparents, William Robertson or James Small, or when they came to America, and had taken no particular interest in my ancestry. I wrote to some of my relatives to see if I could find out something about the early history of the family, and found that Miss Jennie M. Patten, of Yuma, Colorado, had collected the records of the Robertson family from the time that William Robertson came to America to about 1894. I wrote to her and she kindly sent me the records she had collected. Through her I learned the early history in this country of William Robertson, Archibald Livingston, Alexander McNaughton and their families, with some hints of an illustrious ancestry of these families in Scotland, which induced me to search the libraries. In this search I found so much of interest, which I did not know, and I presume that few of the relatives know, that I thought it would be appreciated by all members of the family if it were written up so that all could know the origin of different branches of their ancestry. I also set to work collecting the records of the Robertson and Small families from the time our ancestors came to America to date. In this I have succeeded beyond my expectations, having collected the records of almost every descendant of William Robertson and James Small.

Miss Patten's work very materially assisted me in the collection of the Robertson data, though I have personally written to almost every family in that line to bring the records down to date. On the Small side it was months before I could get any tangible clew to the descendants of James Small, but by persistence and patience I finally succeeded in getting an almost complete record of his descendants.

Believing that it would be impossible for any one, after the present generation has passed away, to collect as complete records as I have done, which has been quite difficult to do even in this generation, I felt that it was the duty of some one in this generation to put these records in shape for preservation for the benefit of future generations, especially as several lines of our ancestors in Scotland were illustrious, and have taken upon myself this task. I have pursued this work as a recreation from the arduous duties of a busy practice and feel that the pleasure I have derived from it has fully compensated me for the work performed, and I trust that my work will be appreciated by every member of our very large family.

I was surprised, and I presume that many of my relatives will be surprised, at the number of lines in our ancestry running back to kings—seven on the Robertson side and six on the Small side. The last few pages of the work will show this in a condensed form, and through the body of the work can be found references to the authorities I have examined, and anyone who will take the trouble to consult these authorities can find the proof of every statement I have made.

I would like to have given more biographical sketches of the relatives in this country. I have asked for them but, through modesty, I presume, they have not been sent. I have, however, included as many biographical sketches as I could get.

It would be a pleasure to me to believe that some member of each family, with this collection of records as a basis, would carefully record and preserve the records of their family to be handed down and kept up through succeeding generations, so that the knowledge of their ancestry may not be lost.

INTRODUCTION.

As frequent reference will be made in this work to the Scottish kings, we shall give a list of them, and date of reign, from Malcolm II to James VI.

As the Robertson family, as well as a long line of Scottish kings, had their origin in Athol, we shall give a description of Athol.

The Robertson family, or rather the ancestors of that family, before the surname of Robertson was assumed, was the Royal Family of Scotland for three hundred years, from Duncan I. to Alexander III. on the male line, and down to James VI. on the female line.

We shall next trace the origin and history of the Robertson family, which family descended from the ancient Celtic Earls of Athol, who were descendants of Duncan II., and trace the different branches of the family in Scotland.

As our immediate ancestor, John Robertson of Peterhead, Aberdeenshire, Scotland, married Anne Hamilton, we shall give a sketch of the Hamilton family in Scotland from its origin in the thirteenth century.

William Robertson, of Argyle, New York, the first of our line of Robertsons in America, married Mary Livingston, daughter of Archibald and Eleanor (McNaughton) Livingston, whose family we shall trace in Scotland from Livingus, who came to Scotland about 1068, down through the seven Lord Livingstons, Earls of Linlithgow and Calender, to about 1850. We shall also give a sketch of a branch of that family, descendants of the fifth Lord Livingston—the Hudson River Livingstons—who took a prominent part in the early history of this country. We shall also trace some of the descendants of Archibald Livingston in this country.

Mary Livingston's mother was Eleanor (McNaughton) Livingston, daughter of Alexander McNaughton and his wife, Mary MacDonald. We shall trace the McNaughton clan back to the tenth century and show that the clan descended from the ancient Pictish kings, the first of whom reigned as early as 455.

The MacDonald clan, from whom Mary MacDonald descended, has been traced back to the sixth century, and was a very ancient and powerful clan in Scotland, a sketch of which will next be given.

As the MacDonald and MacDougall clans both sprang from the same ancestor, Somerled, and as Jeannette Robertson, daughter of William and Mary (Livingston) Robertson, was married to James MacDougall, a descendant of the MacDougall clan, we shall give a sketch of the MacDougall clan in Scotland.

We shall next give the lineage of the Robertsons from Duncan II. down to and including the branch of our line of that family still remaining in Scotland, with an almost complete record of all the descendants of William and Mary (Livingston) Robertson in this country, including biographical sketches of many of them.

As there have been several marriages between the Robertsons and Smalls in this country, we have thought it appropriate to include the Small records in this work, and shall trace the lineage of James Small, the first of our line in this country, back in Scotland to Robert II., and also give the lineage of his wife, Ann Beveridge, with an almost complete record of all the descendants of James and Ann (Beveridge) Small in this country, with biographical sketches of many of them.

The last few pages of the work will give the lineage, in a condensed form, of the Robertsons and Smalls.

KINGS OF SCOTLAND.

MALCOLM II., 1004-1033, after a vigorous reign was succeeded by his grandson,

DUNCAN I., the "Gracious Duncan" of Shakespeare, who was murdered by Macbeth in 1040. Duncan was the son of Bathoc, daughter of Malcolm II., and of her husband, Crinan, Lord, or Earl, of Athol. Duncan married a sister of Siward, Scandinavian Earl of Northumberland.

MACBETH, 1040-1057, was defeated and slain in 1057.

MALCOLM III., 1057-1093 (Malcolm Canmore), son of Duncan I., married the Saxon Princess, Margaret, a sister of Edgar Atherling, heir to the Saxon line.

DUNCAN II., 1093-1095, son of Malcolm III., by his first wife, Ingioborge, widow of Thorfinn, the Scandinavian Earl of Orkneys.

DONALD BANE, 1095-1098, son of Duncan I.

EDGAR, 1098-1107, son of Malcolm III.; died without issue,

ALEXANDER I., 1107-1124, son of Malcolm III.; died without issue.

DAVID I., 1124-1153, son of Malcolm III., married Maud, daughter of the Earl of Waltheof.

MALCOLM IV., 1153-1165, son of David I.; died without issue.

WILLIAM the LION, 1165-1214, son of David I., married Ermengarde, daughter of V. Beaumont.

ALEXANDER II., 1214-1249, son of William the Lion, married first, Joanna, daughter of John of England; second, Mary de Couci.

ALEXANDER III., 1249-1286, son of Alexander II., married, first, Margaret, daughter of John of England; second, Iolande of Dreux.

JOHN, 1292-1296, son of John Balliol. Deposed; died 1314.

ROBERT I. (Bruce), 1306-1329, great-grandson of Robert Bruce and son of Isabella, great-granddaughter of David I., married first, Isabella, daughter of the Earl of Mar; second, Mary, daughter of the Earl of Ulster.

DAVID II., 1329-1370, son of Robert I., married Joanna, daughter of Edward III., of England.

ROBERT II. (Stewart), 1370-1390, son of Walter Stewart, great-grandson of Walter, Steward of Scotland, and Margaret, daughter of Robert I. (Bruce), married Elizabeth Muir.

ROBERT III., 1390-1406, son of Robert II., married Annabella.

JAMES I., 1406-1437, son of Robert III., married Juan, daughter of John Beaufort, Earl of Somerset.

JAMES II., 1437-1460, son of James I., married Mary, daughter of Arnold, Duke of Guilders.

JAMES III., 1460-1488, son of James II., married Margâret, daughter of Christian I., of Denmark.

JAMES IV., 1488-1513, son of James III., married Margaret, daughter of Henry VII., of England.

JAMES V., 1513-1542, son of James IV., married Mary of Guise.

MARY, Queen of Scots, 1542-1567, daughter of James V., married Henry, Lord Darnley, who was murdered in 1567.

JAMES VI., 1567-1625, son of Mary. King of England as James I., 1603-1625.—Hereford B. George, M. A., F. R. G. S., Fellow of New College, Oxford.

ATHOL.

Athol, Atholl, or Athole, earls of, an ancient title, formerly possessed by the royal family of Scotland, subsequently in right of marriage by Thomas de Galloway and his son, and after him by David de Hastings, afterwards by the Strathbogie family, then after being held by a Campbell and a Douglas, it was conferred on a scion of the royal house of Stewart, and through a second creation in the house of Stewart, it came latterly to be possessed by a branch of the noble family of Murray. It is the name of a mountainous and romantic district in the north of Perthshire, which, from a remote period, has preserved its boundaries unaltered. It was the original patrimony of the family which gave kings to Scotland from Duncan to Alexander III., and it is the earliest district in Scotland mentioned in history. The name signifies "pleasant land," and Blair Athol, its principal valley, "the field or vale of Athol." "Its chief interest," says Skene, "arises from the strong presumption which exists that the family which gave a long line of kings to Scotland, from the eleventh to the fourteenth century, took their origin from this district, to which they can be traced before the marriage of their ancestor with the daughter of Malcolm II. raised them to the throne."

When Thorfinn, the Norwegian Earl of Orkney, conquered the north of Scotland, in the early part of the eleventh century, the only territory of the Northern Picts which remained unsubdued was the district of Athol and part of Argyle. The Lord of the Isles had been slain in an unsuccessful attempt to preserve his insular dominions, and the King of the Scots, with the whole of the nobility, had also fallen in the short but bloody campaign which preceded the Norwegian conquest. In their disastrous condition the Scots had recourse to Duncan, the son of Crinan, Abbot of Dunkeld, by Beatrice (or Bathoc), the daughter of Malcolm II., the last Scottish king. Duncan came to the vacant throne in 1034, but after a reign of six years, he was slain in an attempt to recover the northern districts from the Norwegians, and his sons were driven out by Macbeth, who for a time ruled over the south, whilst the Norwegians possessed the north of Scotland. After the overthrow of Macbeth, December 5, 1056, and the establishment of Malcolm Canmore on the throne, the Lowlands of Scotland were, according to the Saxon polity, divided into earldoms, all of which were granted to the different members of the royal family. These earldoms consisted of the country inhabited by the Scots, with the addition of the district of Athol, and from this circumstance it has, not unreasonably, been presumed that Athol was the original possession of the royal race. This is further confirmed by the designation which early Scottish historians apply to Crinan, the father of Duncan. Besides being abbot of Dunkeld, he is styled by Fordun, "Abthanus de Dull ac Seneschallus Insularum." (Abthane of Dull and Steward of the Isles.) Pinkerton has denied that such a title as Abthane was ever known or heard of, but Mr. Skene has most conclusively shown, not only that there was such a title as Abthane in Scotland, but that the very title of Abthane of Dull, which is the name of a district in Athol, existed until comparatively a late period.

By King Edgar, the whole of Athol, except Breadalbane, was erected into an earldom, and conferred upon his cousin Madach, the son of King Donald Bane. Madach married a daughter of Haco, Earl of Orkney. He was a witness to the foundation charter of Alexander I., of the monastery of Scone, in 1114, and he was himself afterwards a benefactor to the abbey. On the death of Madach towards the end of the reign of David I., the earldom of Athol was obtained by Malcolm, the son of Duncan, the eldest son of Malcolm Canmore, by Ingioborge, the widow of Thorfinn, earl of Orkney, whose descendants were excluded from the throne by the king's younger sons. The earldom was thus bestowed on Malcolm, "either," Skene says, "because the exclusion of that family from the throne could not deprive them of the original property of the family, to which they were entitled to succeed, or as a compensation for the loss of the crown." His son Malcolm, the third earl of Athol, gave in pure alms to the monks of the Scone the church of Logen Mabed, with four chapels thereunto belonging, and to the abbey of Dumfermline the tithes of the church of Moulin. He also made a donation to the priory of St. Andrews of the patronage of the church of Dull. His son Henry succeeded to the earldom, and on his death, in the beginning of the thirteenth century, his granddaughters, by his eldest son who predeceased him, carried it into the families of Galloway and Hastings.

"When the Celtic earls of Athol became extinct," says Skene, "and, in consequence, the subordinate clans in the district of Athol assumed independence, the principal part of that district was in the possession of the clan Donachie or the Robertsons."—Scottish Nation. By Anderson.

It is from Athol that the royal dynasty emerged, which terminated with Alexander III., the founder of the house having been Crinan, Abbot of Dunkeld, and from his son, Duncan, proceeded not only the kings of Scotland, but likewise the ancient earls of Athol.

The reign of Alexander II. witnessed the termination of the line of Celtic earls of Athol. The earldom seems to have been an appendage of the family from whom sprang the kings of the race of Duncan, the son of Crinan, and its earls were descended from a younger son and younger brother of Malcolm Canmore. The last of this line was Henry, Earl of Athol, who died before 1215, and the earldom passed to the eldest of two sisters, Isabella and Forflissa, who married Thomas, Earl of Galloway.—Celtic Scotland. Skene, pp. 270, 288.

ROBERTSON.

The Robertsons of Strowan are unquestionably one of the oldest and most eminent families in Scotland, being the sole remaining branch of that royal house which occupied the throne and kingdom during the eleventh, twelfth and thirteenth centuries, and from which they can distinctly trace their descent.

It has in general been held that the Robertsons are a branch of the great clan of McDonald, "but," says Skene, "although there may be a remote connection between the two clans, it is now undoubted that the Robertsons are descended from the ancient Earls of Athol, which house sprung from Duncan, King of Scotland, eldest son of Malcolm III., surnamed Canmore." (Cean, head or chief; Mor, great—Ceanmor, great head or chief.)—Dictionary of Landed Gentry. J. B. Burke. 1850 edition.

The ancient Celtic Earls of Athol were the ancestors of the Robertsons of Strowan. They were the Robertson family before the name Robertson was assumed. Crinan, Lord, or Earl of Athol, Abbot of Dunkeld and Abthane of Dull, married Bathoc (or Beatrice), daughter of King Malcolm II. Crinan and Bathoc were the ancestors of all the Scottish kings from Duncan I. to Alexander III., on the male line, except Macbeth.

Robert I. (Bruce), was the son of Isabella, great-granddaughter of David I., and thus the Robertson blood runs through all the Scottish kings down to James VI. (See list of Scottish Kings.)

The Scottish kings, as descendants of Crinan, were of the Robertson blood.

The Robertsons of Strowan can also be traced back through the ancient Celtic Earls of Athol to Duncan II., son of Malcolm III.

By King Edgar, Athol was erected into an earldom, and conferred upon Madach, son of King Donald Bane. On the death of Madach, towards the end of the reign of David I., the earldom was obtained by Malcolm, son of Duncan II., son of Malcolm III., by Ingioborge, widow of Thorfinn, Earl of Orkney. Malcolm's son, Malcolm, was the third Earl of Athol, and his son, Henry, was the fourth and last of the ancient Celtic Earls of Athol, at the beginning of the thirteenth century.

Robertson, the name of a Highland clan, called in Gaelic the clan Donachie, of which the Robertsons of Strowan, in Perthshire, is the chief. Tradition claims for the clan Donachie a descent from the great sept of the McDonalds, their remote ancestor being said to have been Duncan the Fat, son of Angus Mor, Lord of the Isles, in the reign of William the Lion. Skene, however, in his History of the Highlanders, traces them from Duncan II., King of Scotland, eldest son of Malcolm III., their immediate ancestor being Conan, second son of Henry, fourth and last of the ancient Celtic Earls of Athol. This Conan, in the reign of Alexander II., received from his father the lands of Glenerochy, afterwards called Strowan, in Gaelic Struthen, that is, streamy. His son, Ewen Fiz Conan, who had several sons, from whom descended the families of Skene and others. He was succeeded by his eldest son Angus, who obtained from Robert I. a charter of several lands in Perthshire. He was succeeded by his son Andrew, styled of Athol, de Atholia, which was the uniform designation of the family, indicative of their descent from the ancient Earls of Athol. Andrew was succeeded by his son Duncan de Atholia, who obtained various charters to his different possessions, in all of which he is styled "Duncanus filius Andreoe de Atholia," and it was he who gave the clan their distinctive appellation of the clan of Donachie, or the children of Duncan.

Duncan de Atholia, Earl of Athol (so described in a charter

by David II). They are known among Highlanders of Scotland as clan Donachie, children or descendants of Duncan.

Duncan married first, a daughter of a certain Callum Rua, or Malcolm the red-haired, who, being styled Leamnach, is supposed to have been connected with the Earls of Lennox, and by his wife he acquired a considerable accession of territory, including the southern division of the glen or district of Rannoch. The clan Donachie were adherents of Bruce, and on one of the two islands in Rannoch a MacDougal of Lorn, taken prisoner in one of their clan battles, was confined for some time, but contrived to make his escape.

By his first wife he had a son:

Robert de Atholia.

Duncan married secondly, the co-heiress of Ewen de Insulis, thane, of Glenilt, and got the east half thereby. By her he had:

(1) Patrick de Atholia, first of Lude.

(2) Thomas de Atholia, of Strowan.

(3) Gibbon, who had no legitimate issue.

Duncan was succeeded by his eldest son,

Robert de Atholia, who married first, a daughter of Sir John Stirling of Glenesk, and obtained with her part of her father's property, which their daughter, Jean, received on her marriage with Alexander Menzies of Fothergill.

Robert married secondly, one of the daughters and co-heiresses of Fordell, and had an only son,

Duncan.

In the celebrated foray which the Highlanders made into Angus in 1392, the clan Donachie acted a conspicuous part. It was on this occasion that it appeared for the first time as a distinct tribe.

Thomas, the second son of the second marriage of Duncan, had a daughter, who obtained part of her father's possessions on marrying Alexander, second son of Patrick of Lude, but the estate of Strowan went, probably by marriage of an elder daughter of Thomas, to Duncan, the son of Robert, who is mentioned in the Routli Scotiae as Duncanus de Atholia, dominus de Ranagh, or Rannoch. From his son,

Robert Riach (grizzled), who succeeded him, the clan derive their name Robertson.

This Robert was noted for his predatory excursions into the Lowlands, and is historically known as the chief who arrested and delivered up to the vengeance of the government, Robert Graham and the master of Athol. two of the murderers of James I., for which he was rewarded with a crown charter. dated 1451, erecting his whole lands into a free barony. He also received the honorable augmentation to his arms of a naked man manacled under the achievement, with the motto, "Virtutis gloria merces (meaning, glory is the reward of bravery). He was mortally wounded in the head near the village of Auchtergaven, in a conflict with Robert Forrester of Torwood, with whom he had a dispute regarding the lands of Little Dunkeld. Binding up his head with a white cloth, he rode to Perth, and obtained from the king a new grant of the lands of Strowan. On his return home, he died of his wounds. He died during the time of James II.

Robert married Lady Margaret Stewart, by whom he had three sons:

(1) Alexander, his heir.

(2) Robert, of Dalcobon, ancestor of Sir Alexander Robertson, who assumed the surname Colyear, and was created a Baronet in 1677. He was succeeded by his son, Sir David Colyear, Bart., a military officer of reputation; was elevated to the Scottish Peerage as Earl Portmore, a dignity which remained with his descendants until the demise, issueless, of the late Earl of Portmore.

(3) Patrick.

Alexander, Robert's son (son of Robert), origin of the name Robertson, which from this date became the designation of the family.

Alexander Robertson married first, Elizabeth, daughter of Patrick, Lord Glammis, grandson of Lady Jane Stewart, daughter of Robert II., by whom he had four sons and a daughter:

(1) Duncan, who predeceased his father, leaving a son, William.

(2) Robert.

(3) Andrew, progenitor of the Robertsons of Ladykirk, and other families of the name.

(4) James, ancestor of the Robertsons of Auchleeks. etc.

(5) Mary, married to Andrew Moray, of Ogilvie and Abercairney, and had issue.

He married secondly, Lady Elizabeth Stewart, daughter of John, Earl of Athol, "uterine brother of James II.," by whom he had two sons and a daughter:

(1) Alexander, ancestor of the Robertsons of Faskally.

(2) JOHN ROBERTSON, of Muirton, Elginshire, Gladney, etc., from whom was descended the Robertsons of Kinlochmoidart. Inverness-shire [and who is believed to be the ancestor of our line of Robertsons.—Ed.].

(3) Margaret, married to George, sixth Earl of Errol.

Alexander Robertson died in, or shortly prior to, 1507, and was succeeded by his grandson, William. This chief had some dispute with the Earl of Athol concerning the marches of their estates, and was killed by a party of the earl's followers, in 1530. Taking advantage of a wadset, or mortgage, which he held over the lands of Strowan, the earl seized nearly the half of the family estate, which the Robertsons could never again recover. Robert Robertson of Strowan, who being an infant when his father was killed, was, in consequence of his long minority unable to recover that portion of his property which had been wrested from his father. By his wife, Marion, daughter and heiress of John M'Ian, of Ardwamurchan, he had two sons:

(1) William, his successor. Died without issue.

(2) Donald, who carried on the line of the family.

Donald Robertson, of Strowan, married Janet, daughter of Neil Stewart. of Foss, by whom he had one son:

Robert Robertson, of Strowan, tenth laird of Strowan. He sold a considerable part of the estate, but the sale was reduced by a decree of recognition, and a grant thereof given to John Robertson, merchant in Edinburgh, a near relation of the family. The latter got a charter under the great seal, dated August 7, 1606, but he reconveyed the same, under a strict entail, to the said Robert Robertson of Strowan, and his heirs male.

Robert married Agnes, daughter of MacDonald of Keppoch, and had:

(1) Alexander, his heir.
(2) Donald, called the tutor of Strowan.
(3) Duncan Mor, of Drumaehune, who carried on the line.
(4) James.
(5) Mary, married to M'Intosh, of Strone.

Duncan Mor. of Drumachune, married Dorothy, daughter of Neil Stewart, of Foss, and had four sons:

(1) John, his heir, of Drumachune, who married in 1677, Cecilia, eldest daughter of Robert Stewart, of Fincastle, and was succeeded by his son,

Alexander Robertson, of Drumachune, who married in 1703, Margaret, eldest daughter of Patrick Robertson, of Fascalzie, and had two sons and a daughter, viz.:

Duncan, of whom hereafter as inheritor of Strowan.

Alexander, Lieutenant-Colonel in the service of the States-General.

Emelia, married to Captain Donald Robertson.

(2) Donald Robertson, whose son, Robert Bane, was father

(with a daughter, Margaret, married to John Robertson, Esq.) of two sons:

Donald, Captain in the French service, who married Emilia, daughter of Alexander Robertson, of Drumaçhune.

Duncan was father of Alexander Robertson, who succeeded to Strowan, and of whom hereafter.

(3) Duncan.

(4) Patrick.

(I) The eldest son, Alexander Robertson, of Strowan, married Margaret, daughter of George Graham, of Inbraikie, and died in 1636, leaving an infant son, Alexander, in whose minority the government of the clan devolved upon his uncle, Donald, the tutor of Strowan. Devoted to the cause of Charles I., the latter raised a regiment of his name and followers and was with the Marquis of Montrose in all his battles. Montrose's commission to him as colonel of his regiment is dated June 10, 1646. From Montrose, from Charles II., in his exile, and from General Middleton and others, he received several letters which are still preserved. After the Restoration the king settled a pension upon him.

His nephew, Alexander Robertson, of Strowan, was served heir to nine of his predecessors, February 22, 1681, namely, up to Duncan de Atholia, designed Dominus de Rannoch, before mentioned.

He married, first, Catherine, daughter of Sir James Drummond, of Mathany, and by her had:

(1) Robert, who predeceased him.

(2) Anne, married to Hugh, second son of Sir James MacDonald, of Slate.

He married secondly, Marion, daughter of General Baillie of Latham, by whom he had two sons and a daughter, Margaret:

(1) Alexander, his heir.

(2) Duncan, who died in 1718, leaving an only daughter, Margaret, who died unmarried. Duncan served in Russia, with distinction, under Peter the Great.

Alexander died in 1688, and was succeeded by Alexander, the elder son by his second marriage.

Alexander, the elder son of the second marriage, was the celebrated Jacobite chief and poet. Born about 1670, he was destined for the church, and sent to the University of St. Andrew; but his father and brother by the first marriage dying within a few months of each other, he succeeded to the family estate and chiefship in 1688. Soon after, he joined the Viscount Dundee, when he appeared in arms in the Highlands for the cause of King

James, but though he does not appear to have been at Killiecrankie, and was still under age, he was, for his share in this rising, attainted by a decreet of parliament in absence in 1690, and his estate forfeited to the crown. He retired, in consequence, to the court of the exiled monarch at St. Germains, where he lived for several years, and served one or two campaigns in the French army. In 1703, Queen Anne granted him a remission, when he returned to Scotland, and resided unmolested on his estates, but neglecting to get the remission passed the seals, the forfeiture of 1690 was never legally repealed. With about 500 of his clan he joined the Earl of Mar in 1715, and was taken prisoner at the battle of Sheriffmuir, but rescued. Soon after, however, he fell into the hands of a party of soldiers in the Highlands, and was ordered to be conducted to Edinburgh, but, with the assistance of his sister, he contrived to escape on the way, when he again took refuge in France. In 1723, the estate of Strowan was granted by the government to Margaret, the chief's sister, by a charter under the great seal, and in 1726 she disponed the same in trust for the behoof of her brother, substituting, in the event of his death without lawful heirs of his body, Duncan, son of Alexander Robertson of Drumachune, her father's cousin, and next lawful heir male of the family. Margaret died unmarried in 1727. Her brother had returned to Scotland the previous year, and obtaining, in 1731, a remission for his life, took possession of his estate. In 1745 he once more "marshalled his clan" in behalf of the Stuarts, but his age preventing him from personally taking any part in the rebellion, his name was passed over in the list of prescriptions that followed. He died in his own house of Cairie in Rannoch, April 18, 1749, in his eighty-first year, without lawful issue, and in him ended the direct male line. A volume of his poems was published after his death. An edition was reprinted at Edinburgh in 1785, 12mo., containing also the "History and Martial Achievements of the Robertsons." He is said to have formed the prototype of the Baron of Bradwardine in Scott's Waverly.

The portion of the original estate of Strowan which remained, devolved upon Duncan Robertson, of Drumachune, a property which his great-grandfather, Duncan Mor (who died in 1687), brother of Donald the tutor, had acquired from the Athol family. As, however, his name was not included in the last act of indemnity passed by the government, he was dispossessed of his estate in 1752, when he and his family retired to France. He married Mey, daughter of William, Lord Nairn, and had, with a daughter, Margaret, married to Lawrence Oliphat, of Gask, and a younger son, Walter-Philip-Colyear, who died without issue, an elder son and heir,

Colonel Alexander Robertson, to whom the estate was restored in 1784, but who died, unmarried, in 1822.

Duncan Mor's second son, Donald, had a son, called Robert Bane, whose grandson, Alexander Robertson, now succeeded to the estate.

The son of the latter, Major-General George Duncan Robertson of Strowan, C. B., passed upwards of thirty years in active service, and received the cross of the Imperial Austrian Order of Leopold. He was succeeded by his son, George Duncan Robertson, born July 26, 1816, at one time an officer in the Forty-second Highlanders.

The force which the Robertsons could bring into the field was estimated at 800 in 1715, and 700 in 1745. The principal seat of Robertson of Strowan was formerly the castle of Inverack; it is now Mount Alexander in Rannoch.

For the information contained in the above, acknowledgment is made to the following authorities:

1. Scottish Nation. By William Anderson.
2. Dictionary of Landed Gentry. By J. B. Burke. 1850 edition.
3. Highlanders of Scotland. Skene.
4. Douglas' Peerage.

ROBERTSON ARMS.

Arms—Gules, three wolves' heads, erased, argent, armed and languid, azure. Lying under the arms a wild man, chained, for a compartment.

Crest—A dexter arm and hand erect, holding a regal crown, all proper.

Supporters—Dexter, a serpent; sinister, a dove; the heads of each encircled with rays.

Motto—Virtutis gloria merces.

Seat—Mount Alexander, County Perth, formerly, Rannoch.

The family badge of the Robertsons is Dluith Fraoch, Fine Leaved Heath. This is said to be the oldest badge.

Anderson and Skene give the badge as the Fern or Braken.

ROBERTSONS OF LUDE.

Of the branches of the family, the Robertsons of Lude in Blair-Athol are the oldest, being of contemporary antiquity to that of Strowan.

Patrick de Atholia, eldest son of the second marriage of Duncan de Atholia, received from his father, at his death, about 1358, the lands of Lude. He is mentioned in 1391, by Wyntoun, as one of the chieftains and leaders of the clan. He had, with a daughter, married to Donald, son of Farquhar, ancestor of the Farquharsons of Invercauld, two sons, Donald and Alexander. The latter, known by the name of Rua or Red, from the color of his hair, acquired the estate of Strathloch, for which he had a charter from James II., in 1451, and was ancestor of the Robertsons of Strathloch, Perthshire. His descendants were called the Barons Rua. The last male heir of the family was General John Reid, who left his large fortune to found a music chair in the University of Edinburgh. (General John Reid of Strathloch, the founder of the professorship of music in the University of Edinburgh, adopted that surname in preference to his patronymic, Robertson. He was the son of Alexander Robertson of Strathloch, a property in Perthshire, whose forefathers for more than three centuries were always called Baron Rua, Roy, or Red, from the first of the family having red hair.)

Donald, the elder son, succeeded his father. He resigned his lands of Lude into the king's hands on February 7, 1447, but died before he could receive his infeftment. He had two sons, John, who got the charter under the great seal, dated March 31, 1448, erecting the lands of Lude into a barony, proceeding on his father's resignation; and Donald, who got as his patrimony the lands of Strathgarry. This branch of Lude ended in an heiress, who married an illegitimate son of Stewart of Invermeath. About 1700, Strathgarry was sold to another family of the name of Stewart.

By his wife, Margaret, daughter of Sir John Drummond, ancestor of the earls of Perth, John Robertson of Lude had two sons, Donald, his successor, and John, ancestor of the Robertsons of Guay. "Robertson of Guay" joined the insurgents in 1715, was taken prisoner, and confined in Newgate in 1716, when the estate was forfeited.

Donald, the elder son, the next laird of Lude, died in 1476.

Charles, his son, married Lillias, daughter of Sir John Lamont, chief of the name. This lady brought with her a curious harp, called the "Lamont Harp," which has been in the possession of the family for several centuries, and is mentioned in Gunn's historical work on the "Performance of the Harp." He had a son, John, called M'Charlick, son of Charles, and a daughter, Marion, who married Alexander Red, eldest son of Alexander Red of Strathloch.

The son, John M'Charlick, also called Tarloson, married Margaret, daughter of Sir James Ogilvie of Inchmartin, of the family of Findlater.

His son, also named John, succeeded while still a minor, and was afterwards induced by his mother and her brother, Sir Patrick Ogilvie, of Inchmartin, to resign the barony of Lude in favor of the latter, reserving his leferent. The estate was not entirely recovered from the Ogilvies till the time of his grandson, and then only by the payment of a large sum of money. In 1563, Queen Mary presented John's wife, Beatrix Gardyn, widow of Finla More, ancestor of the Farquharsons of Invercauld, with her own harp, which has been carefully preserved as a family heirloom. John had, with one daughter, Marjory, married to Farquharson of Invercauld, two sons, Alexander, and John of Monzie.

Alexander, the elder son, the first of them who ceased to add the Christian name of his father to that of Robertson, the family surname, was served heir in 1565. He married Agnes, daughter of Alexander Gordon of Abergeldie, and died in 1615. With five daughters he had three sons:

(1) Alexander, his successor.

(2) Donald, who got from his father the lands of Kincraigie, and was ancestor of that family.

(3) John, who got the lands of Inver. The latter, with his brother, Donald, greatly assisted Montrose in bringing the Athol men to the royal standard in 1644. By Montrose, John of Inver was made captain and keeper of Blair Castle. Numerous letters to him from the great Marquis are printed in Napier's "Memoirs of Montrose." His son, Donald, acquired the estate of Tullybelton, and from him descends, in a direct line, Major-General Richardson Robertson, C. B., of Tullybelton, Perthshire (1862). Isabel, third daughter of Alexander Robertson of Lude, married Alexander Forbes of Newe.

The eldest son, Alexander, a zealous protestant, assisted, in 1627, in raising 3,000 men for the service of Gustavus Adolphus, King of Sweden. He married Beatrix, daughter of George Graham of Inchbraco, now Inchbraikie, and had, with a daughter, two sons, Alexander, his successor, and John, of Fowlis, afterwards tutor of Lude. He died suddenly in 1639, at Dalcobon, the seat of the Earl of Portmore.

The elder son, Alexander, was a minor at his father's death, and his uncle, Patrick Graham of Inchbraikie, known as "Black Pate," became his guardian, and commanded the Athol Highlanders under Montrose. Though quite a youth, Alexander Robertson of Lude also joined Montrose, in "Highland weed," and was with him at Tippermuir. His house was burned by Cromwell's troops, and a fine levied on the estate. He died in 1673. He was three times married. By his first wife, Jean, daughter of Sir Alexander Menzies of that ilk, he had a daughter, wife of Alexander Robertson of Faskally. By his second wife he had no issue. By his third wife, Catherine, sister of the first Earl of Breadalbane, he had three sons and a daughter.

His eldest son, John, in 1716, gave up part of his lands to save the life of his brother, who was taken prisoner for having been engaged in the cause of the Stuarts.

He was succeeded by his only son, also John, served heir in November, 1730. He was only a few years in possession, and at his death left two sons and a daughter.

The eldest son, James, succeeded when only four years old, and was served heir to his father in 1758. He married his cousin-german, Margaret Mercer of Aldie, eldest daughter of Hon. Robert Mairne and Jean Mercer, heiress of the ancient family of Aldie and Meikleour, in the counties of Kinross and Perth, and had six sons, of whom five entered the army, two were killed in actions, one at Seringpatam and the other in India, and one died in the West Indies. He himself died in 1802. This laird was sixty-two years in possession.

He was succeeded by his eldest son, General William Robertson of Lude. This gallant officer entered the army at fifteen years of age, served in the American war, and in Holland, and also at the taking of St. Lucia, and several of the West India Islands. In 1794 he raised a regiment of infantry called the Perthshire Fencibles, and in 1804 a corps of volunteers. In 1805 he accompanied the expedition to the coast of Spain under Sir James Murray Pulteney, was subsequently appointed to the staff in Scotland and served in that capacity, as a commanding officer in the Channel Islands and in various districts in England, until the end of 1813, when he was promoted to the rank of lieutenant-general. He married first, Margaret, eldest daughter of George Haldane of Gleneagles, Perthshire (represented by the Earl of Camperdown), and Hon. Margaret Drummond, eldest daughter of James, Viscount of Strathallan; issue, two sons, of whom the younger died in 1814, at a very early age. General Robertson married secondly, Miss Menzies of Culdares, without issue.

His eldest son, Colonel James Alexander Robertson, formerly of the eighty-second regiment, is now the representative of the family. In 1860 he printed, for private circulation, an account of the Comitatus de Atholia, the Earldom of Athol. Its boundaries stated, also, the extent therein of the Possessions of the Family of de Atholia, and their Descendants, the Robertsons. With Proofs and a Map. The estate was sold, in 1821, to a gentleman of the name of M'Inroy.

The Robertsons of Inshes, Inverness-shire, are descended from Duncan, second son of Duncan de Atholia, dominus de Ranagh, above mentioned. One of this family, John Robertson, Burgess of Inverness, called, from his great strength and courage, "Stalwart John," was standard-bearer to Lord Lovat at the battle of Lochy-Lochy in 1544. From William, his third son, sprung the Robertsons of Kindeace, Ross-shire, which branched off about 1544, and from James, William's younger brother, came the Robertsons of Shipland. Another of the family, William Robertson, the second styled of Inshes, was bred to the law, and studied at Leyden with the celebrated Sir George Mackenzie of Rosenhaugh. He was employed in several confidential political negotiations by the government of his time. A letter from him to the Duke of Hamilton, led, it is stated, to the terms of Union.

Arthur John Robertson of Inshes, the fifth in descent from him, possessed in Upper Canada and the United States an extensive territory, derived through marriage with a Canadian lady, his first wife. By her he had two sons and two daughters. Arthur Masterson, the elder son, was born January 9, 1826; Thomas Gilzean, the second son, in 1827. By a second marriage he had a daughter. His estates in Upper Canada are held under a singular old original grant, signed by the hieroglyphics of eighteen Indian chiefs, March 15, 1796, and certified officially May 12, 1797. Captain A. Robertson, Fourth Dragoon Guards, is a son of Robertson of Inshes.

The Robertsons of Kindeace descend from William Robertson, third son of John, ancestor of the Robertsons of Inshes, by his wife, a daughter of Fearn of Pitcullen. He obtained from his father, in patrimony, several lands about Inverness, and having acquired great riches as a merchant, purchased, in 1615, the lands of Orkney, Nairnshire, and in 1639, those of Kindeace, Ross-shire; the latter becoming the chief title of the family.

Charles Robertson, Esq., of Kindeace, Greenyards, and Glencabre, born July 26, 1790, lieutenant-colonel in the army, formerly in the Seventy-eighth and Ninety-sixth Regiments; a justice of the peace and deputy lieutenant of Ross-shire; succeeded his father in 1844; married, in 1816, Helen, fourth daughter and co-heir of Patrick Cruikshank, born May 17, 1817, two other sons and two daughters.

The family of Robertsons of Auchleeks, Pertshire, descend from James Robertson of Calvine, second son of the fifth Baron of Strowan, who died in 1505, Donald, the first of Auchleeks, being his second son.

Charles, an ancestor of this family, called Charlich nan Jead, that is, "Charles of the strings," from his great skill as a harper, married Beatrix Robertson, of the family of Lude.

In 1661, Duncan Robertson of Auchleeks was a commissionery of supply for Perthshire. In 1821, Duncan Robertson of Auchleeks sold the estate to his cousin, Robert Robertson, ninth proprietor. born February 7, 1777. In 1827 this gentleman purchased the estate of Membland, Devonshire. In 1836 he was high sheriff of Devon. A justice of the peace and deputy lieutenant. He married in 1816, Bridget, daughter of George Atkinson, Esq., of Temple Sowerby, Westmoreland; issue, five sons and six daughters.

The Robertsons of Kinlochmoidart, Inverness-shire, are descended from John Robertson of Muirton, Elginshire, second son of Alexander Robertson of Strowan, by his wife, Lady Elizabeth, daughter of the Earl of Athol. [This is believed to be the family from which our line is descended.—Ed.]

The fifth in succession, the Rev. William Robertson, one of the ministers of Edinburgh, was father of Principal Robertson, and of Mary, who married the Rev. James Syme, and had an only child, Eleanor, mother of Henry Lord Brougham. The principal had three sons and two daughters.

David, the eldest son, born in 1764, a lieutenant-colonel in the army, raised the first Malay regiment in Ceylon. He married, in 1799, Margaret MacDonald. of Kinlochmoidart, sister and heiress of Lieutenant-Colonel Donald MacDonald. Governor of Tobago, and assumed the name of MacDonald. By her he had three sons, and was succeeded by his eldest son, William, of whom below.

William, the second son of Principal Robertson, was a judge of the Court of Session. Born in December, 1745, he passed advocate in 1775. In 1779 he was chosen procurator of the Church of Scotland, and in 1805 was appointed a lord of session, when he took the title of Lord Robertson. He was retired from the bench in 1826, and died November 20, 1835. He was twice married, but left no children by either of his wives.

Lieutenant-General James Robertson, the third son, distinguished himself under Lord Cornwallis in India. His elder daughter married Patrick Brydone, Esq., of Lennel House, author of "A Tour Through Sicily and Malta;" and the younger became the wife of John Russell, Esq., writer to the Signet.

William Robertson of Kinlochmoidart, born May 26, 1802, the eldest son of Colonel David Robertson, married, in 1828, Sarah Adams, daughter of James Beck, Esq., of Prior's Hardwick, Warwickshire; issue, three sons. William James, the eldest, born June 10, 1829, married in 1857, a daughter of Frederick Sydney Crawley, Esq.

The Robertsons of Ladykirk, Berwickshire, descend from a branch of the Robertsons of Strowan. David Marjoribanks, youngest son of Sir John Marjoribanks of Lees, Bart., married in 1834, Mary Sarah, eldest daughter of Sir Thomas Haggerston, Bart. of Ellingham, Northumberland, and co-heir of her mother Margaret, only child and heir of William Robertson of Ladykirk, with issue, and assumed the name of Robertson, on succeeding to the estates of his wife's maternal grandfather. Born April 2, 1797, elected M. P. for Berwickshire in May, 1859.

The family of Robertson-Glasgow of Mountgreen, Ayrshire, traditionally claims descent from the Robertsons of Strowan, Perthshire, and in the female line, represents the Setons of Monkmylne, Haddingtonshire, lineally descended from Sir Christopher Seton and Christian Bruce, sister of Robert I.

In 1624, William Robertson purchased from Alexander Meirns certain lands and heritages in the parish of Eyemouth, Berwickshire. Dying in 1638, he was succeeded by his eldest son, John Robertson. The latter died before 1668.

His eldest son died previous to September 10, 1686. His son, William, married Margaret Seton, heiress of Robert Seton of Monkmylne, and was, in consequence, designated of that place. His sister, Margaret, married Andrew Home of Fairneyside, and had an only daughter, Elizabeth, of Fairneyside.

William Robertson of Monkmylne died in 1720. He had two

sons, William, who succeeded him, and Robert, of whom afterwards, and a daughter, Isabella, wife of William Graeme, Esq., of Jordanstown.

The elder son of William Robertson of Monkmylne, also named William, died without issue, August 7, 1738.

He was succeeded by his brother, Robert Robertson of Prenderguest and Brownsbank, born November 4, 1713, married first, in 1743, Margaret, daughter of Rev. George Hume of Chirnside, second son of Alexander Hume of Kennetsidehead, one of the martyrs of the Covenant. This lady was cousin-german of David Hume, the historian. He married secondly, in 1761, Anne Martin of Headrigg, Berwickshire, and thirdly, in 1778, his cousin-german, Elizabeth Home of Fairneyside. He died July 30, 1788, having had issue only by his first wife, two sons, Alexander, born in 1748, and William Robert, of Eyemouth, born in 1761, died July 7, 1833. The latter married in 1801, Margaret, daughter of John Jameson, Esq., sheriff-clerk of Clackmannanshire; issue, three sons and six daughters. Sons:

(1) Robert, born in 1802, passed advocate in 1823; sheriff-substitute of Stirlingshire; married, in 1827, Alicia Catherine, eldest daughter of Rev. Charles Eustace of Robertstown, County Kildare, heir-male and representative of the ancient viscounts of Baltinglass; issue, two sons and two daughters.

(2) John James, of Gledswood, County Dublin, born in 1804; issue, four sons and three daughters.

(3) Rev. William Robertson, minister of New Graftfriers parish, Edinburgh, born in 1805: married, in 1834, Georgiana Touchet, daughter of John Cossins, Esq., of Weymouth, by his first wife, Hon. Elizabeth Susana, a daughter of George, eighteenth Lord Audley: issue, four sons and a daughter.

Jean, the third daughter of Robert Robertson of Prenderguest and Brownsbank, married Thomas Potts, Esq., grandson maternally of Haig of Bemersyde; issue, a son, Thomas, of the Daison, Torquay, Devonshire.

Alexander Robertson of Prenderguest, the elder son of Robert Robertson of Prenderguest and Brownsbank, died in 1804.

The eldest of his six sons, Robert Robertson of Prenderguest, Brownsbank and Gunsgreen, married, in 1804, Anne, daughter of Robert Glasgow, Esq., of Mountgreenan, Ayrshire, and having thereby acquired that estate, and also the property of Glenarback, Dumbartonshire, he assumed the name of Glasgow only. He died January 27, 1845.

He was succeeded by his only surviving son, Robert Robertson-Glasgow of Mountgreenan, born in 1811; died September 20,

1860. By his wife, Mary Wilhelmina, daughter of John Campbell, Esq., of Stonefield, Argyleshire, he had two sons and a daughter.

His eldest son, Robert Bruce Robertson-Glasgow, born April 3, 1842, succeeded him; an ensign in the Twenty-seventh Regiment of foot.

Another judge who assumed the title of Lord Robertson, was Patrick Robertson, the son of James Robertson, writer to the signet. Born in Edinburgh, in 1794, he passed advocate in 1815, and the clearness of his intellect, with the readiness and versatility of his powers, enabled him in a short time to attain considerable practice both in the Court of Session and at the bar of the General Assembly of the Church of Scotland. His real strength lay in his powers of wit and humor, united with acute perception and knowledge of human nature. In sheer power of ridicule no one approached him, and his convivial and social qualities were of the highest order. He was a croupier at the famous Edinburg Theatrical Fund dinner in 1827, when Sir Walter Scott announced himself the author of Waverly, and took his seat as chairman after Scott had left the room. In November, 1842, Mr. Robertson was chosen dean of the faculty of advocates, and a year afterwards, on the resignation of Lord Meadowbank, he was promoted to the bench. In 1845 he astonished the literary world by the publication. at London, of a volume entitled "Leaves from a Journal, and other Fragments, in Verse," eight volumes; and in 1847 appeared his "Gleams of Thought, Reflected from the Writing of Milton: Sonnets and Other Poems," Edinburgh, eight volumes. In 1848 he was elected by the students lord rector of Marischal College and University of Aberdeen, and in 1849 he published "Sonnets, Reflective and Descriptive, and Other Poems," Edinburgh, eight volumes. As a poet his attainments were not nearly so brilliant as were those he possessed as a lawyer and a judge. Lord Robertson died suddenly by a stroke of apoplexy, January 10, 1855. In Lockhart's "Life of Sir Walter Scott" there will be found various interesting notices of his lordship.—Scottish Nation. By William Anderson.

The Lord Robertson, (James Patrick Bannerman Robertson, P. G.,) of Fortviot, Perthshire, D. L., born August 10, 1845. Created Peerage, November 14, 1899, is a descendant of the Strowan Robertsons. The motto on his coat of arms is: "Virtutis gloria merces."—Burke's Peerage.

Our own Patrick Henry's grandmother was a Robertson.

(1) James II., of Scotland, married Lady Mary, daughter of Arnold, Duke of Guelders, of the House of Egmond, and had:

(2) Princess Margaret Stuart, who married, first, William, third Lord of Crighton, who forfeited Crighton in 1483-1484, and had:

(3) Sir James Crighton, of Frendraught, eldest son, who married Lady Catherine, daughter of William, Lord Bostwick, and had:

(4) Lady Margaret Crighton, who married John Robertson, first Laird of Muirton, Elgin, second son of Alexander Robertson, fifth Baronet of Strowan, by his second wife, Lady Isobel. (Elizabeth) daughter of Sir John Stewart, of Baloing, Earl of Athol (a descendant of Edward I., King of England) and his second wife, Lady Eleanor Sinclair, daughter of William, Earl of Orkney, and a descendant of James I., of Scotland, had:

(5) Gilbert Robertson, of Muirton, who married Janet, daughter of John Reid, of Ackenhead, and had:

(6) David Robertson, of Muirton, who married —— Innes, and had:

(7) William Robertson, of Muirton, who married Isabel Petrie, and had:

(8) Rev. William Robertson, of Edinburgh, married Pitcairn of Dreghorn, and had:

(9) William Robertson, Royal Historiographer, and

(10) Jean Robertson, married to Alexander Henry, of Aberdeen, and had:

(11) Colonel John Henry, who removed to Virginia in 1730, and was rested at "Studley" and "The Retreat," in Hanover County; married Sarah, widow of Colonel Syme, and daughter of Isaac Winston, and had:

(12) PATRICK HENRY, of Redhill, Charlotte County, Virginia, first Governor of Virginia; born 1736; died 1799, who married first, 1754, Sarah Shelton of Hanover Court House, Virginia, and married secondly, Dorothia Dandridge, also of Royal descent. (See Pedigree CXXVII.) He had by his first wife:

(1) Martha Henry, married John Fontaine, and had:

William Winston Fontaine, married Martha Dandridge, also of Royal descent, (See Pedigree CXXVII.) issue:

(2) Ann Henry, married Judge Spencer Roane, and had:

(1) Senator William H. Roane, issue:

(2) Fayette and two daughters,

(3) Elizabeth Henry, married Philip Aylitt, of Virginia, issue:

(4) John.

(5) William.—Americans of Royal Descent. Browning.

Please notice that the JOHN ROBERTSON from whom Patrick Henry was a descendant is the same JOHN ROBERTSON from whom our line of Robertsons is descended.

WILLIAM EWART GLADSTONE'S mother was a Robertson, descendant of the Ross-shire Robertsons.

William Ewart Gladstone was of purely Scottish parentage. His father, born in Leith, was descended from a Lanarkshire farmer, and his mother, Ann Robertson, belonged to the Ross-shire Robertsons. (Note. John Gladstanes, of Toftcombs, near Bigger, in the upper ward of Lanarkshire, was a small farmer, who married Janet Aitken; their son, Thomas, who died in 1809, settled in Leith, where he was a prosperous merchant, and where he married Helen Neilson, of Springfield; their son, John, born in 1764, married, 1800, Ann Robertson, daughter of Andrew Robertson, a native of Dingwall, in Ross-shire; John and his wife settled in Liverpool, where, in 1809, their son, William Ewart Gladstone, was born.)—Scotch-Irish. By Hanna.

Sir John Gladstone was twice married; first, in 1792, to Jane, daughter of Mr. Joseph Hall, of Liverpool, who died in 1798, without issue; and secondly, April 29, 1800, to Anne, daughter of Mr. Andrew Robertson, for many years provost of Dingwall. By this lady, who died September 23, 1835, he had, with two daughters, four sons, namely, Thomas, second baronet; Robertson Gladstone, born in 1805, an eminent merchant of Liverpool, and chairman of the Financial Reform Association of that town, married, with issue; John Neilson Gladstone, born in 1807, a commander R. N. M. P. for Walsall and subsequently for Devizes, married with issue; and the Right Honorable William Ewart Gladstone, born in 1809, was educated at Eton and Christ Church, Oxford, where he attained a double first class in 1831, and received honorary degree of D.C.L. in 1848. In 1832 he was elected M. P. for Newark, which place he represented till January, 1846. He was Lord of the Treasury in December, 1834, and under Secretary for the colonies from January to April, 1835. In September, 1841, he was appointed vice-president of the Board of Trade and master of the mint, and sworn a privy councillor. In May, 1843, he became president of the Board of

Trade, retaining the mastership of the mint, but resigned both offices in February, 1845. In December of that year he was appointed Secretary of State for the colonies, which office he held till July, 1846. Elected in 1847 M. P. for the University of Oxford; Chancellor of the Exchequer, December, 1852, till February, 1855. In 1858, Lord-High Commissioner Extraordinary to the Ionian islands; in June, 1859, reappointed Chancellor of the Exchequer. The same year he was elected Rector of the University of Edinburgh. He married in 1839 the eldest daughter of Sir Stephen R. Glynn, Bart. of Hawarden Castle. Flintshire, with issue. Author of "The State in its Relation with the Church," London, 1838, eight volumes. "A Manual of Prayers from the Liturgy," 1845. "An Examination of the Official Reply to the Neapolitan Government," 1852. "Studies on Homer and the Homeric Age," Oxford, 1858; and several political and official papers, letters, and addresses.

The eldest son, Sir Thomas, second Baronet, born at Annfield near Liverpool, in 1804, was M. P. for Queensborough in 1830; for Portarlington from 1832 to 1835; for Leicester from 1835 to 1838; and for Ipswich from June, 1842, to August in the same year, when he was unseated on petition. A deputy lieutenant of Kincardineshire. He married in 1835, Louise, daughter of Robert Fellowes, Esq., of Shottsham Park, Norfolk, with issue. Heir. his son, John Robert, born in 1852.—Scottish Nation. By William Anderson.

In June, 1859, W. E. Gladstone was appointed Chancellor of the Exchequer in the Cabinet of Palmerston. * * * He continued to represent Oxford University until 1865, when he was defeated by the Tory candidate. After the death of Lord Palmerston he became the leader of the House of Commons, and retained the office of Chancellor of the Exchequer under Earl Russell.

He became Prime Minister, December 4, 1868.

In 1874 the Liberal party was defeated at the polls, and Mr. Gladstone, with his Cabinet, retired from office. Mr. Disraeli, who succeeded him, remained premier until 1880, when the unpopularity of his foreign policy, particularly in regard to the Eastern question, led to the defeat of his party and the restoration of the Liberals.

Mr. Gladstone again accepted the premiership, and his first step was to put an end to the war between his government and the Boers of South Africa. He was author of "Juventus Mundi: Gods and Men of the Heroic Ages in Greece" (1869), a pamphlet on "The Vatican Decrees in Their Bearing on Civil Allegiance" (1874), and "Gleanings from Past Years" (1878), a collection of essays and reviews. He died Thursday, May, 19, 1898.—Lippincott's Pronouncing Biographical Dictionary. Thomas.

William Ewart Gladstone was born December 29, 1809, at 62 Rodney Street, Liverpool.—G. W. E. Russell.

Lord John Russell and Henry Lord Brougham, (on the maternal side) Rev. William Robertson, D. D., the eminent Edinburgh divine, and William Robertson, Royal Historiographer, were descendants of the same JOHN ROBERTSON from whom our line of Robertsons descends, viz.:

JOHN ROBERTSON, first Laird of Muirton, Elginshire, second son of Alexander Robertson, fifth Baron of Strowan, by his second wife, Lady Elizabeth, daughter of Sir John Stewart, of Baloing, Earl of Athol, (a descendant of Edward I., King of England,) and his second wife, Lady Eleanor Sinclair, daughter of William, Earl of Orkney, and a descendant of James I., King of Scotland.

JOHN ROBERTSON married Lady Margaret Crighton, whose descent below:

(1) James II., of Scotland, married Lady Mary, daughter of Arnold, Duke of Guilders, of the House of Egmond, and had:

(2) Princess Margaret Stuart, who married first, William, third Lord Crighton, who forfeited Crighton in 1483-1484, and had:

(3) Sir James Crighton, of Frendraught, eldest son, who married Lady Catherine, daughter of William Lord Bostwick, and had:

(4) Lady Margaret Crighton, who married JOHN ROBERTSON.—Burke's Peerage. Anderson's Scottish Nation. Americans of Royal Descent. Browning.

William Robertson, of Inches, Aberdeenshire, was a member of the Scottish Parliament in 1665. There are seven other Robertsons listed as having been members of Parliament in Scotland, viz.: Alexander, James, James, John, John, Thomas and Walter.

In 1861, there were 37,572 MacDonalds in Scotland, the largest number of any surname. There were at that time 32,600 Robertsons, being the fourth largest number of surnames.—Scotch-Irish. By Hanna.

HAMILTON LINEAGE.

From the New York Genealogical and Biographical Record, April, 1889, page 62:

THE LINEAGE OF ALEXANDER HAMILTON.

By Pierce Stevens Hamilton, of Yarmouth, Nova Scotia.

I have never seen any publication of the genealogy of Alexander Hamilton, so famed from the Revolutionary epoch of the United States history. So far as I have seen, at least, all his biographers merely state that he was of Scottish lineage, or that he belonged to the family of "Hamilton of Grange." It might be of interest to the readers of the Record to see the genealogy of Alexander Hamilton, so far as it is traceable. I therefore submit for publication the following genealogy of that distinguished man, from reliable records in my possession.

Tracing back, or upwards, then:

ALEXANDER HAMILTON, born on the island of Nevis, West Indies, on the 11th January, 1757; was the son of

JAMES HAMILTON, described as "a proprietor in the West Indies:" who was the fourth son of

ALEXANDER HAMILTON, of Grange, Scotland; who was the son of

JOHN HAMILTON, of Grange, retoured heir to his father, 31st January, 1677: who was the son of

JOHN HAMILTON, of Grange, who was the son of

ALEXANDER HAMILTON, of Grange, retoured heir to his father, 10th January, 1616; who was the son of

DAVID HAMILTON, Ladleton,—acquired the lands of Grange from his father in 1571; who was the second son of

JOHN HAMILTON, of Cambuskeith, heir to his father in the lands of Cambuskeith in 1561; who was the son of

WILLIAM HAMILTON, of Cambuskeith, retoured heir to his father in 1546; who was the son of

JOHN HAMILTON, of Cambuskeith, had a charter to him and his wife of the mill and mill-lands of Cambuskeith, 21st of September, 1532; who was the son of

ALEXANDER HAMILTON, of Cambuskeith, served heir to his father in 1489; who was the son of

JOHN HAMILTON, of Cambuskeith, who was the son of

JAMES HAMILTON, of Cambuskeith, served heir to his father in 1436; who was the son of

DAVID HAMILTON, of Cambuskeith, had a charter of lands confirmed on 29th January, 1411; who was the son of

WALTER DE HAMILTON, who was the second son of

SIR DAVID DE HAMILTON, Lord of Cadyow, Lanarkshire, mentioned as one of the Scottish Magnates who met at Scone, on the 27th March, 1371; who was the son of

SIR WALTER DE HAMILTON, upon whom King Robert I. (the Bruce) conferred the lands and Castle of Cadyow (now Hamilton), Lanarkshire, and other extensive estates; and who was the son of

SIR GILBERT DE HAMILTON, who is the common ancestor of the Dukes of Hamilton, the Dukes of Abercorn, Earls of Haddington, Viscounts Boyne, Barons Belhaven, several extinct peerages, and of all the Scottish and Irish Hamilton families. This Gilbert De Hamilton made the funeral oration upon King Robert Bruce. He was the son of

WILLIAM DE HAMILTON, who took his designation from the manor of Hambledon, in Buckshire, England, where he was born. He was the third son of

ROBERT DE BLANCHEMAINS, third Earl of Leicester, who figured prominently in the contention between Henry II. and his son. He died in 1190; and was the son of

ROBERT DE BELLOMONT, surnamed BOSSU, second Earl of Leicester, was Chief Justiciary of England for fifteen years, died in 1167; and was the son of

ROBERT, EARL OF MELLENT, created by Henry I., Earl of Leicester,—commanded the right wing of the infantry at the battle of Hastings,—died in 1118, having married Elizabeth Isabella, daughter of

HUGH MAGNUS, Earl of Vermandois, a younger son of King Henry I., of France; and was the son of

ROGER, surnamed DE BELLOMONT, created Earl of Warwick, by William the Conqueror, in 1076; married Adelina, only daughter and heiress of Count of Mellent, and thus assumed the title; was the son of

HUMPHREY, surnamed DE VETULIS, married Albreda de la Haye Auberie; was the son of

TOROLPHE, Lord of PONTAUDEMAR, in the right of his mother, married Woevia, sister to Duchess of Normandy; was the son of

TURFUS, or TURLOFUS, who gave name to the town of

Tourville, in Normandy; married Emerberga de Brigenberg, in 955; was the son of

BERNARD, a near kinsman of Rollo, or Rolf-ganger, the first Duke of Normandy. Rollo, previously to his deeease, named him Governor to his son, Duke William. In the year 912, Bernard married Sphreta de Burgundia.

Thus we find that General Alexander Hamilton, of the United States Revolutionary Army, was the twenty-seventh in direct and unbroken descent from Bernard, the near relative, trusted friend, and brother Viking of the celebrated Northman, or Norman leader of men, Rollo, or Rolf-ganger.

Whilst the subject is in hand, let us try Hamilton's genealogy in another direction. Note above the name of Elizabeth Isabella, Countess of Mellent, wife of Robert Earl of Mellent and first Earl of Leicester, the common ancestress of all the Hamiltons and all the Beaumonts. Let us trace back her genealogy. The historian Gibbon is here my authority:

ELIZABETH ISABELLA, Countess of Mellent, was the daughter of

HUGH, surnamed MAGNUS, Earl of Vermandois, Valois, Chaumont, and Amiens; who was a younger son of

HENRY I., King of France, and his QUEEN; which latter was the daughter of

JEROSLAUS (YAROSLAV), Czar of Russia; who was the son of

PRINCESS ANNE, and of WOLODOMIR, (VLADIMIR) Czar, or Grand Duke of Russia, and also the Apostle who first rudely and summarily converted his Russian subjects to Christianity. The Princess Anne was the second daughter of

ROMANUS II., Emperor of the Eastern or Graeco-Roman Empire. He was the son of

CONSTANTINE VII., Emperor as above; who was the son of

LEO VI., Emperor: who was the son of

BASIL I., Emperor, known in history as "the Macedonian," and founder of a dynasty of Roman Emperors.

On the paternal side, according to Gibbon ("Decline and Fall of the Roman Empire"), this Emperor Basil was a descendant of the Royal Parthian family of the Arsacides. The mother of Basil "was pleased to count among her ancestors the GREAT CONSTANTINE; and their royal infant was connected by some dark affinity of lineage, or country, with the Macedonian Alexander." If Basil was a son of the Parthian dynasty of the Arsacides—as would seem to be the case according to Gibbon's authorities—this would carry back his genealogy, and that of all who claim descent from him, to nearly three hundred years before the Christian era.

Let us try again—Note the name Wolodomir, (Vladimir) Czar of Russia, named above. This

WOLODOMIR (VLADIMIR) was the son of

SWATOSLAUS (SVIATOSLAV); who was the son of

IGOR; who was the son of

RURICK; who was really of the same race as Rollo, Bernard, and the other Normans more particularly so-called; and who was the founder of the first Russian monarchy.

PARTHIA.

The old kingdom of Parthia, reduced for centuries to subordination, first to Persia, afterwards to the successors of Alexander, lay in comparative obscurity. But the time had now arrived for an emergence by rebellion into light and life and action. At this epoch the actual history of Parthia as an independent power begins. All the rest is, as it were, the setting of the picture. From this time forth the movement, first toward freedom, and then to greatness, is rapid and direct.

The administration of Antiochus the Divine was of precisely the kind to furnish the opportunity and the suggestion of a revolt. About six years before the conclusion of his reign, Theodotus, or Diodotus, the Greek satrap of Bactria, perceived in the distance between himself and Antioch and in the effeminate administration of the King the hint of successful rebellion. He accordingly at once threw off the yoke, gave himself the title of Basileus, and entered upon an independent administration. Thus did Bactria lead the way in renouncing the sovereignty which had been accepted since the Alexandrian conquest. It appears that Antiochus had neither the ambition nor the courage to chastise his rebellious governor, and Theodotus was accordingly permitted to take his undisturbed course to independence.

The example was contagious. The neighboring satrapies felt the shock of the Bactrian revolution, and soon adopted a similar method. Parthia was the first to follow in the wake of the neighboring revolt. In this country, however, the movement took on a wholly different character. In Bactria the revolution could hardly be said to be national. The Greek Governor was simply permitted to raise himself to the rank and title of King; but in Parthia the revolt had a different source. Here the spring of action was a national sentiment against the rule of the Europeans in any form. The feeling was against the Greek

Dynasty *in toto,* so that instead of following the lead of the Governor in making himself independent of Antiochus, the Parthians rose against the Governor himself, and the whole system of foreign domination which he represented.

The circumstances and details of the revolt have been differently told by different authors. It has been narrated that a certain ARSACES—which name the leader of the revolution certainly bore—appeared out of Bactria, from which country he had fled from the jealousy of Theodotus. Coming into Parthia, he induced the people to accept him for their leader in a rebellion against their own Greek Governor. Successful in this, he was made King of Parthia and founder of the dynasty. Another account says that Pherecles, satrap of Parthia under Antiochus the Divine, offered an insult to Arsaces, who, according to this tradition, was a native of Parthia, son of Phriapites, and that he—Arsaces—and his brother Tiridates drew five of their fellow noblemen into a conspiracy and slew the satrap. This done, the people were easily induced to rise and throw off the foreign domination altogether. They then chose Arsaces for their King. Still another account makes Arsaces to have been a Scythian of the nation called Dahae, who came by hostile invasion into Parthia overthrew the Greek government, and made their leader King. It is sufficient for historical purposes to say that the rebellion against the Greeks was led by a patriot named Arsaces, who was, perhaps, of Scythian extraction; that the foreign officers were expelled; that the pride of the nation was gratified by the success of the insurrection; and that its leader was made King of Parthia, with the title of ARSACES I. These events are assigned to the year B. C. 256, but some have moved the event forward to 250, being the year of the death of Antiochus Theos.

It appears that the name ARSACES was at once adopted as the designative title of the Dynasty, which is known in history as the ARSACIDAE.

More than any other name among Parthian monarchs is that of Mithridates known to the people of the West. Those historians who are willing to allow to individual agency the general results which in the aggregate go by the name of history, have been wont to ascribe to Mithridates the place among his countrymen which the same writers assign, each in his respective sphere, to Alexander and Caesar. More properly we may regard this sixth representative of the Arsacid Dynasty as the personal expression of the historical growth and purpose of the Parthian nation in his age. To him undoubtedly great abilities and great ambitions must be ascribed. His courage and strength were equally manifested in civil administration and in war. His reign, covering a period of thirty-seven years, is the most important and interesting of Parthian history. His career as a ruler was so extraordinary as to impress itself strongly upon the Greeks and Romans, whose historians have done tolerable justice to the builder of the Parthian Empire.

Parthia was a rival of Rome and the only nation which Rome, in her palmiest days, could not subdue.

This ARSACIDES DYNASTY extended from B. C. 256 to 226 A. D., and ended with Artabanus IV., the thirtieth of the line.

The Parthians were great cavalrymen and their main reliance in war was on the cavalry.—Ridpath.

ROME.

BASIL I., AND THE ROMAN DYNASTY FOUNDED BY HIM.

The genealogy of Basil the Macedonian exhibits a genuine picture of the revolution of the most illustrious families. The Arsaeides, the rivals of Rome, possessed the sceptre of the East near four hundred (five hundred) years; a younger branch of these Parthian Kings continued to reign in Armenia; and their royal descendants survived the partition and servitude of that ancient monarchy. Two of these, Artabanus and Chlienes, escaped or retired to the court of Leo the First; his bounty seated them in a safe and hospitable exile, in the province of Macedonia; Adrianople was their final settlement. During several generations they maintained the dignity of their birth; and their Roman patriotism rejected the tempting offers of the Persian and Arabian powers, who recalled them to their native country. But their splendor was insensibly clouded by time and poverty; and the father of Basil was reduced to a small farm, which he cultivated with his own hands; yet he scorned to disgrace the blood of the Arsacides by a plebian alliance; his wife, a widow of Adrianpole, was pleased to count among her ancestors the GREAT CONSTANTINE; and their royal infant was connected by some dark affinity of lineage or country with the Macedonian Alexander. No sooner was he born, than the cradle of Basil, his family, and his city, were swept away by an inundation of Bulgarians; he was educated a slave in a foreign land; and in this severe discipline, he acquired the hardiness of body and flexibility of mind which promoted his future elevation. In the age of youth or manhood he shared the deliverance of the

Roman captives, who generously broke their fetters, marched through Bulgaria to the shores of the Euxine, defeated two armies of Barbarians, embarked in the ships which had been stationed for their reception, and returned to Constantinople, from whence they were distributed to their respective homes. But the freedom of Basil was naked and destitute; his farm was ruined by the calamities of war; after his father's death, his manual labor, or service, could no longer support a family of orphans; and he resolved to seek a more conspicuous theater, in which every virtue and every vice may lead to the paths of greatness. The first night of his arrival at Constantinople, without friends or money, the weary pilgrim slept on the steps of the Church of St. Diomede; he was fed by the casual hospitality of a monk; and was introduced to the service of a cousin and namesake of the Emperor Theophilus; who, though himself a diminutive person, was followed by a train of tall and handsome domestics. Basil attended his patron to the government of Peloponnesus; eclipsed, by his personal merit, the birth and dignity of Theophilus, and formed a useful connection with a wealthy and charitable matron of Patras. Her spiritual and carnal love embraced the young adventurer, whom she adopted as her son. Danielis presented him with thirty slaves; and the produce of her bounty was expended in the support of his brothers, and the purchase of some large estates in Macedonia. His gratitude or ambition still attached him to the service of Theophilus; and a lucky accident recommended him to the notice of the court. A famous wrestler, in the train of the Bulgarian Ambassadors, had defied, at the royal banquet, the boldest and most robust of the Greeks. The strength of Basil was praised; he accepted the challenge; and the Barbarian champion was overthrown at the first onset. A beautiful but vicious horse was condemned to be hamstrung; it was subdued by the dexterity and courage of the servant of Theophilus; and his conqueror was promoted to an honorable rank in the Imperial stables. The public administration had been abandoned to the Caesar Bardas, the brother and enemy of Theodora; but the arts of female influence persuaded Michael to hate and to fear his uncle; he was drawn from Constantinople, under the pretence of a Cretan expedition, and was stabbed in the tent of audience, by the sword of the chamberlain, and in the presence of the Emperor. About a month after this execution, Basil was invested with the title of Augustus and the government of the Empire. He supported this unequal association till his influence was forfeited by popular esteem. His life was endangered by the caprice of the Emperor; and his dignity was profaned by a second colleague, who had rowed in the galleys. Yet the murder of his benefactor must be condemned as an act of ingratitude and treason; and the churches which he dedicated to the name of St. Michael were a poor and puerile expiation of his guilt.

The different ages of Basil the First may be compared with those of Augustus. The situation of the Greek did not allow him in his earliest youth to lead an army against his country, or to proscribe the noblest of her sons; but his aspiring genius stooped to the arts of a slave; he dissembled his ambition and even his virtues, and grasped, with the bloody hand of an assassin, the Empire which he ruled with the wisdom and tenderness of a parent. A private citizen may feel his interest repugnant to his duty; but it must be from a deficiency of sense or courage, that an absolute monarch can separate his happiness from his glory, or his glory from the public welfare. The life or panegyric of Basil has indeed been composed and published under the long reign of his descendants; but even their stability on the throne may be justly ascribed to the superior merit of their ancestor. But the most solid praise of Basil is drawn from the comparison of a ruined and a flourishing monarchy, that which he wrested from the dissolute Michael, and that which he bequeathed to the Macedonian dynasty. The evils which had been sanctioned by time and example, were corrected by his master hand; and he revived if not the national spirit, at least the order and majesty of the Roman Empire. His application was indefatigable, his temper cool, his understanding vigorous and decisive; and in his practice he observed that rare and salutary moderation, which pursues each virtue, at an equal distance between the opposite vices. His military service had been confined to the palace; nor was the Emperor endowed with the spirit or the talents of a warrior. Yet under his reign the Roman arms were formidable to the Barbarians. As soon as he had formed a new army by discipline and exercise, he appeared in person on the banks of Euphrates, curbed the pride of the Saracens, and suppressed the dangerous though just revolt of the Manicheans. His indignation against a rebel who had long eluded his pursuit, provoked him to wish and to pray, that, by the grace of God, he might drive three arrows into the head of Chrysochir. That odius head, which had been obtained by treason rather than by valor, was suspended from a tree, and thrice exposed to the dexterity of the Imperial archer: a base revenge against the dead, more worthy of the times than of the character of Basil. But his principal merit was in the civil administration of finances and of the laws. After reforming the luxury, he assigned two patrimonial estates to supply the decent plenty of the Imperial table; the contributions of the subjects were reserved for his defense; and the residue was employed in the embellishment of the capitol and provinces. A taste for building, however costly, may deserve some praise and much excuse; from thence industry is fed, art is encouraged, and some object is attained of public emolument or pleasure; the use of a road, an aqueduct, or a hospital, is obvious and solid; and the hundred churches that arose by the command of Basil were consecrated to the devotion of the age. In the character of a judge he was assiduous and impartial; desirous to save, but not afraid to strike; the oppressors of the people were severely chastised; but his personal foes, whom it might be unsafe to pardon, were condemned, after the loss of their eyes, to a life of solitude and repentance. The change of language and manners demanded a revision of the obsolete jurisprudence of Justinian; the voluminous body of his Institues, Pendects, Code, and Novels, was digested under forty titles, in the Greek idiom; and the *Basilics*, which were improved and completed by his son and grandson, must be referred to the original genius of the founder of their race. This glorious reign was terminated by an accident in the chase. A furious stag entangled his horns in the belt of Basil, and raised him from his horse; he was rescued by an attendant; but the fall, or the fever, exhausted the strength of the aged monarch, and he expire in the palace amidst the tears of his family and people. If he struck off the head of a faithful servant for presuming to draw his sword against his sovereign, the pride of despotism, which had lain dormant in his life, revived in the last moments of despair, when he no longer wanted or valued the opinion of mankind.

LEO VI., Emperor of the Graeco-Roman Empire, was the son of Basil I.

CONSTANTINE VII., Emperor as above, was the son of Leo VI.

ROMANUS II., Emperor as above, was the son of Constantine VII.

ANNE, second daughter of Romanus II., was married to Wolodomir, (Vladimir) Czar or Emperor of Russia.

The dynasty founded by Basil I. was established 867 A. D., and was ended with Constantine IX., son of Romanus II., in 1028 A. D.

Romanus II. left two sons, Basil II., and Constantine IX., and two daughters, Theophano and Anne. The elder sister was given to Otho II., Emperor of the West; the younger became the wife of Wolodomir, (Vladimir) great Duke and apostle of Russia, and, by the marriage of her granddaughter with Henry I., King of France, the blood of the Macedonians, and of the Arsacides, still flows in the Bourbon line.—The Decline and Fall of the Roman Empire. Gibbon.

RUSSIA.

THE FIRST RUSSIAN MONARCHY, FOUNDED BY RURIC.

Soon after the Slavic tribes gained the ascendency they founded the towns of Novgorod and Kiev, which became the capitals of the two divisions of the country. In the course of a century the former principality was invaded by the Rus out of the North, and both Slavs and Finns were reduced to a tributary relation. Several times the Slavic tribes revolted; but finally, despairing of success, they invited the great Rus Prince, RURIC, to come to Novgorod and be their King. In the year 862 he came with his brothers Sinaf and Truver, and then and there was founded the Russian Empire.

From this time until nearly the middle of the eleventh century the family of Ruric occupied the throne. On the death of the great chieftain, in 879, the succession passed to his cousin, Oleg, who reigned for twenty-three years. During this time the principality of Kiev was conquered and added to that of Novgorod. The Khazars between the Dnieper and the Caspian were also subdued, and the Magyars were driven out of Russia in the direction of Hungary. Oleg next made war on the Byzantine Empire, and pressed upon the Greeks with such force that in 911 the Emperor was obliged to consent to a peace in every way advantageous to the Rus.

After the death of Oleg, in the following year, Igor, son of Ruric, came to the throne, and reigned for thirty-three years. His career was that of a warrior. He first put down a revolt of the Drevlians on the Pripet, and then vanquished the Petchenegs, who had their seats on the shores of the Black Sea. Afterwards, in 941, he engaged in a war with the Greek Emperor, but was less successful than his predecessor. In a second conflict with the Drevlians he was defeated and slain, and the crown passed to his son, Sviatoslav, under the regency of Olga, his mother. This princess became a convert to Christianity, and the new faith gained a footing at Kiev.

The Emperor, however, remained a pagan, and devoted himself to war. He made campaigns against the same nations that had felt the sword of his father and grandfather. The Bulgarians also were at one time his enemies, and were defeated in battle. While returning from an unsuccessful expedition against the Greeks of Constantinople Sviatoslav was attacked and killed by the Petchenegs, through whose country he was passing. On his death, in 972, the Empire, which was now extended to the Sea of Azov, was divided among his three sons, Yaropolk, Oleg, and Vladimir. The first received Kiev, the second the country of the Drevlians, and the third Novgorod. The brothers soon quarreled and went to war. Oleg was slain and Vladimir fled. Yaropolk gained possession of the whole country, but Vladimir gathered the Rus tribes to his standard, returned against his brother, put him to death, and secured the Empire to himself. He then conquered Red Russia, Lithuania, and Livonia. He became a Christian, married the sister of the Greek Emperor, and received the title of the Great. Under his influence and example Russia turned from paganism to Christianity. Churches rose on every hand; schools were founded, and new cities gave token that the night of Barbarism was lifting from the great power of the North.

Vladimir (married to Anne, second daughter of Romanus II.) left twelve sons to contend for the crown. On his death civil war broke out among them, and several of the claimants were slain. At length Sviatopolk, son of Yaropolk, himself an adopted son of Vladimir, hewed his way to the throne over the bodies of three of his foster brothers. Yaroslav, one of the surviving sons of the late Emperor, allied himself with Henry II. of Germany and returned to the contest. The struggle continued until 1019, when a decisive battle was fought, in which Sviatopolk was signally defeated. He fled from the field and died on his way to Poland.

After this crisis the Empire was divided between Yaroslav and Metislav, but the latter presently died, and the former became sole ruler of Russia.

To this epoch belongs the beginning of art and learning in the Northern Empire. The works of the Greeks began to be translated into Slavic. Learned institutions were founded in various cities, and scholars were patronized and honored. The Russian customs and usages were compiled into a code of laws, and amicable relations were established with foreign States. Three of the daughters of Yaroslav were taken in marriage by the Kings of Norway, Hungary, and France (Anne was married to Henry I. of France)—a clear recognition of the rank of the new Russian Empire among the kingdoms of the earth.

In the year 1051 Yaroslav established the succession on his son, Izaslav, but portions of the Empire were to go to the three brothers of the heir expectant. They were to acknowledge the eldest as their sovereign. In the same year the Emperor died, and the four brothers took the inheritance. The result was that the unity of the Empire was broken. Each of the rulers became independent; the feudal principle came in, and Russia was reduced to a confederation. Thus weakened, the frontiers were successfully assailed by the Poles, Lithuanians, Danes, and Teutonic Barons. Such was the condition of affairs when Europe forgot her own turmoils and sorrows in a common animosity against the Infidels of the East.—Ridpath.

FRANCE.

THE CAPETIAN DYNASTY, FOUNDED BY HUGH CAPET.

The Carlovingian family were soon opposed by national princes who had courage and talent; and after a struggle which went on during the latter part of the ninth and nearly the whole of the tenth century, they were finally deprived of their hereditary throne. Previous to this a new race, the Normans, had established themselves in Northwest of France. They had carried on a system of piracy along the coast as early as the reign of Charlemagne, and since then they had several times pushed their incursions into the very heart of the country. The weak Charles the Simple, at last had recourse to concessions to check their continued attacks, and in 912 the lands situated west of the lower Seine were ceded to Rollo, the chief of a large horde of these Northmen, and Normandy soon became one of the most flourishing and best regulated provinces in France. Its dukes held the first rank among the feudal princes, when Hugues or Hugh Capet, the Duke of France, on the death of Louis V., was made King of France, founding the Capetian dynasty, which ruled continuously more than 800 years through several collateral branches, and is still represented by the Bourbon family.

Hugh Capet, King of France and founder of the Capetian dynasty, was born about 940, and died October 24, 996. When still a child he inherited from his father, Hugh the Great, the Duchy of France and the County of Paris, thus taking rank among the most powerful princes of his country.

On the death of Louis V., the last of the Carlovingian Kings, a number of nobles and bishops from all parts of the country assembled at Senlis to settle the succession, and selected Hugh Capet in preference to the Carlovingian Duke, Charles of Lorraine, the uncle of the late King. Hugh was consequently crowned at Noyon, July 3, 987, by the archbishop of Rheims. Notwithstanding this election, Charles supported his claims to the crown of France by the sword, and after four years' hostilities was apparently on the point of succeeding, when he was treacherously made prisoner by Adalberon, bishop of Laon, who delivered him to his rival. The unfortunate prince was sent to Orleans, where he soon breathed his last in a dungeon. Hugh, having thus secured possession of the crown, associated his son Robert in the government, which he settled on the principle of hereditary succession.

HENRY I., the third French King of the Capetian dynasty, was born about 1011, and died August 4, 1060. As early as 1027 he was associated in the government by Robert, his father, whom he succeeded in 1031, notwithstanding the rebellion raised against him by his stepmother, Constance. This he quelled through the assistance of Robert the Devil, Duke of Normandy.

By Anna, daughter of Yaroslav, Grand Duke of Russia, Henry had Philip, who was his successor, and Hugh, who became Count of Vermandois.—The American Cyclopaedia.

Hugh of Vermandois was the leader of the French Knights of the Crusaders.—Ridpath.

ELIZABETH ISABELLA, daughter of Hugh Magnus, Earl of Vermandois, a younger son of Henry I., of France, was married to

ROBERT, Earl of Mellent, who was created Earl of Leicester, by Henry I.: commanded the right wing of the infantry at the battle of Hastings; died in 1118; he was the son of Roger, surnamed De Bellomont, who was the son of Humphrey, surnamed De Vetulis, who was the son of Torolphe, Lord of Pontaudemar, who was the son of Turfus, who was the son of Bernard, near kinsman of Rollo, first Duke of Normandy.

ROBERT DE BELLOMONT, surname BOSSU, second Earl of Leicester, son of Robert, Earl of Mellent and Elizabeth Isabella, was Chief Justiciary of England for fifteen years; died in 1167, and was the father of

ROBERT DE BLANCHEMAINS, third Earl of Leicester, who figured prominently in the contention between Henry II. and his son. He died in 1190 and was the father of

WILLIAM DE HAMILTON, who took his designation from

the manor of Hambledon, in Buckshire, England, where he was born. He was the third son of Robert De Blanchemains, and was the father of

SIR GILBERT DE HAMILTON, who is the common ancestor of the Dukes of Hamilton, the Dukes of Abercorn, Earls of Haddington, Viscounts Boyne, Barons Belhaven, several extinct peerages, and of all the Scottish and Irish Hamilton families. This Gilbert de Hamilton made the funeral oration upon King Robert Bruce. This Gilbert de Hamilton was the common ancestor of Alexander Hamilton and of our great-great-grandmother,

ANNE HAMILTON, who was married to

JOHN ROBERTSON, and they were the parents of

WILLIAM ROBERTSON, our great-grandfather, the first of this line to come to America, in 1772.

Thus four dynasties were founded by this line: The Parthian Arsacides dynasty, founded by Arsaces, B. C. 256, and ending with Artabanus IV., the thirtieth of the line, 226 A. D.; the Graeco-Roman dynasty founded by Basil I., 867 A. D., and ending with Constantine IX., in 1028; the first Russian dynasty, founded by Ruric, 862 A. D., and ending with Yaroslav, in 1051, who was father of Anna, wife of Henry I., of France; the Capetian dynasty of France, founded by Hugh Capet in 987, and which ruled continuously for more than 800 years through several collateral branches, and is still represented by the Bourbon family.

RECAPITULATION.

The ARSACIDES dynasty of Parthia was founded by ARSACES B. C. 256, and ended with Artabanus IV., the thirtieth of the line, 226 A. D.

BASIL I., Emperor of the Graeco-Roman Empire, a descendant of the Royal Arsacides family of Parthia, founded a Graeco-Roman dynasty in 867, which ended with Constantine IX. in 1028.

LEO VI., Emperor as above, son of Basil I.

CONSTANTINE VII., Emperor as above, son of Leo VI.

ROMANUS II., Emperor as above, son of Constantine VII., was father of ANNE, who was married to Vladimir, Czar or Emperor of Russia.

The first Russian monarchy was founded by

RURIC in 862 A. D., and ended with Yaroslav in 1051

IGOR, Czar or Emperor of Russia, son of Ruric.

SVIATOSLAV, Czar or Emperor of Russia, son of Igor.

VLADIMIR, Czar or Emperor of Russia, son of Sviatoslav; married

ANNE, second daughter of Romanus II., Emperor of Rome.

YAROSLAV, Czar or Emperor of Russia, son of Vladimir and Anne, had

ANNE, who was married to Henry I., King of France.

HUGH CAPET, King of France, founder of the Capetian dynasty in 987, which ruled continuously for more than 800 years through several collateral branches, and is still represented by the Bourbon family.

ROBERT, King of France, son of Hugh Capet.

HENRY I., King of France, son of Robert;married

ANNE, daughter of Yaroslav. Czar or Emperor of Russia.

HUGH MAGNUS, Earl of Vermandois, a younger son of Henry I. and Anna.

ELIZABETH ISABELLA, daughter of Hugh Magnus, was married to

ROBERT, Earl of Mellent, created by Henry I., Earl of Leicester. He was the son of

ROGER, surnamed De Bellomont, created Earl of Warwick by William the Conqueror, in 1076; married Adelina, only daughter and heiress of Count of Mellent, and thus assumed the title; was the son of

HUMPHREY, surnamed DE VETULIS, married Albreda de la Haye Auberie; was the son of

TOROLPHE, Lord of Pontaudemar, in right of his mother, married Wocvia, sister to Duchess of Normandy; was the son of

TURFUS, or TURLOFUS, who gave name to the town of Tourville, in Normandy; married Emerberga de Brigenberg, in 955; was the son of

BERNARD, a near kinsman of Rollo, First Duke of Normandy.

ROBERT DE BELLOMONT, surnamed BOSSU, Second Earl of Leicester, was the son of Robert, Earl of Mellent and Elizabeth Isabella. He was Chief Justiciary of England for fifteen years, and was father of

ROBERT DE BLANCHEMAINS, Third Earl of Leicester; died in 1190; was the father of

WILLIAM DE HAMILTON, who took his designation from the manor of Hambledon, in Buckshire, England, where he was born; was the third son of Robert de Blanchemains. He was the father of

SIR GILBERT DE HAMILTON, who is the common ancestor of the Dukes of Hamilton, the Dukes of Abercorn, Earls of Haddington, Viscounts Boyne, Barons Belhaven, several extinct peerages, and of all the Scottish and Irish Hamilton families, including Alexander Hamilton and our great-great-grandmother,

ANNE HAMILTON, who was married to

JOHN ROBERTSON, and had

WILLIAM ROBERTSON, born January 24, 1752, in Peterhead, Aberdeenshire, Scotland; went to Kilkenny, Ireland, in 1762; came to America in 1772 and settled in Washington county, New York; married Mary Livingston, September 24, 1775; died February 19, 1825.

THE HAMILTONS IN SCOTLAND.

The Hamilton family in Scotland dates from the thirteenth century. The first person of the name in Scotland that can be relied upon was Walter de Hamilton, usually designated Walterus filius Gilberti, or Walter Fitz-Gilbert, and from him the ducal family of Hamilton are descended.

In the chartulary of Paisley he appears as one of the witnesses of confirmation by James, a great steward of Scotland, to the monastery of Paisley, of the privilege of a herring fishery in the Clyde in 1294; and in 1292, and again in 1296, we find him among the barons who swore fealty to King Edward I., for lands lying in Lanarkshire and different other countries. During the contest which ensued for the succession to the Scottish crown he adhered to the English or Baliol interest. By Edward II. he was appointed governor of the castle of Bothwell, and he held that important fortress for the English at the period of the battle of Bannockburn. He is mentioned by Barbour as "Schyr Walter Gilbertson." He seems soon after to have been taken into favor with Robert Bruce, as that monarch bestowed on him the barony of Cadyow in Lanarkshire, and several other lands and baronies in that county, and in Linlithgowshire and Wigtonshire. He continued faithful to King David Bruce, the son of his great benefactor, and during his minority he accompanied the regent Douglas to the relief of Berwick, then threatened with a siege by the English. He was also present at the battle of Halidon-hill, where he had a command in the great body of the army under the young Stewart. He was twice married. His second wife was Mary, only daughter of Adam de Gordon, ancestor of all the Gordons in Scotland. He had two sons, Sir David and John de Hamilton, who, marrying Elizabeth, daughter of Alan Stewart of Dreghorn, got with her the lands of Ballencrief, etc. Of him are descended the Hamiltons of Innerwick, the Earls of Haddington, and others. Sir Walter had two brothers, Sir John de Hamilton de Rossaven, and Hugo de Hamilton. The former had a charter from his nephew, Sir David de Hamilton de Cadyow, of the barony of Fingaltoun in Renfrewshire, dated in 1339. He was ancestor of the Hamiltons of Fingaltoun and Preston, from whom are sprung the families of Airdrie and Ellershaw, and from the latter are said to be descended the Hamiltons of Cairnes, and the Hamiltons of Mount Hamilton in Ireland.

Sir David de Hamilton was knighted by Robert II., who, in 1377, made him a grant of the lands of Bothwell muir. He died before 1392. He married Janet or Johnetta de Keith, only daughter and heiress of the gallant Sir William Keith of Gaston, and the ancestrix, not only of the noble family of Hamilton, but of their cousins, the Stewards of Darnley, from whom James I. of England, and the subsequent monarchs of the house of Stewart were lineally descended.

James Hamilton was created a Lord of Parliament by royal charter, on July 3, 1445, under the title of Lord Hamilton of Cadyow. He married, secondly, Princess Mary, eldest daughter of James II., King of Scotland, and widow of Thomas Boyd, Earl of Arran; and during nearly a century the head of the house of Hamilton was, after the Royal Family, heir to the Scottish crown. By her he had a son,

James, Second Lord Hamilton, and a daughter, Elizabeth, married to Matthew, Second Earl of Lennox.

King James made James, Second Lord Hamilton, a grant of the island of Arran, and at the same time created him earl thereof, by letters patent, dated August 11, 1503. He also gave him a charter or commission of justiciary within the island. He married, thirdly, Janet, daughter of Sir David Bethune of Creich, comptroller of Scotland, niece of Cardinal Bethune, and widow of Sir Thomas Livingston of Easter Wemyss, and by her had, with four daughters, two sons:

James, Second Earl of Arran, Regent of Scotland, and Duke of Chatelherault. He married Lady Margaret Douglas, eldest daughter of the Third Earl of Morton, and by her had:

(1) James, Third Earl of Arran.

(2) John, First Marquis of Hamilton, born in 1532, had the commendatory of the rich abbey of Aberbrothwick conferred on him in 1541.

(3) Lord David Hamilton, who died without issue.

(4) Lord Claud, ancestor of the Earls of Abercorn.

James, Third Earl of Arran, succeeded his father in 1545.

The dukedom of Chatelherault, having been resumed by the crown of France, did not descend to him.

He was in the castle of St. Andrew when Cardinal Bethune was assassinated in 1546, and was detained a prisoner there by the conspirators. As his father was the presumptive heir to the crown, on August 14, 1546, the Estates of the Kingdom passed an act declaring him to be secluded as long as he happened to be in the hands of those that committed the slaughter of the cardinal, or of any enemies of the realm. He was released on the surrender of the conspirators to the French, and in 1555 he went over to France, where he obtained the command of the Scottish Guards.

In 1560 the Scottish Estates proposed the Earl of Arran as a husband to the Princess Elizabeth, but with great professions of regard she declined the alliance.

The following year, on the arrival from France of his own sovereign, Queen Mary, he openly aspired for her hand, and on her part she showed great partiality for him, but by his most imprudently opposing the exercise of her religion, he forfeited her favor altogether. He died, without issue, March 16, 1609, and was succeeded by his nephew,

James, Second Marquis of Hamilton, born in 1589, succeeded his father in 1604, and his uncle, the Earl of Arran, in May, 1609, in his estates and in the hereditary office of sheriff of Lanarkshire. And here it becomes necessary to correct an "historical error" that is almost universally held, namely, that after the present royal family, the house of Hamilton is heir to the Scottish crown, and of consequence to the throne of Great Britain, as by the act of Union it is forever provided that whoever is heir to the throne of Scotland shall be heir also to the throne of the United Kingdom, and vice versa.

During the period of nearly a century (previous to the birth of children of the marriage of the Princess Elizabeth, which took place in 1613) the head of the Hamilton family was undoubtedly the next heir to the Scottish crown. As such, in the year 1542, an act was passed in the Estates of Scotland, by which "all the lordis sperituale, and commissaris of burrowis, representand the thre estatis of parliament, declarit and declaris James, Earl of Arran, Lord Hamilton, (ancestor of the Duke of Hamilton) secound persoun of this realme, and narrest to succede to the crown of the samin, falyeing of our souirant lady (Queen Mary) and the barnis lauchfullie to be gotten of her body." And again, in 1546, as already stated, the three estates solemnly recognized the eldest son of the Earl of Arran as "the third persoun of the realm," and acknowledged "all his rychtis of successionis alsweill of the crowne as of others."

The head of the house of Hamilton remained in this distinguished position of "second person of the realm," or heir presumptive to the crown, until the birth of King James VI. interposed a third person between him and the throne. After the dethronement of Queen Mary, the house of Hamilton again reverted to its pre-eminence of being next heir to the crown, and held that high position until the numerous issue of King James VI. removed them to a distance in the order of succession.

The Second Marquis of Hamilton died at Whitehall, London, March 2, 1625; in his 36th year, a few days before King James. With three daughters, he had two sons:

James, Third Marquis, and First Duke of Hamilton, and

William, Earl of Lanark, Second Duke of Hamilton.

Duke of Hamilton, a title in the peerage of Scotland, conferred with that of Marquis of Clydesdale, in 1643, on James, Earl of Arran, the elder son of the Second Marquis of Hamilton, and now held by the Douglas family, through the marriage of Anne, Duchess of Hamilton, niece and successor of the second duke, with the Earl of Selkirk. The first duke having only surviving daughters, was succeeded by his brother, William, Earl of Lanark.

William, second Duke of Hamilton, was born at Hamilton, December 4, 1616. On the last day of March, 1639, he was created a Scottish peer by the titles of Earl of Lenark, Lord Machanshyre and Polmont, and in 1640 was made Secretary of State for Scotland. He died September 12, 1651. He had married in 1638, Lady Elizabeth Maxwell, eldest daughter and co-heiress of James, Earl of Dirleton, and by her had:

James, Lord Polmont, who died an infant, and five daughters.

The Dukedom of Hamilton, with the titles and estates, devolved on his niece, Anne, Duchess of Hamilton, born about 1636. She married Lord William Douglas, eldest son of William, first Marquis of Douglas, who died April 18, 1694. Anne, Duchess of Hamilton, died in 1717. She resigned her titles in favor of her eldest son, the Earl of Arran, who was accordingly created Duke of Hamilton, with the original precedency.

They had four daughters, and seven sons, the eldest,

James, fourth Duke of Hamilton and first Duke of Brandon.

James, fifth Duke of Hamilton and second Duke of Brandon, born in 1702, succeeded his father when only ten years old. He was installed a Knight of the Thistle at Holyroodhouse, October 31, 1726, and appointed, in 1727, one of the lords of the bedchamber to King George II., but resigned that office in 1733, not approving of the measures of Sir Robert Walpole's administration. At the general election in 1734, he was a candidate to represent the Scottish peerage, in opposition to the court list, and died at Bath, March 9, 1743, in his forty-first year. He was thrice married; first, to Lady Anne Cochrane, eldest daughter of the three beautiful daughters of John, fourth Earl of Dundonald; secondly, to Elizabeth, fourth daughter of Thomas Strangeways, of Melbury Samford, Dorsetshire; and, thirdly, to Anne, daughter and co-heir of Edward Spenser, of Rendlesham, in Suffolk. By his first duchess he had a son, James, sixth Duke of Hamilton, and by his third, a daughter, Anne, Countess of Donegal, and two sons, Archibald, ninth Duke of Hamilton, and Lord Spenser Hamilton, colonel in the guards and one of the gentlemen of the bedchamber to the Prince of Wales, who died March 20, 1791, in his forty-ninth year.

James, sixth Duke of Hamilton, and third of Brandon, born in 1724, and was invested with the order of the Thistle, March 14, 1755.

James-George, seventh Duke of Hamilton and fourth of Brandon, born at Holyroodhouse, February 18, 1755, succeeded his father when only three years old.

Douglas, eighth Duke of Hamilton, and fifth of Brandon, born July 24, 1756, succeeded his brother in 1769; died August 2, 1799.

Archibald, ninth Duke of Hamilton, and sixth Duke of Brandon, born July 15, 1740, inherited through his mother and grandmother, extensive property in the County of Suffolk, and in Lanarkshire, and Staffordshire, died February 16, 1819. Married Lady Harriet Stewart, fifth daughter of the sixth Earl of Galloway, and by her, who died before her husband's accession to the ducal titles, he had three daughters and two sons;

Alexander, tenth Duke of Hamilton, and

Lord Archibald Hamilton.

Alexander, tenth Duke of Hamilton, and seventh of Brandon, born October 3, 1767. succeeded his father in 1819; died in 1854, and was succeeded by his son,

William Alexander Anthony Archibald, eleventh Duke of Hamilton, and eighth Duke of Brandon, born February 15, 1811. He married in 1843, the Princess Mary Amelia Elizabeth Caroline. (born 1818) daughter of the Grand Duke of Baden. and cousin-german of Napoleon III., Emperor of the French. Issue, two sons and one daughter.

(1) William Alexander Louis Stephen, Marquis of Douglas and Clydesdale, born in 1845.

(2) George Archibald, born in 1847.

(3) Lady Maria Victoria, born in 1850.

His grace is hereditary keeper of Holyroodhouse, premier peer of Scotland and Knight Marischal of Scotland, 1846, appointed Lord Lieutenant of Lanarkshire and colonel of its militia, 1852.

The Dukes of Hamilton have never relinquished their right to the title of Duke of Chatelherault, in France, conferred on the Regent Earl of Arran, in 1548. The title is also claimed by the Marquis of Abercorn, as male representative of the House of Hamilton.

The most ancient cadet of the House of Hamilton is the family of Hamilton of Preston, East-Lothian, and Fingaltoun, Renfrewshire, which possesses a baronetcy of Scotland and Nova Scotia, conferred in 1673, on Sir William Hamilton, born 1647, the thirteenth from the original progenitor of this line.—Scottish Nation. By William Anderson.

LIVINGSTON.

The Scottish historian, Buchanan, says the family descended from Livingus, a Hungarian Nobleman, who accompanied Margaret Atherling from Hungary to Scotland, 1067, when Margaret became the second wife of Malcolm Canmore. (Canmore is from Gaelic, cean, head—mor, big—bighead.) Margaret was the daughter of Edward, son of Edmund Ironsides, Saxon King of England. Canute, King of Denmark, conquered England. The Atherlings had to leave. Margaret and her brother Edgar went to Germany, and then to the Court of Hungary; probably Livingus came back with them after Canute and his son died. Buchanan says it is a Saxon name, and that he got lands in West Lothian, and named his place Livingston, i. e., the dwelling place of Livingus.

His son, Thurstanus, witnessed the charter of Holyrood House, 1127. He had two sons, Alexander and William. Alexander was the first to take the name Livingston, from the name of his place; a regular Scandinavian custom. Thurstanus is a Scandinavian name, from Thor, God of Thunder.

Thurstanus and Livingus are Latinized forms of Teutonic names.

That the Hudson River Livingstons are descended from the above is a matter of fact, I believe. Father and Philip Livingston (one of the Hudson River Livingstons) who were members of the Legislature together, [New York Legislature, 1820] and great friends, came to the conclusion that they were distantly connected.—James Livingston.

It is said by some antiquaries that the head of this noble family was a Hungarian gentleman who came to Scotland with Margaret, Queen of Malcolm Canmore, about 1070. Their immediate ancestor, Livingus, flourished in the reign of Alexander I. and of his brother, David I. He possessed a considerable estate in West Lothian, called Livingston. His son, Thurstanus, "filius Livingi," witnessed the foundation charter of Holyrood House, 1128, and was father of Alexander Livingston, who first assumed the surname, Livingston. He left a son, Sir William Livingston, who had three sons:

(1) William Livingston, from whom descended the Livingstons of Livingston, the last of whom, Sir Bartholomew Living-

ston, fell at Floddon, in 1513, leaving three daughters and co-heirs.

(2) Sir Archibald Livingston, of whom we treat.

(3) Adam Livingston.

Sir Archibald Livingston was father of:

Sir William Livingston, who married a daughter of Sir John Edskine, and left a son and heir:

Sir William Livingston, who accompanied King David II. in his expedition to England in 1346; was knighted under the royal banner; and taken prisoner at the battle of Durham, October 17, 1346. He had a grant of the Barony of Calender, whose only daughter and heir, Christian, he married. His only remaining son and successor,

Sir William Livingston, died during the time of King Robert II., leaving a son,

Sir John Livingston, of Calender, who married, first, a daughter of Menteth of Carse, and had issue:

(1) Sir Alexander Livingston, his heir.

(2) Robert Livingston, ancestor of the Livingstons of Westquarter, and the Livingstons of Kynnaird, Earls of Newburgh.

(3) John Livingston, ancestor of the Livingstons of Bonton.

He married, secondly, Agnes, daughter of Sir James Douglas, of Dalkeith, and by her had a son,

(4) William Livingston, ancestor of the Viscounts Kilryth.

The eldest son,

Sir Alexander Livingston, of Calender, having passed through numerous political troubles and suffering imprisonment, was eventually restored to royal favor and appointed Justiciary of Scotland, and sent as Ambassador to England in 1449. He married a daughter of Dundas, of Dundas, and was succeeded by his eldest son,

Sir James Livingston, of Calender, County Stirling, who had the appointment of Captain of the Castle of Stirling, with the tuition of the young King James II. committed to him by his father, and was afterwards (previous to August 30, 1450,) created a peer of Scotland as Lord Livingston. He died about 1467. He had issue:

(1) James Livingston, second Lord Livingston.

(2) Alexander Livingston, father of John Livingston, third Lord Livingston.

(3) Elizabeth, married to John, Earl of Ross, Lord of the Isles.

(4) Eupheme, married, first, Malcolm, son and heir of Robert, Lord Fleming; secondly, to William Fleming of the Bord.

The elder son,

James Livingston, second Lord Livingston, married, first, a daughter of Sir John Erskine, of Kinnoul; secondly, a daughter of Sir Robert Crighton; thirdly, Agnes Houston, but dying without issue, was succeeded by his nephew,

John Livingston, third Lord Livingston, who married, first, Elizabeth, daughter of Robert, Lord Fleming, by whom he had a son,

William, fourth Lord Livingston.

He married, secondly, a daughter of Sir John Houston, of Houston, by whom he had another son,

Alexander, ancestor of the Livingstons, of Glentirran, whose male line is extinct.

Lord Livingston died before 1510, and was succeeded by his son,

William Livingston, fourth Lord Livingston, who married Agnes, daughter of Adam Hepburn, the youngest of Hales, by whom he had a son and two daughters:

(1) Alexander Livingston, the fifth Lord Livingston.

(2) Margaret Livingston, married to John, fourth Lord Hay of Yester.

(3) Isobel Livingston, married to Nicol Ramsey, of Dalhousie.

The son and heir,

Alexander Livingston, fifth Lord Livingston, was appointed an extraordinary Lord of Sessions in 1542, and accompanied Queen Mary to France, in 1548, and died there in 1553. He married, first, Janet Stewart, who died without issue; and, secondly, Lady Agnes Douglas, daughter of John, second Earl of Morton, by whom he had seven children:

(1) John, Master of Livingston; slain at Pinkie; died without issue.

(2) William, sixth Lord Livingston.

(3) Thomas, ancestor of the Livingstons of Haining.

(4) Elizabeth, married to John Buchanan.

(5) Janet, married to Sir Archibald Bruce of Airth.

(6) Magdalan, married, first, to Sir Alexander Erskine of Gogar; secondly, to John Scrymgeour of Gloster.

(7) Mary, maid of honor to Queen Mary, and "one of the four Maries," married in 1567, to John Sepill of Beltrees.

The elder surviving son,

William Livingston, sixth Lord Livingston, fought for Queen

Mary at Langside. He married Agnes Fleming, second daughter of Malcolm, third Lord Fleming, and had issue:

(1) Alexander, his heir.

(2) John, died young.

(3) Henry, died young.

(4) George of Ogleface, County Linlithgow, created in 1625 a Baronet of Nova Scotia. (Now extinct.)

This family succeeded to the representation of the Earls of Linlithgow and Calender.

(5) William of Westquarter.

(6) Joe.

(7) Margaret.

Lord Livingston died in 1592, and was succeeded by his son,

Alexander Livingston, seventh Lord Livingston, who was created Earl of Linlithgow, Lord Livingston and Calender, 1600. He married Lady Eleanor Hay, only daughter of Andrew, seventh Earl of Erroll, and had issue:

(1) John, Master of Livingston.

(2) Alexander, who succeeded his father as Earl of Linlithgow.

(3) James, who was created Earl of Calender.

(4) Anne, married to Alexander, sixth Earl of Eglington.

(5) Margaret, married to John, second Earl of Wigton.

The Earl died April 2, 1622, and was succeeded by his son,

Alexander, second Earl of Linlithgow, who was appointed an extraordinary Earl of Sessions, January 13, 1610. He married, first, Lady Elizabeth Gordon, second daughter of George, first Marquis of Huntley, and by her, who died in childbed of her son, at Edinburgh, July, 1616, had issue:

George, his heir.

He married, secondly, Lady Mary Douglas, eldest daughter of William, tenth Earl of Angus, by whom also he had issue:

(1) Alexander, who succeeded his uncle as second Earl of Calender under the special remainder of his Patent.

(2) Margaret, married to Sir Thomas Nicholson, of Carnock; secondly, to Sir George Stirling of Kier; thirdly, to Sir John Stirling of Kier.

(3) Eleanor, died unmarried.

The elder son,

George Livingston, third Earl of Linlithgow, born July, 1616, was implicated in Sir James Montgomery's plot for the restoration of the abdicated royal family. He married, July 30, 1650, Lady Elizabeth Maule, second daughter of Patrick, first Earl of Panmore, dowager of John, second Earl of Kinghorn, and by her (who died at Castle Huntley, in October, 1659) had issue:

(1) George, fourth Earl of Linlithgow.

(2) Alexander, succeeded his uncle as third Earl of Calender, which uncle had also inherited from an uncle, the title of Calender being thus borne by the second son of this family for three generations in succession.

(3) Henriet, married in July, 1666, to Robert, second Viscount of Oxford.

The Earl died February 1, 1690, and was succeeded by his son,

George Livingston, fourth Earl of Linlithgow, who was sworn a privy councillor in 1692, and appointed one of the Commissioners of the Treasury. He married Henriet Sutherland, but had no issue. He died August 7, 1695, when his title succeeded to his nephew,

James Livingston, fourth Earl of Calender, son of Alexander Livingston, third Earl of Calender. Engaging in the rebellion of 1715, the Earl of Linlithgow and Calender was attainted of high treason, and his estate and honors forfeited to the crown. He married Lady Margaret Hay, second daughter of John, twelfth Earl of Erroll, and by her had a son,

James, Lord Livingston, who died April 13, 1715, and a daughter,

Anne, who was married to William, fourth Earl of Kilmarnock, and their eldest son, James, succeeded in her right to the Earldom of Erroll.

The great Calender property (first sold to the York Buildings Company, a London corporation) was purchased eventually, about 1780, by William Forbes, Esq.

Though "the strongholds of the Livingstons are in ruins in Scotland," a flourishing branch of the family still remains in high honor and distinction in the United States of America.—Burke's Extinct Peerage.

Sir Alexander Livingston, of West quarter, County Stirling, succeeded as eleventh baronet, on the decease of his uncle, April 1, 1853.

Sir Alexander is Keeper of the Royal Palace of Linlithgow and of the Castle of Blackness, and is heir representative of the attainted Earl of Linlithgow.

LINEAGE.

William, the sixth Lord Livingston, died in 1592. His fourth son,

(1) The Hon. George Livingston, of Ogleface, County Linlithgow, was created a Baronet of Nova Scotia, May 30, 1625, and was succeeded by his eldest son,

(2) Sir William Livingston, who was succeeded by his son,

(3) Sir Alexander Livingston, who was succeeded by his only son,

(4) Sir Alexander Livingston, designated of Bedlermie, who married Susanah Walker, heir of Bedlermie, and was succeeded by his only son,

(5) Alexander Livingston. This gentleman married Henrietta, daughter of Alexander Scott, Esq., by whom he had seven sons and three daughters, and was succeeded by his eldest son,

(6) Sir George Livingston, at whose decease without issue, in 1729, the baronetcy devolved upon his brother,

(7) Sir Alexander Livingston, who died unmarried in 1766, and was succeeded by his brother,

(8) Sir William Livingston, designated of Westquarter and Bedlermie. This gentleman, dying without issue, in 1769, was succeeded by his nephew,

(9) Sir Alexander Livingston, who married, first, Anne, daughter of John Atkinson, Esq., of London, by whom he had seven sons and one daughter, Ann, (who married the Rev. John Fenton, rector of Ousby and Torpenhow, Cumberland, and had issue: 1, John; 2, Alexander; 3, Robert; 4, George, in holy orders; 5, Anne, married William-Henry Clarke, Esq., of Hexham House, Northumberland, and had two sons, Clement-Henry and Livingston; 6, Caroline, married to her cousin, Robert Fenton, Esq.; 7, Mary.)

Sir Alexander married, secondly, Jane, daughter of the Hon. Captain Cranston, son of Lord Cranston, by whom he had two sons and a daughter.

Sir Alexander Livingston died in 1795, and was succeeded by the third, but eldest, surviving son of his first marriage,

(10) Sir Thomas Livingston, Admiral of the White; married in 1809, Janet, only surviving daughter of the late Sir James Stirling, Bart. of Mansfield, by whom (who died in 1831) he had no issue. Sir Thomas Livingston died April 1, 1853, and was succeeded by his nephew,

(11) Sir Alexander Livingston, of Westquarter, as above. —Burke's Peerage and Baronetcy. 1855.

Sir Alexander, the ninth baronet, designated of that ilk, Westquarter and Bedlermie, in 1784, laid before Lord Kenyon, then Attorney-General, a case respecting his claim to the attainted conjunct titles of Earl of Linlithgow and Earl of Calender. He was twice married. By his first wife he had, with one daughter, seven sons, and by his second, two sons and one daughter. He died in 1795. Two of his sons, George-Augustus and David, were killed in battle. Sir Thomas, his third son, became the tenth baronet. He entered the navy in 1782, and commanded the Diadem in the expedition against Quiberon and Belleisle in 1800. In 1806-7 he was employed in the Mediterranean. In 1848 he attained the rank of Admiral of the Blue. He was appointed Keeper of the Royal Palace of Linlithgow and the Castle of Blackness, by the King, in consideration of his being the male heir and representative of the hereditary governors of these places. He married, in 1809, the daughter of Sir James Stirling, baronet, and died April 1, 1853, without issue.

His brother, Thurstanus Livingston, born in 1770 or 1772, went to sea, as common sailor, both in the merchant service and in the navy, and was discharged in 1797, in consequence of his wounds. Taking up his residence at Bethnal Green, London, he married, the same year, Susanah Brown, a widow, who died in 1806. Two years afterwards he married her sister, Catherine Ann Ticehurst, also a widow. By the latter he had a son, Alexander, born in 1809, who, on the death of his uncle, in 1853, assumed the title of Sir Alexander, as eleventh baronet, and took possession of the estates. The tenth baronet's sister, the wife of Rev. John Fenton, rector of Ousby, and vicar of Torpenew, in Cumberland, instituted two suits in the Court of Session, disputing Sir Alexander's legitimacy and his right to the succession, on the ground that, according to the law of Scotland, the marriage of his father with his deceased wife's sister was not lawful. The court held that the domicile of Thurstanus Livingston, during both his marriages, having been in England, the legitimacy of his son must be decided by the laws of England. The case was appealed to the House of Lords, by Mr. John Fenton, Mrs. Fenton's son, that lady having died July 15, 1859, when their lordships reversed that judgment, and remitted to the Court of Session to decide the question according to the law of Scotland. The case again came before the Court of Session January 18, 1861, when it was unanimously decided that the marriage of Alexander's parents was incestuous and illegal, and giving a decree for the pursuer. Sir Alexander Livingston died at Edinburgh, January 20, 1859.—Anderson's Scottish Nation.

LIVINGSTON, the name of a family various members of which have been distinguished in American history. John Livingston, born in 1603, the common ancestor of the family, and a lineal descendant of the fifth Lord Livingston, ancestor of the Earls of Linlithgow and Calender, was an energetic preacher of the Reformed Church in Scotland, and, having been banished in 1663 for nonconformity to prelatical rule, took refuge in Rotterdam, where he died in 1672. Of his seven children, his son Robert, born in 1654, (born in Ancrum, Scotland, December 13, 1654; died in Albany, New York, April 20, 1725) emigrated to New York about 1675, and in 1686 received from Governor Dongan a grant of a large tract of land, which was in 1715 confirmed by a royal charter of George I. erecting the manor and lordship of Livingston, with the privilege of holding a court leet and a court baron, and with the right of advowson to all the churches within its boundaries. This tract embraced large portions of what are now the counties of Dutchess and Columbia, N. Y., and is still known as the Livingston manor, though the greater part of it has long since passed out of the hands of the family. He was a man of influence in the colony, and procured the fitting out of the ship with which Captain Kidd undertook to restrain the excesses of the pirates. He was connected by marriage with the Schuyler family, ("Robert Livingston married Alida, widow of Rev. Nicholas Van Rennsselaer and daughter of Philip Pieterson Schuyler, by whom he had three sons, Philip, Robert and Gilbert") and had three sons, Philip, Robert, and Gilbert, from whom the most distinguished members of the family in America are descended.

(1) PHILIP LIVINGSTON, a signer of the Declaration of Independence, son of Philip, and great-grandson of John Livingston, born in Albany, N. Y., January 15, 1716, died in York, Pennsylvania, June 12, 1778. He graduated at Yale College in 1737, subsequently embarked in business in the city of New York, and in 1754, and several years afterward, served in the capacity of alderman. In 1758 he was returned to the Colonial House of Assembly from the city of New York, and continued a member of that body till 1769, when in consequence of his strong Whig views he was unseated by the Tory majority. He was chosen a member of the first and second Continental Congresses. He subsequently served in the New York Provincial Congress, in the State Assembly and Senate. and at the time of his death was a delegate from New York to the Continental Congress, then sitting in York.

(2) WILLIAM LIVINGSTON, Governor of New Jersey, brother of the preceding, born in the province of New York, in September, 1723, died in Elizabethtown, New Jersey, July 25, 1790. He graduated at Yale College in 1741, and subsequently became an eminent member of the bar in New York and New Jersey. He was elected a delegate to the First Continental Congress from the latter province in 1774, and after the deposition of William Franklin in 1776, succeeded to the office of Governor, which he retained to the close of his life. During the period in which the Jerseys were the principal seat of war he was indefatigable in his efforts to keep the militia in a state of efficiency. In 1787 he was a delegate to the convention which framed the Federal constitution. He was the author of a poem called "Philosophical Solitude," a funeral oration on President Burr, of Princeton College, and a variety of political and miscellaneous tracts.

(3) BROKHOLST LIVINGSTON, a soldier and jurist, son of the preceding, born in New York, November 25, 1757, died in Washington, March 18, 1823. He graduated at Princeton College in 1774, and in 1776 became a member of the family of General Schuyler, whom he attended as aide-de-camp during the operations of the army in the North. He was subsequently attached to the suite of General Arnold with the rank of major, was present at the surrender of Burgoyne, and before leaving the army was promoted to a colonelcy. In 1779 he went to Spain as private secretary to Mr. Jay, who had married his sister. Returning home after three years' absence, he studied law, was admitted to the bar in 1783, was appointed judge of the Supreme Court of the State of New York in January, 1802, and in November, 1806, was raised to the bench of the United States Supreme Court.

(4) ROBERT R. LIVINGSTON, a statesman and jurist, grandson of the second Robert Livingston, born in the city of New York, November 27, 1746, died February 26, 1813. He graduated at King's (now Columbia) College in 1765, studied and practiced law in New York, and in 1773 was appointed recorder of that city, a judicial office of which he was soon deprived on account of his participation in revolutionary measures. He was a member of the Second Continental Congress, and was one of the committee of five appointed to draft the Declaration of Independence. He was prevented from signing that instrument by a necessary absence from Philadelphia; but he furthered the cause with zeal and efficiency throughout the

war, being a member of Congress again in 1780, and Secretary of Foreign Affairs for two years commencing in August, 1781. He was also a leading member of the Kingston convention which framed the first constitution of the State of New York, adopted in April, 1777. He was appointed the first Chancellor of the State, and held the office till 1801, administering the oath of office taken by Washington on first assuming the duties of President, April 30, 1789. In February, 1801, he was appointed Minister Plenipotentiary to France; and in April, 1803, he completed the purchase from that country of the territory of Louisiana. Mr. Monroe had been dispatched as special envoy to assist him in the negotiation, but it was so far advanced before the arrival of the latter that the treaty of cession was signed a few days afterward. Mr. Livingston resigned his post in 1804, and, after traveling over the continent, returned home the next year. During the remainder of his life he was actively engaged in introducing into the State of New York several improvements in agriculture, and in measures for the encouragement of a taste for the fine arts among his countrymen; and he was associated with Robert Fulton in the early experiments in steam navigation.

(5) EDWARD LIVINGSTON, brother of the preceding, an American jurist and statesman, born in Clermont, Columbia county, New York, May 26, 1764, died in Rhinebeck, May 23, 1836. He graduated at Princeton College in 1781, studied law at Albany, and on his admission to the bar in 1785 commenced practice in the city of New York, where at an early age he attained high rank as a jurist and advocate. In 1794 he was elected a representative in Congress from the district including the city of New York, and was re-elected to the following two Congresses, in which he was an opponent of the administration of Washington and Adams upon the various party questions of the period. In March, 1801, he was appointed by Mr. Jefferson United States District Attorney for the State of New York, then composing but one judicial district. He was also elected mayor of the city of New York for two years, commencing in 1801. By virtue of the latter office he was at the same time judge of an important municipal court of record. A volume of reports of his judicial opinions, delivered in that court during the year 1802, edited by himself, was published at New York in 1803. During his mayoralty the city was visited by yellow fever, when his benevolence and intrepidity in remaining at his post nearly cost him his life. He now found his private affairs so

involved, through the fault of others, it is said, that he was unable to pay his debts, including a considerable balance due to the general government. He promptly resigned his office and removed to New Orleans, in hopes to retrieve his fortune by fresh exertions in a new field. In this he succeeded thoroughly, paying his debt to the government in full, principal and interest, and making head against great difficulties, not the least of which was a severe controversy respecting the title which he had acquired to some lands at New Orleans formed by gradual deposits from the annual inundations of the Mississippi River, and called the Batture; a controversy in which, among other opposition, he encountered that of the Federal government under the personal management of Mr. Jefferson himself. This matter was the subject of a special message to Congress of March 7, 1808, and of a pamphlet by the President, as well as of a pamphlet by Mr. Livingston in reply. The latter eventually triumphed in the courts, though the complete pecuniary fruits of the victory only came to his family long after his death. Many years later Mr. Livingston and Mr. Jefferson became heartily reconciled. Soon after his arrival in the territory the Legislature of Louisiana commissioned him to prepare a system of judicial procedure, which was adopted in 1805, and continued in force till 1825, when it was superseded by the new and elaborate code of practice. In 1823 he was appointed, conjointly with Mr. Louis Moreau-Lislet, to revise the civil code of Louisiana, a work which was completed the next year, and substantially ratified by enactment. In 1821 Mr. Livingston had been intrusted solely with the task of preparing a code of criminal law and procedure. The next year he made a report of his plan for this work, which was soon afterward reprinted in London and Paris. The work itself was submitted to the Legislature in 1826, but was never directly acted upon by that body, although by a joint resolution of March 21, 1822, the plan had been approved and its completion "earnestly solicited." However, the author derived from its publication great celebrity, both in America and in Europe. It was published at Philadelphia in 1833, in I vol. 8vo. He had completed his draft in 1824, and a copy had been made for the printer, when both copies were destroyed by fire. The next day, at the age of sixty years, he commenced the reconstruction of the work, and in two years more it was again complete. Upon this performance the best part of Mr. Livingston's fame rests. It is a comprehensive code, or series of codes, of crimes and punishments, of evidence, of procedure, of reform, of prison discipline, and of definitions, and is characterized throughout by the simplicity of its arrangement and by the wisdom and philanthropy of its provisions. It has visibly influenced the legislation of several countries, and portions of it have been enacted entire by the Republic of Guatemala. All these judicial works were required to be prepared in both French and English, and called for the exercise of profound and philosophical knowledge, not only of the laws of England and the United States, but of the French, the Spanish, and the civil law. In 1823, on his retiring from the bar, Mr. Livingston was elected a Representative in Congress from Louisiana, which office he held till 1829, when he was made a United States Senator from the same State. In 1831 he succeeded Mr. Van Buren as Secretary of State of the United States, and in 1833 was appointed by President Jackson Minister to France, where he resided till 1835, managing with success several affairs of more than ordinary importance and difficulty. On his return home he retired to Rhinebeck in his native county. An eloquent eulogy upon his life and works was pronounced by M. Mignet in 1838 before the French Academy of Moral and Political Sciences, of which he had been chosen an associate a few years before. Mr. Livingston was a man of very social tastes, great gayety of manners, and perfection of temper. Amiability and goodness of heart were always the terms first employed in describing his character by those who remembered him. His life by C. H. Hunt, was published in New York in 1864, and his "Complete Works on Jurisprudence," in two volumes, in 1873.

(6) JOHN H. LIVINGSTON, grandson of Gilbert Livingston, born in Poughkeepsie, New York, May 30, 1746, died in New Brunswick, New Jersey, January 20, 1825. He graduated at Yale College in 1762, and began the study of law; but resolving to devote himself to the ministry, he studied theology at Utrecht in Holland, where he received the degree of D. D. in 1770. In the autumn of that year he returned to America, and at once became pastor of the Dutch Church in New York city. In 1775 he was married to his third cousin, the daughter of Philip Livingston; and in 1776, having removed from New York on the occupation of that city by the British, he accepted a call to Albany, where he remained three years. He then preached successively at Kingston and Poughkeepsie, and at the close of the war returned to New York. In 1784 he was appointed by the general synod of America their professor of divinity, but it

was not till 1795 that a regular seminary was opened under his direction at Bedford, Long Island. This establishment was closed after two years for lack of support, and he resumed his labors in New York. In 1807 the professorate was united to Queen's College, New Brunswick, New Jersey, and Dr. Livingston was appointed president and professor of theology. He removed to New Brunswick in 1810, and there passed the rest of his life. His published writings comprise "A Funeral Service;" "Incestuous Marriage," a dissertation on marriage with a sister-in-law (1816); and some occasional pieces. There is a memoir of his life by the Rev. Alexander Gunn (New York, 1829).—The American Cyclopaedia.

ARCHIBALD LIVINGSTON, the ancestor of our branch of the Livingston family in America, was born about 1730, on the Isle of Islay, Argyleshire, Scotland. He was a descendant of the seventh Lord Livingston, Earl of Linlithgow and Calender. He went to the north of Ireland with his parents, and when a young man, about 1751, came to America. He settled in Tappan, Rockland County, New York, where he remained until the spring of 1765, when he moved, with his family, to Washington County, New York, where his family was prominent among the early settlers of that county. He died September 2, 1792, near East Greenwich, Washington County, New York, and is buried in the McNaughton family graveyard, near the residence of Mr. Christie in Greenwich.

Archibald Livingston and Eleanor McNaughton were married November 23, 1756, in Tappan, Rockland County, New York, where their two elder children were born.

Eleanor McNaughton, daughter of Alexander and Mary (McDonald) McNaughton, was born May 5, 1735, on the Isle of Islay, Argyleshire, Scotland; came to America with her father's family in 1738; and died March 7, 1817, at the home of her daughter, Mrs. James Shaw, in East Greenwich, Washington County, New York.

Archibald and Eleanor (McNaughton) Livingston had:

(1) MARY LIVINGSTON, born September 26, 1756; died August 7, 1793.

(2) MARGARET LIVINGSTON, born May 30, 1759; died December 7, 1839.

(3) JEANETTE LIVINGSTON, born February 2, 1767; died February 20, 1853.

(4) ALEXANDER LIVINGSTON, born June 8, 1769; died October 23, 1863.

(5) MOSES LIVINGSTON, born March 2, 1772; died August 24, 1793.

(6) MARIANNE LIVINGSTON, born June 29, 1774; died February 12, 1842.

(7) ELEANOR LIVINGSTON, born August 10, 1777; died April 24, 1855.

(1) MARY LIVINGSTON, eldest daughter of Archibald and Eleanor (McNaughton) Livingston, was born September 26, 1756, at Tappan, Rockland County, New York; was married to William Robertson, of Argyle, Washington County, New York, September 24, 1775; and died August 7, 1793, in Argyle, Washington County, New York.

The descendants of William and Mary (Livingston) Robertson will be given under the head of William Robertson.

(2) Margaret Livingston, second daughter of Archibald and Eleanor (McNaughton) Livingston, was born May 30, 1759, at Tappan, Rockland County, New York, and died December 7, 1839, in Argyle, New York.

John Taylor and Margaret Livingston were married.

John Taylor was a son of Duncan Taylor, Sr., and his wife, Mary Gillis; the latter emigrated from the Isle of Islay, Argyleshire, Scotland, to America in 1738. He died April 16, 1813, aged sixty-five years.

John and Margaret (Livingston) Taylor had:

(1) Duncan Taylor, who married Sarah, a daughter of the Rev. George Mairs, Sr., and had, George M. Taylor, who married a daughter of Henry Warren, of Troy, and his wife, Maria Wilson, of Hebron, New York; John J. Taylor, now a merchant at Argyle, unmarried; Sarah Taylor, who was married to Nathaniel Sylvester, now United States Commissioner at Saratoga Springs, and distinguished for his authorship of "Northern New York," "Valley of the Connecticut," "History of Saratoga County," and other historical works; Mary Elizabeth Taylor, now residing with her brother, John J. Taylor, in the village of Argyle; James Taylor.

(2) John Taylor, Jr., who married Jane Mairs, a sister of the wife of his brother, Duncan, and had two sons, James Taylor, who went into the army of the United States and never returned to Argyle, and John Taylor, now residing at Argyle.

(3) Eleanor Taylor, born January 16, 1786; married to Joseph McCoy, son of William and Nancy McCoy, who was born October 17, 1774, at Salem, New York; died July 17, 1856, and she January 31, 1871, and both are buried in the new cemetery

in the village of Argyle. They had William McCoy, who married a daughter of James Flack, and their son, Taylor McCoy, married a sister of Robert Barkley.

(4) Margaret Taylor, married, first, to David Robertson, and, secondly, to Robert G. Hall.

(5) Jane Taylor, married, first, to John McCoy, and had, Margaret McCoy; John McCoy, Jr.; Archibald McCoy and Mary McCoy. She married, secondly, John Stevenson.

(3) Jeannette Livingston, third daughter of Archibald and Eleanor (McNaughton) Livingston, was born February 2, 1767, at East Greenwich, Washington County, New York, and died February 20, 1853, at Cambridge, Washington County, New York. She was married, first, to James Shaw, of East Greenwich, New York, who died November 24, 1822.

James and Jeannette (Livingston) Shaw had:

Margaret Shaw; Mary L. Shaw; Eleanor L. Shaw.

She married, secondly, William Stevenson, of Cambridge, but had no children by him.

(4) HON. ALEXANDER LIVINGSTON, eldest son of Archibald and Eleanor (McNaughton) Livingston, was born June 8, 1769, in East Greenwich, Washington County, New York, and died October 23, 1863 in the ninety-fifth year of his age. All his life was spent on the farm which had been granted to his father, Archibald Livingston. He was a man of extraordinary ability, and occupied a distinguished position in that county. He was three times elected to the New York Legislature, viz.: 1809, 1812 and 1818, and was a member of the State Constitutional Convention of 1821.

About 1820 he met Philip Livingston of the Hudson River family in Albany, New York; they were both members of the New York Legislature at that time and great friends; they discussed the subject of their relationship and decided that they were distant cousins.

Hon. Alexander Livingston married Elizabeth McDougall, daughter of William and Sarah McDougall, who died February 28, 1853, and had by her:

(1) Sarah Livingston, born August 10, 1807; died.

(2) Robert Livingston, unmarried; died in 1895.

(3) Margaret Livingston, unmarried; died February 17, 1862, aged forty-eight.

(4) Eleanor Livingston, unmarried; died.

(5) Eliza Livingston, unmarried; died December 22, 1881.
(6) James Livingston, unmarried; died in 1895.
(7) Jane Livingston, was married to Isaac Shaw.

(1) Sarah Livingston, daughter of Hon. Alexander and Elizabeth (McDougall) Livingston, was born August 10, 1807, in Washington County, New York, and died in Kansas City, Mo.

Peter Alexander and Sarah Livingston were married January 30, 1834.

Peter Alexander, son of James Alexander, was born February 7, 1806, in Washington County, New York, and died November 28, 1884, in Kansas City, Mo. He with his family arrived in Chicago from Washington County, New York, June 5, 1849; settled in Wheatland, Will County, Illinois; moved from Wheatland to Monmouth, Illinois, in the spring of 1860; moved from Monmouth to Kansas City, Mo., about 1870.

Peter and Sarah (Livingston) Alexander had:

(A) William Alexander, born August 13, 1836; died May 22, 1863.

(B) Edward Livingston Alexander, born February 28, 1838; died September 27, 1891.

(C) James Alexander, born September 9, 1841.

(D) Mary Elizabeth Alexander, born October 14, 1843.

(E) John Miller Alexander, born October 2, 1845; died April 15, 1852.

(F) Isaac S. Alexander, born July 18, 1848.

(A) William Alexander, son of Peter and Sarah (Livingston) Alexander, was born August 13, 1836, in Washington county, New Work. He enlisted in the Union Army in the spring of 1861, Company "F," Seventeenth Infantry. He was killed at the siege of Vicksburg, Miss., May 22, 1863.

(B) Edward Livingston Alexander, son of Peter and Sarah (Livingston) Alexander, was born February 28, 1838, in Washington County, New York, and died September 27, 1891, at Garrison, Montana. Remains buried at Deer Lodge, Montana. He enlisted in the Union Army in the spring of 1861, Company "F," Seventh Illinois Infantry. He was discharged from service on account of sickness. He entered the railway postal service in 1866 and remained in the service until his death.

(C) James Alexander, son of Peter and Sarah (Livingston) Alexander, was born September 9, 1841, in Washington County,

New York. He was long in the railway service in Galesburg and Chicago, and now lives on the "Sunnyside Farm," Greenwood, Missouri.

(F) Isaac S. Alexander, son of Peter and Sarah (Livingston) Alexander, was born July 8, 1848, in Washington County, New York, and now lives at 3928 Belleview avenue, Kansas City, Missouri.

Isaac S. Alexander and Celia Greene were married January 19, 1872, in Monmouth, Illinois.

Celia Green, daughter of Rev. James and Margaret E. (McNair) Greene, was born June 27, 1852.

Isaac S. and Celia (Greene) Alexander had:

(a) William Graham Alexander, born February 9, 1873.

(b) Edward Livingston Alexander, born October 11, 1875; was graduated from the Commercial College in Kansas City in 1896.

(c) James Richard Alexander, born March 10, 1878; was graduated from the Kansas University in 1899; later from the Kansas City Law School.

(d) Roy McNair Alexander, born December 20, 1881.

(e) Marguerite Eleanor Alexander, born January 25, 1886; was graduated from the Kansas City High School in 1904.

(V) Moses Livingston, second son of Archibald and Eleanor (McNaughton) Livingston, was born March 2, 1772, and died August 24, 1793, and is buried with his father and mother in the family burying ground of the McNaughtons, near Christie's, in Greenwich.

(VI) Marianne Livingston, daughter of Archibald and Eleanor (McNaughton) Livingston, was born June 29, 1774, and died February 12, 1842.

Alexander Shaw and Marianne Livingston were married April 7, 1801.

Alexander Shaw, brother of James Shaw, was born in Scotland, and died March 23, 1843, aged seventy-seven years. He owned, lived and died on the farm about half a mile below East Greenwich, and he and his wife are buried in the churchyard at South Argyle. They had:

(1) John Shaw, who married Jennie Harsha. He died at Argyle, August 9, 1844, aged forty-one years. He had one daughter, Jennie, who married Rev. Mr. Anderson, of Pennsylvania.

(2) Archibald Shaw, who married Eliza Cowan, sister of Moses Cowan, of Lake, and of Martha, wife of Anthony McKellor. Their children were: James C. Shaw, former sheriff; Alexander Shaw; Isaac Shaw; Archibald Shaw, Jr.; Jeannette Shaw, who was married to Robert Stewart, of Lake; and Mary Ann Shaw, who died young.

(3) Eleanor Shaw, who was married to Robert G. Hall, and had: Mary Ann Hall, who was married to Robert Shaw; and Margaret Hall, who was married to John Barkley.

(4) Margaret Thompson Shaw, who was married to Simon Newcomb Pratt, September 24, 1863; no issue.

(5) Jeannette Shaw, who was married to William D. Robertson.

(6) Mary Shaw, twin sister of Jeannette Shaw, who was married to Thomas Robertson, son of Archibald Robertson.

(7) James Shaw, who married Anna McCollum.

(8) Isaac Shaw, who married Jane Livingston, youngest daughter of Hon. Alexander Livingston. They had no children and are both dead.

(VII) Eleanor Livingston, youngest daughter of Archibald and Eleanor (McNaughton) Livingston, was born August 10, 1777, at the home of Duncan Taylor, Sr., of Argyle, New York, where the family had stopped on its way home from Burgoyne's Camp. She died April 24, 1855, at East Greenwich.

William McDougall, Jr., and Eleanor Livingston were married August 6, 1798 at East Greenwich.

William McDougall, Jr., son of William McDougall, Sr., of Wigton, Galloway, Scotland. William McDougall, Jr., died June 17, 1819.

William and Eleanor (Livingston) McDougall, Jr., had:

(1) Moses McDougall; died in 1871.

(2) Robert McDougall; died young.

(3) Robert McDougall; second.

(4) Elizabeth McDougall.

(5) Alexander McDougall.

(6) William McDougall; died in Pennsylvania in 1881.

(7) Jane McDougall, who was married to Alexander Robertson, of Salem.

(8) Andrew McDougall; died in 1882, aged sixty-one years.

(9) Archibald McDougall, born July 9, 1817. Lawyer in Salem, N. Y., Colonel of the One-Hundred-Twenty-third New York State Volunteers. Wounded in battle of Dalles, Georgia, May 25, 1863; died June 23, 1863.

Archibald McDougall was educated at the Washington Academy; went to his brother William's, in Pennsylvania; was appointed deputy surveyor by the Surveyor-General of that State on January 31, 1841; studied law in the office of Wilson & Leste, esquires, and was admitted to the practice of law in that State on February 9, 1841, and pursued the practice of his profession at that place till his removal to Salem, New York, in the spring of 1844. On March 15, of the latter year, he was admitted to the bar and commenced the practice of law at Salem. On September 11, 1848, he married Mary Blanchard, born December 19, 1826, daughter of John Blanchard and his wife, Susan Wright, and granddaughter of Hon. Anthony I. Blanchard and his wife, Maria, a daughter of General John Williams and his wife, Susanah Thomas (Turner). He continued to reside in Salem, and became exceedingly active as a member of the Democratic party. He remained in that affiliation till September, 1856, when he joined in the organization of the Republican party, signing the call and attending the convention held at Greenwich on September 22, for that purpose, and to send delegates to the State convention. He became a very active Republican and at the November election, 1856, was elected to the office of District Attorney of Washington County, which position he held till his resignation in 1862, to enter the military service for putting down the rebellion.

He was commissioned as colonel of the One-Hundred-Twenty-Third Regiment New York State Volunteers, and continued such till severely wounded at the battle of Dalles, in Georgia, on May 25, 1863, from which he died on June 23, 1863. He had for a considerable time before his death been in command of the first brigade, first division, of the Twelfth Army Corps, to which his regiment was attached. As colonel and acting brigadier, he had won the respect and affection of all associated with him and was regarded by his superiors and by the administration as among the most energetic and fearless officers in his corps.

Colonel McDougall was survived by his wife, Mary, and four children, viz.:

(A) William McDougall, born March 23, 1854; died February 12, 1886.

(B) Mary McDougall, born March 31, 1856, now residing with her mother at Cambridge.

(C) Jennie McDougall, born August 22, 1859; married Charles M. Davison, Esq., of Saratoga Springs, a son of John M. Davison, of the latter place, and his wife, Sarah S. Walworth, and grandson, on his mother's side, of the distinguished Chancellor Walworth. He and his wife are residing at Saratoga, where he is practicing law.

(D) Grace McDougall, born May 24, 1861; married to Ellsworth Law, son of George Law and his wife, Margaret Scrimger, who was born May 25, 1861. His father, George Law, was the only son of Robert R. Law.—Graves and Graveyards of Washington County, New York. By Hon. James Gibson.

MACNAUGHTON.

The name Nectan is Pictish and comes from nig, wash. It is clear that the MacNaughtons are intruders into Argyle from Pictland.—Alexander MacBain.

The original name of Nectan or Nechtan is Pictish and has been gradually changed to McNaughton. First Nechtan, then Nachtan, then MacNachtan (son of Nachtan), then MacNaughton, then McNaughton.

There were three Pictish Kings named Nechtan.

Nechtan I., 455-479.

Nechtan II., 597-617.

Nechtan III., 709-724; resigned, 724; returned, 728; died, 729.

MACNAUGHTON—Lineage—The genealogy contained in the manuscript discovered by Skene in the collection of the Faculty of Advocates, confirms the ancient origin of this family and puts it beyond a doubt that they were one of the three clans descended from the old Maormors of Moray, sovereigns of the Pictish race, which from the earliest time occupied the district of Moray.—Burke's Peerage. 1900.

MACNAGTON, or MACNAUGHTON, the name of great antiquity in the West of Scotland (Argyleshire), the badge of which was the trailing azalia. The manuscripts of 1450 deduces the descent of the heads of this clan from Nachtan Mor, who is supposed to have lived in the tenth century. The Gaelic name Neachtain is the same as the Pictish Nectan, celebrated in the Pictish Chronicle as one of the great Celtic divisions in Scotland, and the appellation is among the most ancient in the north of Ireland, the original seat of the Cruthen Picts. The parish of Dunnichen, in Forfarshire, derived its name from the Gaelic dun, a hill, and the word Nechtan, the name of a Pictish chief who is traditionally reported to have resided in the parish. According to Buchanan, of Auchmar, the heads of this clan were from ages thanes of Loch Tay, and possessed all the country between the south side of Loch-Fyne and Lochawe, parts of which were Glenira, Glenshira, Glenfine, and other places, while their principal seat was Dunderraw on Loch-Fyne.

In the reign of Robert III., Maurice or Morice MacNaughton had a charter from Colen Campbell of Lochow of sundry lands in Over Lochow, but their first settlement in Argyleshire, in the central parts of which their lands latterly wholly lay, took place long before this. The MacNaughtons are said to have been originally a branch of the tribes of the province of Moray, when united under its maormors. These maormors were the most powerful chiefs in Scotland during the middle ages. When Malcolm the Maiden attempted to civilize the ancient province of Moray, by introducing Norman and Saxon families, such as the Bissets, the Comyns, etc., in the place of the rude Celtic natives whom he expatriated to the south, he gave lands in or near Strathay or Strathspey, to Nachtan of Moray, for those he had held in that province. He had there a residence called Dunnachtan castle. Nisbet describes this Nachtan as "an eminent man in the time of Malcolm IV.," and says that he "was in great esteem with the family of Lochawe, to whom he was very assistant in their wars with the MacDougalls, for which he was rewarded with sundry lands." The family of Lochawe here mentioned were the Campbells.

The MacNaughtons appear to have been fairly and finally settled in Argyleshire previous to the reign of Alexander III., as Gilchrist MacNaughton, styled of that ilk, was by that monarch appointed in 1287, heritable keeper of his castle and island of Frechelan (Fraoch Ellan) on Lochawe, on condition that he should be properly entertained when he should pass that way, whence, a castle embattled was assumed as the crest of the family.

This Gilchrist was father or grandfather of Donald MacNaughton of that ilk, who being nearly connected with the MacDougalls of Lorn, joined that powerful chief with his clan against the Bruce, and fought against the latter at the battle of Dalree in 1306, in consequence of which he lost a greater part of his estates. In Abercromby's "Martial Achievements," (Vol. I. p. 577,) it is related that the extraordinary courage shown by the king in having, in a narrow pass, slain with his own hand several of his pursuers, and amongst the rest three brothers, so greatly excited the admiration of the chief of the MacNaughtons that he became thenceforth one of his firmest adherents.

His son and successor, Duncan MacNaughton of that ilk, was a steady and loyal subject of King David II., who, as a reward for his fidelity, conferred on his son, Alexander, lands in the island of Lewis, a portion of the forfeited possessions of John of the Isles, which the chiefs of the clan MacNaughton held for a time. The ruins of their castle of MacNaughton are still pointed out on that island.

Donald MacNaughton, a younger son of the family, was, in 1436, elected bishop of Dunkeld, in the reign of James I.

Alexander MacNaughton of that ilk, who lived in the beginning of the 16th century, was knighted by James IV., whom he accompanied to the disastrous field of Flodden, where he was slain with nearly the whole chivalry of Scotland. His son, John, was succeeded by his second son, Malcolm MacNaughton of Glenshira, his eldest son having predeceased him. Malcolm died in the end of the reign of James IV., and was succeeded by his eldest son, Alexander.

John, the second son of Malcolm, being of a handsome appearance, attracted the notice of King James VI., who appointed him one of his pages of honor, on his accession to the English crown. He became rich, and purchased lands in Kintyre. He was also sheriff-depute of Argyleshire. His elder brother, Alexander, adhered firmly to the cause of Charles I., and in his service, like all who remained loyal to him, sustained many severe losses. At the Restoration, as some sort of compensation, he was knighted by Charles II., and, unlike many others, he received from that monarch a liberal pension for life. Sir Alexander MacNaughton spent his later years in London, where he died. His son and successor, John MacNaughton, succeeded to an estate greatly burdened with debt, but did not hesitate in his adherence to the fallen fortunes of the Stuarts. At the head of a considerable body of his own clan, he joined the Viscount Dundee, and was slain with him at Killiecrankie. James VII. signed a deed in his favor, restoring to his family all its old lands and hereditary rights, but, as it never passed the seals in Scotland, it was of less value than the paper on which it was written. His lands were taken from him, not by forfeiture, but "the estate," says Buchanan of Auchmar, "was evicted by creditors for sums of money equivalent to its value, and there being no diligence used for relief thereof, it went out of the hands of the family." His son, Alexander, a captain in Queen Anne's guards, was killed in the expedition to Vigo in 1702. His brother, John, at the beginning of the last century was for many years collector of customs at Anstruther in Fife, and subsequently was appointed inspector-general in the same department. The direct male line of the MacNaughton chiefs became extinct at his death.

The chiefship is now in an Irish family, descended from Shane Dhu, grandson of Sir Alexander MacNaughton, slain at Flodden, who went to Ireland in 1580, as secretary to his kinsman, the first Earl of Antrim, and settled there. His son, Daniel MacNaughton, Esq., married Catherine, niece of the celebrated primate, George Dowdall, and their great-grandson, Edmund Alexander MacNaughton, esq., of Beardiville, born August 3, 1762, was M. P. for County Antrim, and lord of the treasury. The clan MacNaughton elected this gentleman and his heirs to the chieftainship. At his decease in 1832, it descended with his family estates to his brother, Sir Francis Workman MacNaughton, born August 2, 1763, educated for the law, and knighted on being appointed a judge of the supreme court of judicature at Madras in 1809. In 1815 he was transferred to that of Bengal, and in 1823 he assumed the additional surname and arms of Workman. He retired from the bench in 1825, and was created a baronet July 16, 1836. He died November 22, 1843. By his wife, the eldest daughter of Sir William Dunkin of Clogher, a judge of the supreme court of judicature, Calcutta, he had six sons and ten daughters. Of the eldest son, in the following paragraph. The second son, William Hay, of the Bengal Civil Service, was created a baronet in 1889. and was assassinated at Cabul, December 25, 1841. Stuart MacNaughton, the youngest son, born June 20, 1815, educated at Edinburgh and Trinity College, Dublin (B. A., 1835), called to the bar at the Middle Temple, 1839; married in 1848, Agnes, daughter of James Eastmont, Esq., of St. Berners, near Edinburgh, and widow of Captain Lewis Shedden.

The eldest son, Sir Edmund Charles Workman MacNaughton of Dunderave, Bushmills, county Antrim, second baronet, born April 1, 1790, M. P. for that county, 1847-1852, married in 1827, Mary, only child of Edward Gwatkin, Esq.; issue, five sons and two daughters. The sons are:

(1) Frances Edmund, major Eighth Hussars, born in 1828.
(2) Edward, barrister-at-law.
(3) William Henry, First Bengal Light Cavalry.
(4) Fergus.
(5) Edmund Charles.

The family spell their name MacNaghton.—Anderson's Scottish Nation.

John MacNaughton, Inverary, member of Scottish Parliament 1685-6.—Scotch-Irish. Hanna.

Clan Nachtan (MacNaughton). Arms. Quarterly. First and fourth—Argent, a hand fess-ways, coupee, proper, holding a cross crosslet, fitchee, azure. Second and third—Argent, a tower embattled, gules. Principal Seat—Dundurraw on Lochfine. Chief. Extinct.—The Highlanders of Scotland. By Skene.

THE ARGYLE GRANT.

It may be well here to give some of the history of the early settlement of Washington county, New York, in which Alexander MacNaughton took a prominent part.

The only move towards counteracting the French advance was an attempt made to settle the territory above the Saratoga patent with a colony of fearless men, who might act as protectors of the lands below. In 1735 a proclamation was issued by the governor inviting "loyal protestant Highlanders" to settle the lands between the Hudson and the northern lakes—the men of the tartan and claymore being considered the best defenders that the province could have. In 1737, Captain Lauchlin Campbell, of Islay, a Highland soldier of distinguished courage, came to America in response to this proclamation, and went over the territory of Washington county to see if a colony could be located there. He was satisfied with the locality, and according to his statement, which was in all probability true, Lieutenant-Governor Clarke (acting governor) promised him a grant of thirty thousand acres for the use of the colony, free of all expense except surveying fees and quitrent.

Campbell returned to Scotland, sold his property there, raised a company of four hundred and twenty-three adults, to come to America, and in 1738 crossed the Atlantic with part of his charge. On his arrival, the governor insisted on his full fees and a share of the land. This Campbell refused to give—the fees he was perhaps unable to give. Governor Clarke pretended to be very anxious to aid the emigrants, and recommended the Legislature to grant them assistance. But the Legislature was, as usual, at war with the governor and refused to vote money to the emigrants, which, they suspected with good reason, the latter would be required to pay to the colonial officials for fees. The members of the colony were obliged to separate to earn their livings.

A full account of this enterprise was set forth by a son of Lauchlin Campbell in a "Memorial to the Lords of Trade," printed in the Documentary and Colonial History of New York, Vol. VII., p. 630, from which the following extract has been made:

To the Right Honorable the Lords Commissioners of Trade, etc., memorial of Lieutenant Donald Campbell of the Province of New York Plantation humbly showeth:

That in the year 1734, Colonel Crosby, being then governor

of the Province of New York, by and with the advice and assent of the Council, published a printed advertisement for encouraging the resort of Protestants from Europe to settle upon the northern frontier of the said province (in the route from Fort Edward to Crown Point) promising to each family two hundred acres of unimproved land out of the one thousand acres purchased from the Indians, without any fee or expense whatever, except a very moderate charge for surveying, and liable only to the King's quitrent of one shilling and nine pence farthing per hundred acres, which settlement would at that time have been of the utmost utility to the province, and these proposals were looked upon as so advantageous that they could not fail of having a proper effect.

That these proposals, in 1737, falling into the hands of Captain Lauchlin Campbell, of the Island of Islay, he the same year went over to North America, and passing through the province of Pennsylvania, where he rejected many considerable offers that were made to him, he proceeded to New York, where, though Governor Crosby was deceased, George Clarke, Esq., then governor, assured him no part of the lands were as yet granted; importuned him and two or three persons that went over with him to go up and visit the lands, which they did, and were very kindly received and greatly caressed by the Indians. On his return to New York, he received the most solemn promises that he should have a thousand acres of land for every family that he brought over, and that each family should have, according to their number, from five hundred to one hundred and fifty acres, but declined making any grant till the families arrived, because, according to the constitution of the government, the names of the settlers were to be inserted in the grant. Captain Campbell accordingly returned to Islay, and brought from thence, at a very large expense, his own family and thirty other families, making in all one hundred and fifty-three souls. He went again to visit the lands, received all possible respect and kindness from the government, who proposed an old fort, Anne, to be repaired, to cover the settlers from the French Indians. At the same time, the people of New York proposed to maintain the people already brought till Captain Campbell could return and bring more, alleging that it would be for the interest of the infant colony to settle upon the lands in a large body; that, covered by the fort, and assisted by the (friendly) Indians, they might be less liable to the incursions of enemies.

That to keep up the spirit of the undertaking, Governor Clarke, by a writing bearing date the fourth day of December,

1738, declared his having promised Captain Campbell thirty thousand acres of land at Wood Creek, free of charges, except the expenses of surveying and the King's quitrent, in consideration of his having already brought over thirty families, who, according to their respective numbers in each family, were to have from one hundred and fifty to five hundred acres. Encouraged by this declaration, he departed in the same month for Islay, and in August, 1740, brought over forty families more; and under the faith of the same promises made a third voyage, from which he returned in November, 1740, bringing with him thirteen families; the whole making eighty-three families, composed of four hundred and twenty-three persons, all sincere and loyal Protestants, and very capable of forming a respectable frontier for the security of the province.

But after all these perilous and expensive voyages, and though there wanted but seventeen families to complete the number for which he had undertaken, he found no longer the same countenance of protection, but on the contrary it was insinuated to him that he could have no land either for himself or the people but upon conditions in direct violation of the faith of the government, and detrimental to those who upon his assurances had accompanied him to America (i. e., that he should bribe the officials for their assistance in securing legislative approval of the grant). The people also were reduced to demand separate grants for themselves, which upon large promises some of them did, yet more of them never had so much as a foot of land, and many listed themselves to join the expedition to Cuba. That Captain Campbell, having disposed of his whole fortune in the Island of Islay, expended the far greatest part of it from confidence in these fallacious promises, found himself at length constrained to employ the little he had left in the purchase of a small farm, seventy miles north of New York, for the subsistence of himself and his family, consisting of three sons and three daughters. He went over again to Scotland in 1745, and having command of a company of Argyleshire men, served with reputation under his Royal Highness, the Duke, against the rebels. He went back to America in 1747, and not long after died of a broken heart, leaving behind him the six children before mentioned, of whom your memorialist is the eldest, in very narrow and distressed circumstances, etc.

In January, 1763, Donald, George, and James Campbell, sons of Lauchlin Campbell, presented a petition asking for a grant of a hundred thousand acres between Batten Kill and Wood

Creek. It is difficult to account for the seeming exorbitance of this request, as under the terms of his contract with Governor Clarke, Lauchlin Campbell would have been entitled to only eighty-three thousand acres. It has been suggested that the Campbells intended, or claimed that they intended, to provide for the descendants of the colonists who had expected to settle under their father's direction. A more probable explanation, in view of what had happened before, would be, that it was designed to use a portion of the grant as a bribe to secure the passage of the act.

The petition was rejected on the ground that the orders of the English government positively forbade the granting of over a thousand acres to any one person. Nevertheless, it was felt that Captain Campbell had been very badly treated, and there was a disposition on the part of the colonial authorities to give some relief to his children. Accordingly, in the autumn of that year, a grant of ten thousand acres in the present township of Argyle, Washington county, was made to the three brothers before named, their three sisters, and four other persons, three of whom were also named Campbell.

On the 2d of March, 1764, Alexander McNaughton and one hundred and six others of the original Campbell immigrants and their descendants petitioned for one thousand acres to be granted to each of them "to be laid out in a single tract between the head of South Bay and Kingsbury, and reaching east towards New Hampshire and westwardly to the mountains in Warren county." The committee and the Council to whom this petition was referred, reported May 21, 1764, recommending that 47,700 acres should be granted to them, between the tract already granted to Schuyler and others (Fort Edward), and the tract proposed to be granted to Turner and others (Salem). The grant was made out in conformity with the recommendation of the Council, and specifies the amount of land that each individual of the petitioners was to receive, two hundred acres being the least and six hundred acres the most that any individual obtained. It also appoints five men as trustees, to divide and distribute the lands as directed. By the same instrument, the tract was incorporated as a township, to be named Argyle, and to have a supervisor, treasurer, collector, two assessors, two overseers of highways, two overseers of the poor, and six constables, to be elected annually by the inhabitants on the first of May.

This grant included a large portion of what is now the northern half of the township of Greenwich, and a portion of the township of Fort Edward.

The townships in which these Scottish Highlanders settled were directly west of what is now Salem township, Washington county. Settlements were made in the latter township early in the year 1762, by James Turner, Alexander Conkey, and others, who had come from the Scotch-Irish colony of Pelham, in Massachusetts, to which reference has already been made. Salem township consists largely of the tract of twenty-five thousand acres granted, August 7, 1764, to James Turner and others. One-half of the land covered by the patent, however, in accordance with a not uncommon custom of the time, became the property of Oliver De Lancy and Peter DuBois, two government officials, whose services presumably aided in securing the grant. DeLancy and DuBois sold their share of the land in 1765 to Rev. Thomas Clarke and his Scotch-Irish congregation, who had emigrated the year before from Ballybay, county Monaghan, Ireland. Mr. Clark, a native of Scotland, was a follower of Ebenezer Erskine, and in 1748 had been called as their minister by a portion of Mr. Jackson's congregation in Ireland, which had seceded from the main body. At Ballybay he is said to have labored with great success, but amid many trials and persecutions. He refused to take an oath by "kissing the book," believing it to be unscriptural; and although he entered the army while a student, and fought against the Pretenders, yet he would not take the Oath of Abjuration, because it recognized the King as the head of the Church. Taking advantage of these things, some of his enemies had him arrested by the civil authorities in 1754, and he was imprisoned in the jail at Monaghan. From his place of confinement he preached every Sabbath to as many of his people as could convene. When the day of his trial came, it appeared that he had been imprisoned on a fraudulent charge, and he was released. In 1763 Mr. Clark received invitations to visit two settlements in America, one in Rhode Island and the other near Albany. Wearied with his contendings he regarded these calls favorably, and his Presbytery gave him leave of absence for one year. But when he came to sail from Newry on May 16, 1764, it was found that the greater part of his congregation, some three hundred persons, were ready to sail with him. They all embarked together, and after arriving in New York settled temporarily at Stillwater. Thence a portion of his parishioners removed to Abbeville district, South Carolina, but a majority of them settled with Mr. Clark at Salem. His pastoral relation had never been disturbed; his church had simply been transplanted; and he continued at Salem as the pastor of the eight ruling elders and one hundred and fifty communicants and their children, who had come with him from Ballybay. He resigned his ministry at Salem in 1782, and three years later removed to Abbeville district, where he was installed as minister of Cedar Spring and Long Cane congregations, dying there in 1792.—Scotch-Irish. By Hanna.

Few families in Washington county can trace a more ancient lineage than the McNaughtons, as it can readily be followed back for more than eight hundred years.

Among the first of the clan to come to this country was Alexander McNaughton of Argyleshire, landing in the city of New York in 1738, being in the company of Lauchlin Campbell, which immigrated that year.

He was the first settler of the name in this country, which he always wrote ALEXANDER M'NACHTEN—this is "Alexander, the son of Nachten"—that being the family name of the race, traced back for more than eight hundred years. He was born in Argyleshire, in Islay, the most southern island of the Hebrides, and immigrated in the first company brought over by Lauchlin Campbell, landing in the city of New York, July, 1738. Not obtaining the promised grant of lands on which to settle in this country, he and family, with many others of his associate colonists, settled at New Windsor in Orange county, and there remained till his removal in 1764 to the Argyle patent.

In the grant of the Argyle patent, as finally made in 1764, a trust was created for the benefit of all the settlers who came to this county in the companies brought over by Lauchlin Campbell in 1738, 1739 and 1740, or the descendants of such of them as had died, or those of their families surviving. In this trust Alexander McNaughton was the presiding trustee and the affairs and management of the trust were largely under his direction. In order to provide for the expenses of the surveying and allotment of the lands, an assessment was made according to the number of acres allotted, and on receiving his deed the grantee would pay his share of the expenses. But as some of the parties or immigrants entitled to shares never came forward to receive their deeds and pay their portion of the expenses, all such shares were sold and conveyances made to the purchasers. In this way, persons not of the original immigrants became owners of shares in the Argyle patent. And indeed there were cases where the conveyance was made, and the expenses paid, but the grantee never claimed the lands, and those who did actually occupy, had possession without title.

In this connection an explanation may be made of how the patent received the name of Argyle. The common statement that it was originally granted to the Duke of Argyle, and that he parcelled it out among his clan, is without the slightest foundation. The Duke of Argyle had nothing whatever to do with the grant of the patent, or with its allotment or settlement. The whole subject is a matter of history and it is difficult to see how such a story originated. The learned and distinguished author of the "History of Washington County" (we refer to Dr. Asa Fitch, now deceased) explained this fable more than forty years ago. (See Fitch's History, Section 76.)

Lauchlin Campbell, a native of Islay, which forms part of Argyleshire in Scotland, had received encouragement from the provincial authorities of New York, that if he would procure the immigration to the province of a number of families from Scotland, those brought over by him should receive a grant of lands, free of expense, sufficient to enable them to obtain a support. The object of the government of New York, in this matter, was to procure the settlement of that portion of this county lying south of what is now Whitehall, and on the borders of Wood Creek, and form a barrier against French and Indian invasion from Canada by way of Lake Champlain. In pursuance of this encouragement, Campbell procured the immigration, in 1738, of a colony from Argyleshire, consisting of thirty-three families and forty-nine single persons, making in all 177 persons. In 1739 he, in like manner, procured an immigration of forty-two families and twenty-four single persons, making in all 193 persons. And in 1740, he obtained fifteen families and forty-six single persons in addition, making together 100 persons. The immigration having been obtained, all solicitude on the part of the Provincial authorities to fulfill the promises made to Campbell in their behalf wholly ceased, and no grant of lands for their settlement was made and they were left to take care of themselves as best they could.

The colonists thus introduced, suffered great hardships for many years, and this seems to have finally shamed those having control to make the grant of lands as originally promised. In the meantime, the lands about Whitehall and Wood Creek had been granted to others, and were included in the Skenesborough and Artillery patents, and could not, therefore, be granted to the Scottish settlers. The lands in the Argyle patent were therefore granted in their place. Thus, after the lapse of over twenty years, the settlers, or their descendants, who came over under the offers made to Lauchlin Campbell, received a grant of those lands in part fulfillment of the original promises made to him. This grant was made by the Governor and Council of the Province of New York, by patent to Alexander McNaughton and others, in trust, to be allotted among those settlers and their descendants. The patent was issued in the usual form of such grants and in the same form and manner as Skenesborough and other patents located in this section were issued.

This much for the story of the Duke of Argyle granting or receiving a grant of the patent. The name of Argyle was given because the settlers were all from the shire of Argyle in Scotland.

Alexander McNaughton settled on that portion of the patent which now lies in the town of Greenwich, and on the farm which was long after occupied by Deacon Samuel Dobbin as a homestead. Here he built a common log house in 1764, and a few years after another of squared logs. He was appointed a justice of the peace, and was the first appointed on the Argyle patent to that office. His only associates in that dignity in the whole territory now composing the county of Washington, were Colonel Skene, at Skenesborough, and John Monro, Esq., Cambridge.

It was while acting as such justice that he was summoned to New Perth, as Salem was then called, to enforce the law against Ethan Allen and his ruffianly associates, who had by force of arms raided the lands granted to Charles Hutchan, Donald Campbell and others in the northwest corner of the present town of Salem and torn off the roofs from their log houses, and by threats compelled the occupants to leave the premises.—Graves and Graveyards of Washington County, N. Y. By Hon. James Gibson.

Alexander McNaughton was born on the Isle of Islay, Argyleshire, Scotland, and in 1738 came to America, accompanied by his wife, Mary (MacDonald) McNaughton, and his children, John, Moses, Jeannette and Eleanor, and settled in Orange county, New York, where they resided several years, then removed to Tappan, Rockland county, New York, where they remained until their removal to Washington county in the same state in 1765.

Alexander McNaughton was one of the five original trustees of the Argyle patent, a grant of nearly fifty thousand acres of land given to the Scotch colonists who settled in Washington county, New York, and he had charge of surveying the land and its division among the colonists.

He was the first Justice of the Peace on the Argyle patent, and an arrest made under a warrant issued by Justice McNaughton was the first civil process ever served in Washington county. His farm of six hundred acres was in that part of Argyle, now the town of Greenwich, where Alexander McNaughton resided until the death of his wife in 1777; the remaining years of his life were spent with his daughter Mary, who was married to Judge Edward Savage, of Salem, New York, where he died about 1786, and was buried in the McNaughton burial ground on his own farm.

[Mary MacDonald, his wife, was married, first, to MacEwen; secondly, to Alexander McNaughton. She was a granddaughter of Sir James MacDonald, second Baronet of Slate, and, I believe, was a daughter of Sir Donald MacDonald, third Baronet of Slate, by his wife, Lady Mary Douglas, daughter of Sir Robert Douglas, tenth Earl of Morton; though she may have been the daughter of one of the other sons of Sir James MacDonald, second Baronet of Slate. See MacDonald, p. 95.—Ed.]

Mary (MacDonald) McNaughton died about August 10, 1777, at the home of Duncan Taylor, Sr., in Argyle, New York, where the family had stopped on its way home from Burgoyne's Camp, whither they had gone for protection after the Indian depredations in Washington county. She was buried beside her daughter, Jeannette Brown, in the Old Argyle Cemetery, and afterwards, Mary Livingston, wife of William Robertson, was laid beside her.

Alexander and Mary (MacDonald) McNaughton had:

(1) John McNaughton, born in Argyleshire, Scotland, and married Margaret, daughter of Duncan Taylor, Sr., of Argyle, New York. She died in December, 1769, leaving a large family. He died in the town of Greenwich, Washington county, New York, about 1800.

(2) Moses McNaughton was the schoolmaster in the family and taught the other children under the supervision of his mother. He died at Tappan before the removal of the family to Washington county.

(3) Jeannette McNaughton was married to Archibald Brown, and died June 22, 1770, leaving no children. Her remains were the first interred in the Old Argyle Cemetery; the land occupied by the cemetery was part of her husband's farm.

(4) ELEANOR McNAUGHTON, born May 5, 1735, in Argyleshire, Scotland, was married to Archibald Livingston, and

their eldest daughter, Mary Livingston, was married to William Robertson, of Argyle, New York.

(5) Mary McNaughton, born in 1742, at New Windsor, Orange county, New York, and was married in December, 1770, to Hon. Edward Savage, of Salem, New York, and their son, John Savage, became Chief Justice of New York.

Edward Savage held various offices. He was Sheriff of Charlotte county; Surrogate of Washington county; Judge of the Court of Common Pleas; member of the Legislature nearly twenty years, and elder in the Presbyterian church nearly forty years. In all, he acquitted himself with honor.—Miss Jennie M. Patten.

In a letter to your publisher, Mrs. Mary H. Field, of New York City, great-granddaughter of the Hon. Edward Savage, writes:

" * * * I, too, am glad to know of a new cousin. To be sure, cousins are not a scarce commodity—a random snap-shot at any crowd I fancy is likely to bring one down—but having no instinct to help in the matter of finding them, we have to go in blissful ignorance.

"In our case, however, we know that our little great-grandmothers 'grew in beauty side by side.' I have a good picture of my great-grandmother, Mary McNaughton Savage, taken in her beautiful old age. I was named for her, and I have my mother's letter written to my venerable ancestress to inform her of the fact. My grandfather, who married Jane Savage, used to tell me that my Great-grandmother Savage was a fine, sensible woman; a spirited talker and a great story-teller; I think her sister Eleanor had the same characteristics. As to my Great-grandfather Savage, my father used to say emphatically, 'He was the best man I ever knew.'

"Of course, you know Dr. O. W. Holmes' 'Dorothy Q.' How admirably he touches in that poem the subtle problems of heredity:

DOROTHY Q.—A FAMILY PORTRAIT.

"O Damsel Dorothy! Dorothy Q.!
Strange is the gift that I owe to you;
Such a gift as never a king
Save to daughter or son might bring—
All my tenure of heart and hand,
All my title to house and land;
Mother and sister and child and wife
And joy and sorrow and death and life!

"What if a hundred years ago
Those close-shut lips had answered No,
When forth the tremulous question came
That cost the maiden her Norman name,
And under the folds that look so still
The bodice swelled with the bosom's thrill?
Should I be I, or would it be
One tenth another, to nine tenths me?

"Soft is the breath of a maiden's Yes;
Not the light gossamer stirs with less;
But never a cable that holds so fast
Through all the battles of wave and blast,
And never an echo of speech or song
That lives in the babbling air sò long!
There were tones in the voice that whispered then
You may hear today in a hundred men.

"O lady and lover, how faint and far
Your images hover—and here we are,
Solid and stirring in flesh and bone—
Edward and Dorothy—all their own—
A goodly record for time to show
Of a syllable spoken so long ago!—
Shall I bless you, Dorothy, or forgive
For the tender whisper that bade me live?"

LORD OF THE ISLES.

Isles, the Lord of, an ancient title, possessed by the descendants of Somerled, thane of Argyle, who, in 1135, when David I. expelled the Norwegians from Arran and Bute, and some other of the islands, appears to have got a grant of them from that monarch. To secure himself in possession, however, he married, about 1140, Effrica, or Ragnhildis, the daughter of Olave the Red, king of Man, from which marriage sprung the dynasty so well known in Scottish history as the Lords of the Isles. By her he had three sons, Dugall, Reginald or Ranald, and Angus. The Chronicles of Man adds a fourth, Olave. By a previous marriage he had one son, Gillecolane. According to the Celtic genealogists, this Somerled (the name is Norse, in Gaelic Somhairle, in English, Samuel) was descended, through a long line of ancestors, from the celebrated Irish king, Conn Chead Chath, or Conn of the Hundred Battles. He assisted his son-in-law, Wimund, the pretended Earl of Moray, when he invaded Scotland in 1141, and on the death of David I., accompanied by the children of Wimund, he landed with a great force in Scotland, November 5, 1153, in order to revenge the wrongs done him. Having, however, encountered a more vigorous opposition than he had anticipated, he found it necessary to agree to terms of accommodation with Malcolm IV., an event which was deemed of so much importance as to form an epoch from which various royal charters were dated.

His brother-in-law, Godfred the Black, King of Man, had acted so tyrannically that Thorfinn, one of the most powerful of the insular nobles, resolved to depose him, and applied to Somerled for his son, Dugall, then a child, whom he proposed to make king of the isles in Godfred's place. Carrying Dugall through all the isles, except Man, Thorfinn forced the inhabitants to acknowledge him as their king, and took hostages from them for their obedience. One of the chief islanders fled to the Isle of Man, and informed Godfred of the plot against him. The prince immediately collected a large fleet, and proceeded against the rebels, then under the guidance of Somerled, with a fleet of eighty galleys. After a bloody but undecided battle (1156) a treaty was entered into, by which Godfred ceded to the sons of Somerled what were afterwards called the South Isles, retaining for himself the North Isles and Man. Two years afterwards,

Somerled invaded the latter island with a fleet of fifty-three ships, and laid the whole island waste, after defeating Godfred in battle.

Somerled's power was now very great, and for some time he carried on a vexatious predatory warfare on the coasts of Scotland, till Malcolm required him to resign his possessions into his hands as sovereign, and to hold them in future as a vassal of the Scottish crown. Somerled refused, and in 1164, assembling a numerous army, he sailed up the Clyde with 160 galleys, and landed his forces near Renfrew, where he was met by the Scots army, under the high steward of Scotland, and defeated, he himself and his son Gillecolane being among the slain. According to tradition, he was assassinated in his tent by an individual in whom he placed confidence. This celebrated chief has been traditionally described as "a well tempered man, in body shapely, of a fair, piercing eye, of middle stature, and of quick discernment." According to the then prevalent custom of gavel king, whilst Gillecolane's son, also named Somerled, succeeded to his grandfather's superiority of Argyle, the insular possessions were divided among his sons descended of the house of Man. Dugall, the eldest of them, got for his share, Mull, Coll, Tiree, and Jura; Reginald, the second son, obtained Isla and Kintyre; and Angus, the third son, Bute. Arran is supposed to have been divided between the two latter. The Chronicle of Man mentions a battle, in 1192, between Reginald and Angus, in which the latter obtained the victory. He was killed in 1210, with his three sons, by the men of Skye, leaving no male issue. One of his sons, James, left a daughter and heiress, Jane, afterwards married to Alexander, son and heir of Walter, High Steward of Scotland who, in her right, claimed the Isle of Bute.

Both Dugall and Reginald were called Kings of the Isles at the time that Reginald, the son of Godfred the Black, was styled King of Man and the Isles; and in the next generation we find in a Norse chronicle, mention made of three Kings of the Isles, of the race of Somerled, existing at one time. It is evident, therefore, says Mr. Gregory, that the word king, as used by the Norwegians and their vassals in the Isles, was not confined, as in Scotland, to one supreme ruler, but that it had with them an additional meaning, corresponding either to prince of the blood, or to magnate. On Dugall's death, the isles that had fallen to his share, instead of descending immediately to his children, were acquired by his brother, Reginald.

From Dugall sprang the great house of the MacDugalls of

Lorn, who styled themselves de Ergadie or of Argyle. He left two sons, Dugal Scrag and Duncan, who, in the northern Sagas, bear the title of the Suderyan kings. Dugal was taken prisoner by Haco, King of Norway, but of the history of Duncan nothing is known, except that he founded the priory of Ardchattan in Lorn.

Reginald had two sons, Donald and Roderick. From Donald, who appears to have inherited the Isles, sprang the great family of Isla, patronymically styled MacDonald.

MacDONALD.

MacDONALD, the name of a numerous and widespread clan, divided into several tribes, which derived its general name from Donald, elder son of Reginald, second son of Somerled of Argyle, King of the Isles.

The distinctive badge of this clan was the bell-heath.

They formed the principal branch of the Siol-Cuinn, or race of Conn, their great founder, Somerled, being supposed by the Sennachies of Celtic genealogists, to have been descended from an early Irish King, called Conn of the Hundred Battles. Although a Norwegian extraction has been claimed for them, their own traditions invariably represent the MacDonalds as of Pictish descent, and as forming part of the great tribe of the Gall-gael, or Gaelic pirates, who in ancient times inhabited the coasts of Argyle, Arran and Man. The latter is Mr. Skene's opinion. (History of the Highlanders. Vol. II, p. 38) The antiquity is undoubted, and one of their own name traces it back to the sixth century. Sir James MacDonald of Kintyre, in a letter addressed, in 1615, to the Bishop of the Isles, declares that his race "has been tenne hundred years Kyndlie Scottismen under the Kings of Scotland."—Anderson's Scottish Nation.

MacDonald Arms. Quarterly. First—Or, a lion rampant, azure, armed and languid, gules. Second—A dexter hand coupee, holding a crown crosslet, fitchee sable. Third—Or, a ship with her sails unfurled, salterwise, sable. Fourth—A salmon naiant, proper, with a chief waved argent.

Badge, Heath. Principal Seat. Isla. Oldest Cadet. MacAlester of Loup, now Somerville Macalister of Lenox. Chief. The Ranaldson MacDonells of MacDonell and Glengarry, are the unquestionable male representatives of the founder of the clan, and therefore, possess the right of blood to the chiefship.—The Highlanders of Scotland. By Skene.

(I) Somerled, ancient Celtic chief, had three sons:
(1) Dugald, ancestor of the MacDougalls of Lorn.
(2) Reginald, ancestor of the MacDonalds.
(3) Angus.
(II) Donald, son of Reginald.
(III) Angus Mor, son of Donald.
(IV) Angus Og, son of Angus Mor.

(V) John, Lord of the Isles, son of Angus Og, married, secondly, Margaret, daughter of Robert, seventh High Steward of Scotland, afterwards King Robert II., by whom he had three sons:

SIR JAMES MACDONALD, second Baronet of Slate, descendant of John, Lord of the Isles, and his wife, Margaret, daughter of Robert II., joined the Marques of Montrose in 1645, and sent some of his men to the assistance of Charles II., when he marched into England in 1651.

He married, first, Margaret, only daughter of Sir Roderick Mackenzie of Coieach, tutor of Kintail, and had:

(1) Donald MacDonald, his heir.
(2) Roderick MacDonald, married and had issue.
(3) Hugh MacDonald of Glenmore.
(4) Somerled MacDonald of Sortle.
(5) Katherine MacDonald, married to Sir Norman Macleod of Bernera.
(6) Florence MacDonald, married to John Macleod of Harris and Dunvegan.

He married, secondly, Mary, eldest daughter of John Macleod, and had another son,

John MacDonald of Backney.

Sir James MacDonald died December 8, 1678, and was succeeded by his eldest son,

Sir Donald MacDonald, third Baronet of Slate, who married Lady Mary Douglas, whose lineage follows:

Sir William Douglas, ninth Earl of Morton, K. G. and Lord High Steward of Scotland, who before the war broke out was one of the richest and greatest subjects in the kingdom, married Lady Anne Keith, daughter of George, fifth Earl Marischal of Scotland.

Sir Robert Douglas, their son, tenth Earl of Morton, married Elizabeth, daughter of Sir Edward Villiers (and niece of George Villiers, Duke of Buckingham) and by her had:

(1) Sir William Douglas, eleventh Earl of Morton.
(2) Robert Douglas.
(3) Lady Anne Douglas.

(4) LADY MARY DOUGLAS, who was married to Sir Donald MacDonald, third Baronet of Slate, and had:

(1) Donald MacDonald, his successor.

(2) James MacDonald, who succeeded as sixth Baronet of Slate.

(3) William MacDonald.

(4) Isabella MacDonald, married to Sir Alexander Bannerman of Elsick, second Baronet.

(5) Barbara MacDonald, married to Colonel MacDonald of Keppoch.

(6) Probably, Mary MacDonald, married to Alexander MacNaughton, though Mary MacDonald may have been the daughter of one of the other sons of Sir James MacDonald, second Baronet of Slate.

Sir Donald MacDonald died February 5, 1695, and was succeeded by his eldest son,

Sir Donald MacDonald, fourth Baronet of Slate, who, joining the rebellion of 1715, was attainted. He married Mary, daughter of Donald MacDonald of Castletown, and died in 1718, leaving issue:

(1) Donald MacDonald, his heir.

(2) Mary MacDonald, married, 1712, to John MacDougall of Dunollie; died 1779.

(3) Margaret MacDonald, married to Captain John MacQueen, by whom she had issue.

(4) Isabella MacDonald, married to Alexander Monro of Auchenbowie, and had issue.

(5) Janet MacDonald, married to Norman Macleod.

Sir Donald MacDonald was succeeded by his son,

Sir Donald MacDonald, fifth Baronet, at whose decease, unmarried, in 1720, the baronetcy reverted to his uncle,

Sir James MacDonald, sixth Baronet, designated of Oransay, who married, first, Janet, daughter of Alexander Macleod of Grishesnish, and had:

(1) Alexander MacDonald, his successor.

(2) Margaret MacDonald, married to Sir Robert Douglas, Bart. of Glenbervie, author of the Peerage of Scotland.

(3) Isabella MacDonald, died unmarried.

(4) Janet, married to Sir Alexander Mackenzie, Bart. of Coul.

He married, secondly, Margaret, daughter of John MacDonald of Castletown, by whom he had a son,

John MacDonald, who died young; and dying in 1723, was succeeded by his son,

Sir Alexander MacDonald, seventh Baronet of Slate, who married, first, Anne, daughter of David Erskine of Dun, and widow of James Lord Ogilvy, by whom he had a son,

Donald MacDonald, born 1734; died young.

He married, secondly, April 24, 1739, Margaret, daughter of Alexander, ninth Earl of Eglinton, and had:

(1) James MacDonald, his successor.

(2) Alexander MacDonald, ninth Baronet and first Lord.

(3) Archibald MacDonald, Lord Chief Baron of the Exchequer in England; created a Baronet in 1813.

He died in 1746, and was succeeded by his eldest son.

Sir James MacDonald, eighth Baronet of MacDonald, one of the greatest scholars and mathematicians of his time, at whose decease, unmarried, on his travels at Rome, July 26, 1766, the title devolved upon his brother,

Sir Alexander MacDonald, first Baron MacDonald, who was elevated to the peerage in Ireland, July 17, 1776, by the title of Baron MacDonald of Slate, County Antrim.

His lordship married in 1768, Elizabeth Diana, eldest daughter of Godfrey Bosville, of Gunthwaite, County York, and granddaughter, maternally, of Sir William Wentworth, Bart. of Bretton, by whom (who died 1789) he had issue:

Alexander Wentworth MacDonald, his successor.—Burke's Peerage.

MacDOUGALL.

MacDOUGALL, or MacDUGALL, a clan who derive their descent and their name from Dugall, the son of Ranald, the son of the famous Somerled. The name Dhu Gall means the dark-complexioned stranger. The chiefs were generally styled De Argadia of Lords of Lorn. The clan badge was the cloudberry bush. The MacDougalls are not mentioned in history till 1284. In the list of those who attended the convention of that year we find the name of Alexander de Ergadia, and it is supposed that his presence was the consequence of his holding his lands by a crown charter. Another form of the name is MacDowall, used especially by those of the race who possessed lands in Galloway, to which the Dhu Galls, or black Gaels, are said to have given its name.

At the time that Robert Bruce asserted his claim to the throne of Scotland the chief's name was Alexander. He had married the daughter of Red Comyn, whom Bruce slew in the Dominican Church at Dumfries, and in consequence he became the mortal enemy of the King. After his defeat at Methven, on June 19,

1306, when Bruce, with only 300 followers, approached the borders of Argyleshire, he was attacked by MacDougall of Lorn, at the head of 1,000 men, part of whom were MacNabs, who had joined the party of John Baliol, and after a severe conflict was compelled to abandon the field. This battle was fought at a place called Dalree, and, in his retreat, one of the MacDougalls, having come up with the King, seized hold of his plaid, which was fixed across his breast by a brooch. In the struggle which ensued the man was killed, but the plaid and brooch were left in his dying grasp. The latter, under the name of "the brooch of Lorn," was long preserved by the chief of the MacDougalls, and after being carried off during the civil war of the Seventeenth century, has been restored to the family.—Anderson's Scottish Nation.

MacDougall Arms. Quarterly. First and fourth—In a field azure, a lion rampant, argent, for MacDougall. Second and third—Or, a lymphad sable, with flame of fire issuing out of the topmast, proper, for Lorn.

Badge. Cypress. Principal Seat. Lorn. Oldest Cadet. MacDougall of Rarey. Chief. MacDougall of Dunolly. Force in 1745, 200.—The Highlanders of Scotland. Skene.

MACDOUGALLS—The MacDougalls of Lorn were anciently Lords of Argyle "De Argandie," and are so designed in very early writs.

Lorn was originally a petty kingdom, the residence of its King being the Castle of Dunolly. It subsequently became a lordship, and was often excepted from truces with England.

At one time it included within its boundaries the west part of Athol. where Mam Lorn still preserves its name.

About the beginning of the twelfth century Somerled ruled Argyle. By a daughter of Olaus, King of Man and the Isles, he had four sons, one of whom was Dougal, who erected his inheritance into a principality. He was grandfather of Alexander MacDougall of Lorn, who fought and defeated King Robert Bruce at the battle of Dalree in Perthshire in 1306. His son, John MacDougall, was succeeded by his son, Ewen MacDougall, father of John MacDougall of Dunolly, whose son, John of Dunolly, entered by charter from Argyle in 1535 and another in 1547. He was father of Dougall MacDougall of Dunolly, who entered to his lands by charter from Argyle in 1562 and 1567.

His son, Duncan MacDougall of Dunolly, obtained a charter

from King James IV., dated September 8, 1598. He was succeeded by his son,

Sir John MacDougall of Dunolly, who married Margaret, daughter of Sir Duncan Campbell of Glenurchy, and left a son and successor,

Alexander MacDougall of Dunolly, who married and had two sons:

Duncan, who died without issue.

Allan, who succeeded his brother and obtained from King James VII. a charter of the greater part of the lands of Lorn, dated at Windsor, September 20, 1686, registered the 13th and sealed August 14, 1688. His son,

John MacDougall of Dunolly, joined the rising in 1715 and suffered forfeiture in consequence. (He married Mary, daughter of Sir Donald MacDonald, fourth Baronet of Slate, by his wife, Mary, daughter of Donald MacDonald of Castletown, in 1712.—Burke's Peerage.) He left two daughters, the elder of whom was married to John Maclean of Lachbuy, and a son and successor,

Alexander MacDougall of Dunolly, who was restored to his father's forfeited estates by charter from the Duke of Argyle in 1745. He married Mary, daughter of Campbell of Barcaldine, County Argyle, and had issue:

(1) John MacDougall, who married the Hon. Isabel Ruthven, second daughter of James, third Lord Ruthven, but had no issue. He died at Bombay, April 27, 1775.

(2) Patrick MacDougall, who succeeded his father.

(3) Duncan MacDougall, who married Jane, daughter of Campbell of Duntroon Castle, County Argyle, and had five sons and five daughters.

(4) ALEXANDER MACDOUGALL, who came to America.

(5) Lucy MacDougall, married to MacDowell, Esq., of Canomills, near Edinburgh.

(6) Mary MacDougall, married to MacNeil of Cransay.

The second son, Patrick MacDougall, Esq., of Dunolly, succeeded his father. He married in 1782, Louisa Maxwell, daughter of John Campbell, Esq., of Achalader, in Perthshire, and had issue:

(1) Alexander MacDougall, Captain in the Fifth Regiment of Foot: killed at the storming of Ciudad Rodrigo, January, 1812. He predeceased his father and died without issue.

(2) John MacDougall, now of Dunolly, present chief of this ancient and distinguished clan.

(3) Patrick MacDougall, lieutenant-colonel in the army.

(4) Allan MacDougall.

(5) Isabella MacDougall, married to Captain Niell MacDougall of the Seventy-fifth Regiment; killed at Castella, in Spain, April 13, 1813, and had issue:

Niel and Louisa Maxwell.

(6) Anne Colina MacDougall, married to Patrick Campbell, Esq., of Baleveolan, County Argyle, and had a son, Douglas Patrick Campbell.

(7) Mary Jane MacDougall, married to Charles Hale Monro, Esq., of Devon, and has three sons and two daughters.

(8) Colina MacDougall.—Landed Gentry. Burke.

LINEAGE OF THE ROBERTSONS.

(I) Crinin, Lord of Athol, Abbot of Dunkeld and Abthane of Dull, married Beatrice, (or Bathoc) daughter of King Malcolm II., from whom descended all the Kings of Scotland, from Duncan I. to Alexander III., except Macbeth.

(II) Duncan I., King of Scotland, 1033-1040, son of Crinan and Beatrice.

(III) Malcolm III. and Donald Bane, sons of Duncan I.

(IV) Madoch, son of King Donald Bane, first ancient Celtic Earl of Athol. (1115.)

(I) Malcolm III., (Malcolm Canmore) King of Scotland, 1057-1093, eldest son of Duncan I.

(II) Duncan II., King of Scotland, 1093-1095, eldest son of Malcolm III., by his first wife, Ingioborge, widow of Thorfinn, Early of Orkney.

(III) Malcolm, son of King Duncan II., second ancient Celtic Earl of Athol.

(IV) Malcolm, son of Malcolm, son of Duncan II., third ancient Celtic Earl of Athol.

(V) Henry, son of the preceding, fourth and last ancient Celtic Earl of Athol. (In the beginning of the thirteenth century.)

(VI) Conan, second son of Henry. (1214-1249.)

(VII) Ewen Fiz Conan, son of Conan.

(VIII) Angus, eldest son of Ewen Fiz Conan.

(IX) Andrew de Atholia, son of Angus.

(X) Duncan de Atholia, son of Andrew de Atholia, who gave the clan their distinctive appellation of the clan Donachie, or children of Duncan.

(XI) Robert de Atholia, Duncanus de Atholia, dominus de Ranagh, or Rannoch, son of Robert de Atholia. (1392.)

(XIII) Robert Riach, (grizzled) son of the preceding, from whom the clan derive the surname Robertson. (1451.)

(XIV) Alexander Robertson, son of Robert, Robert's son, who first bore the surname ROBERTSON. He was the fifth Baron of Strowan. (Died 1507.)

(XV) JOHN ROBERTSON, first Laird of Muirton, Elginshire, second son of Alexander Robertson, by his second wife, Lady Elizabeth, daughter of Sir John Stewart of Baloing, Earl of Athol, (a descendant of Edward I., King of England) and his wife, Lady Eleanor Sinclair, daughter of William Earl of Orkney, and a descendant of James I., King of Scotland.

JOHN ROBERTSON married Lady Margaret Crighton, whose descent follows:

(1) James II., King of Scotland, married Lady Mary, daughter of Arnold, Duke of Guilders, of the House of Egmond, and had,

(2) Princess Margaret Stuart, who was married, first, to William, third Lord Crighton, and had,

(3) Sir James Crighton of Frendraught, eldest son, who married Lady Catherine, daughter of William Lord Bostwick, and had,

(4) Lady Margaret Crighton, who was married to JOHN ROBERTSON.

The above marriage must have occurred about 1500, so that there is a space here of more than two centuries, probably seven generations, that I have not as yet been able to trace fully, though I have many reasons, which I can not state here, for believing that our immediate ancestors sprang from the above marriage of JOHN ROBERTSON and LADY MARGARET CRIGHTON.

(I) JOHN ROBERTSON of Peterhead, Aberdeenshire, Scotland, the immediate ancestor of our line of Robertsons, had three brothers:

(II) ALEXANDER ROBERTSON of Collielaw, near Peterhead, Scotland.

(III) GILBERT ROBERTSON, a bachelor, who went to Kilkenny, Ireland.

(IV) WILLIAM ROBERTSON, who went to Kilkenny, Ireland, and married a daughter of Sir Tichard Jones, and had:

(1) William Robertson.
(2) John Robertson.
(3) Susana Robertson.
(4) Elizabeth Robertson.

Miss Jennie M. Patten has in her possession a letter written by John Robertson, son of William Robertson, from Kilkenny, Ireland, dated May 15, 1816, to his cousin and our great-grandfather, William Robertson, of Argyle, Washington County, New York, which I shall here copy:

Kilkenny, May 15, 1816.

Dear Cousin:

Though disunited by distance, time, and even the failure of recollection, yet, being of the one blood, by so close a tie, I should regret that all trace of our connection should be lost, and shall feel a pleasure in renewing and strengthening it by every opportunity.

It was extremely unfortunate that the breaking out of the late war should have so unexpectedly prevented my enjoying the satisfaction of seeing your son here; he would have found a welcome from our family, which I should hope would prolong his stay and compensate for his absence from home.

The account you gave of the situation of your family afforded me much gratification, and hope that the branch transplanted from us in the other world will long continue to flourish and take such root as to last to the end of time; here, I may proudly say, that the name has ever been coupled with honor, honesty and high estimation, and such I trust it has been with you, and will remain distinguished. It will prove the most solid foundation ever to worthy prosperity, and draw down that blessing from Providence without which every hope is blasted.

Though I suppose you have received my letter informing you of our situation here, yet, as I flatter myself, you will feel an interest in it, I shall repeat: that my father's industry was so successful as to enable him to settle us in good circumstances before his death. My only brother here, William, being the first architect in this country, lives outside the town some short distance, and may be estimated worth about ten thousand pounds. He is married to a cousin of his own, but as yet is without children. My property is much about the same. I still follow the business of nurseryman, and hold the same ground my father did with much more. Am unmarried and mean to continue so. We have two sisters, both married, but without heirs, and in good circumstances.

Of the Jones', my mother's family, which I suppose you must have known. The brothers and sisters are all dead except Tichard, on whom my grandfather's property devolved to the amount of about 1,500 pounds a year. He has been knighted; lives in Clomnell, and has fifteen or sixteen children living, I believe ten sons; two of them in the army; one a Captain in the 21st Dragoons, now at the cape; the other a Lieutenant in the 50th Infantry.

'Tis time for me to tell you that this letter goes by John Stone, once a prentice of yours at Desart. He is going over to a brother-in-law of his at Washington City, one Hobson, an architect, who has been settled there these many years. He takes part of his family with him and hope will do well. He has been always an honest, friendly well-wisher of ours, and is very anxious to see you, but that from the distance you are separated is not likely.

When convenient I should be glad to hear from you, or one of your family, of your and their situation. The letter you last sent . . . has been mislaid.

This country has never known so much distress in my memory as since the conclusion of the peace. The prices of all sorts of grain having fallen so low as to ruin the farmers. Wheat is 20—, and barley and oats 6—6 per barrel; every other crop has suffered in consequence, but now prices are looking up again, and business increasing. Wheat is at 50—, oats and barley 10—.

Combination and assassination of Tythe Proctors and the active magistrates has been disgracefully frequent, but no where more common than in the County Tipporary, and where you lived at Thomastown; it was put under martial law; numbers have been hung and they are now quiet. I remain dear Cousin, yours truly,

JOHN ROBERTSON.

Miss Jennie M. Patten wrote to a minister in Thomastown, Ireland, the place referred to in the above letter as the residence of our great-grandfather, William Robertson, to inquire if any of the Robertsons were still in that locality. The minister happened to know one member of the family, Duncan S. Robertson, who lived in Dublin, and sent the letter to him. In her letter she had enclosed a copy of the above letter from John Robertson to William Robertson, which served for identification.

Duncan S. Robertson kindly answered the letter and through him we have learned the birthplace of our ancestor, William Robertson of Argyle, and the branch of the Robertson family from which our line has descended. He also gave information in regard to our branch of the Robertsons still in Scotland, which I shall here give.

(II) ALEXANDER ROBERTSON of Collielaw, near Peterhead, Aberdeenshire, Scotland, married, December, 1760, Christian Clarke, daughter of William Clarke, a lieutenant of the tenants of the Earl Marischal at Peterhead, in arms for the old chevalier in 1715, and had:

(I) Alexander Robertson, who married Helen Watson, sister of George Watson, Esq., of Aberdeen, Indian merchant; and aunt of the late John Watson, E. G. D. L., of Markford, Aberdeen, and had:

(1) James George Robertson.

(2) Alexander Robertson, banker at Macduff, Aberdeenshire, Scotland.

He held the King's (George III.) commission, first, as lieutenant, and later as a captain, in the Peterhead Fencible Regiment, raised during the long French war.

(1) James George Robertson left Peterhead, Scotland, in 1828, when twelve years old; lived sixty years in Kilkenny, Ireland, and died in Dublin in 1900. He married Wilhelmine Alice Strangways, daughter of William Strangways, Esq., of Suttonsrath, in the County Kilkenny, Ireland, and formerly of the Eighty-third Regiment; served in the Peninsular war and was invalided. The Strangways family has been connected with the County Kilkenny for nearly 300 years; a branch of the Strangways of Lancashire, England, who took a prominent part in the Pilgrimage of Grau, 1536. He had by her:

(A) Duncan S. Robertson.

(B) William Alexander Robertson.

(C) Alice Helen Beatrice Robertson.

(D) Juliet Annie Maria Robertson; died young.

(A) Duncan S. Robertson lived ten years in Australia; was lecturer and tutor at Ormond College, in the University of Melbourne; was also called to the Victoria bar. At present he is not exercising any profession. He married his cousin, Olive Robertson, daughter of his uncle, Alexander Robertson, banker at Macduff, Aberdeenshire, Scotland, and had:

(a) Olive Helen Alexandra Robertson, born in 1903. Mrs. Robertson died when her child was born.

(B) William Alexander Robertson married Anne Elizabeth Lawrence Cassan, daughter of Matthew S. Cassan, J. P., of Sheffield House, Queens County. The Cassans originally called de Cassagne, and were from Caen in Normandy. Their ancestor acquired the estate of Sheffield by marriage, about 1689.

(C) Alice Helen Beatrice Robertson was married to her cousin, Leonard R. Strangways, M. A.

(2) Alexander Robertson, younger brother of James George Robertson, who is a banker at Macduff, Aberdeenshire, Scotland, had:

(A) Alexander Robertson, J. P., for Banffshire and Aberdeenshire.

(B) James G. Robertson.

(C) Helen Watson Robertson.

(D) Olive Robertson, married to Duncan S. Robertson.

In Scotland this family of Robertsons is represented by Alexander Robertson, J. P. for Banffshire and Aberdeenshire, and James G. Robertson, (sons of Alexander Robertson, younger brother of James George Robertson) and their sister, Helen Watson Robertson. There are also numerous descendants of our common ancestor, who cannot be traced, I am afraid, in the female line.

This branch of the Robertsons came from a stronghold of Episcopacy and Jacobitism, Peterhead, which was on the estate of Keith, the Earl Marischal of Scotland.

My great-grandmother's father, William Clarke, was one of the lieutenants of the Peterhead Fencible Force, raised by the Earl Marischal to support Prince James Edward in 1715. Our chapel was burned on that occasion, and again before the battle of Culloden, so, unfortunately, all records are lost. I have a family birth and some old papers which throw a little light on the family history, but not much.

The old Kilkenny Robertsons, when my father came, were William and John, Susana and Elizabeth.

(I) William Robertson married his cousin, Catherine Jones, daughter of Sir Richard Jones of Clonmell.

(II) John Robertson never married.

(III) Susana was married to McCraith, but had no children.

(IV) Elizabeth Robertson was married to T. Newton, Esq., of Kilkenny, who afterwards went to New South Wales, in Australia, and had two children, one of whom was:

(1) John Robertson Newton, of New South Wales, (second cousin of James George Robertson) for some time M. P. for the Williams district in New South Wales. He died in 1875. His landed estate is chiefly owned by

(A) T. Jones-Newton, Esq., but partly by Duncan S. Robertson and his sister, Mrs. Alice Strangways, as residuary legatees.

There are no Robertsons in Kilkenny at present and the only members of the family in Ireland are myself and little daughter, Olive Helen Alexandra Robertson, and my sister, Alice Strangways.

The Kilkenny Robertsons are buried in the churchyard of St. Mary, Kilkenny, and there are stone monuments up to their memory. My mother, brother and sister are buried there, too, and commemorated on a brass inside the church.—Duncan S. Robertson.

From Alexander Robertson of Macduff, Scotland, I am informed that this line of Robertsons is descended from the head of the clan.

It is well known that the descendants of John Robertson of Muirton, Elginshire, settled in Aberdeenshire. The names Alexander, Duncan, Gilbert, John and William, have appeared in every generation of this line that can be traced, so that I have no doubt that our line is descended from JOHN ROBERTSON of Muirton, Elginshire, second son of the second marriage of Alexander Robertson, who first bore the surname ROBERTSON.

Lord John Russell and Henry Lord Brougham, (on the maternal side) Rev. William Robertson, D. D., the eminent Edinburgh divine, and his son, William Robertson, Royal Historiographer, and his daughter, Jean Robertson, grandmother of our own Patrick Henry, are all descended from the same JOHN ROBERTSON of Muirton, Elginshire, as ourselves.

(I) JOHN ROBERTSON of Peterhead, Aberdeenshire, Scotland, the immediate ancestor of our line of Robertsons, descendant of John Robertson, first Laird of Muirton, Elginshire, by his wife, Lady Margaret Crighton, (see lineage) married ANNE HAMILTON, (one of whose ancestors, the first Lord Hamilton, married, 1474, Princess Mary, eldest daughter of

King James II., of Scotland. The Hamilton family has been known in Scotland since the thirteenth century, and has been a ducal family since 1643. During nearly a century the head of the House of Hamilton was, after the Royal Family, heir to the Scottish crown) and had:

(1) WILLIAM ROBERTSON, born January 24, 1752; died February 19, 1825.

(2) ANNE ROBERTSON, died young.

(I) WILLIAM ROBERTSON, son of John and Anne (Hamilton) Robertson, was born January 24, 1752, at Peterhead, Aberdeenshire, Scotland, and died February 19, 1825, aged seventy-three years and 26 days, in Argyle, Washington County, New York, on the Robertson homestead, for many years the home of his grandson, Hon. William D. Robertson, and was buried in the South Argyle cemetery.

William Robertson, when ten years old, (1762) after the death of his father, mother and only sister, Anne, went to Kilkenny, Ireland, to live with his bachelor uncle, Gilbert Robertson. In 1772, accompanied by his uncle, Gilbert, he came to America. The uncle was offered a grant of a tract of land in Cherry Valley, near Albany, New York, but did not like the location, and they settled on the south bank of the Batten Kill, in the town of Jackson, Washington County, New York, not far from the home of Archibald Livingston, whose daughter William Robertson afterwards married. The uncle, Gilbert Robertson, returned to Ireland and died in Kilkenny. He left the farm to William Robertson, who later sold it and moved to Argyle, Washington County, New York, where he spent the remainder of his life. He left his farm to be divided between his two elder sons, Gilbert and Archibald, Gilbert receiving the homestead.

WILLIAM ROBERTSON and MARY LIVINGSTON were married September 24, 1775, by Rev. Thomas Clark, D. D., at the home of Archibald Livingston, near East Greenwich, Washington County, New York.

MARY LIVINGSTON, eldest daughter of Archibald Livingston, (descendant of the seventh Lord Livingston, Earl of Linlithgow and Calender) by his wife, Eleanor McNaughton, daughter of Alexander McNaughton, (whose ancestry runs back to the Pictish Kings, 455) by his wife, Mary MacDonald, granddaughter of Sir James MacDonald, second Baronet of Slate, (whose ancestor, John MacDonald, Lord of the Isles, married

Margaret, daughter of King Robert II.) and, I believe, a daughter of Sir Donald MacDonald, third Baronet of Slate, (though she may have been a daughter of one of the other sons of Sir James MacDonald) by his wife, Lady Mary Douglas, daughter of Sir Robert Douglas, tenth Earl of Morton, who was a son of Sir William Douglas, ninth Earl of Morton, Knight of the Garter, and Lord High Steward of Scotland, who, before the war broke out, was one of the richest and greatest subjects in the kingdom, by his wife, Lady Anne Keith, daughter of George, fifth Earl Marischal of Scotland.

Mary Livingston was born September 26, 1757, at Tappan, Rockland (then Orange) County, New York, and died August 7, 1793, in Argyle, Washington County, New York, on the Robertson homestead, and was buried in the Old Argyle cemetery.

WILLIAM and MARY (LIVINGSTON) ROBERTSON had:

(I) ANNA ROBERTSON, born December 8, 1776; died February 9, 1853.

(II) GILBERT ROBERTSON, born August 24, 1778; died February 10, 1865.

(III) ARCHIBALD ROBERTSON, born March 1, 1780; died December 31, 1849.

(IV) JEANNETTE ROBERTSON, born January 26, 1782; died February 23, 1856.

(V) WILLIAM ROBERTSON, born December 15, 1783; died November 1, 1857.

(VI) JOHN ROBERTSON, born May 2, 1786; died September 2, 1873.

(VII) ALEXANDER ROBERTSON, born October 30, 1788; died January 27, 1852.

(VIII) MOSES ROBERTSON, born April 25, 1791; died February 17, 1869.

(IX) MARY ROBERTSON, born August 7, 1793; died April 6, 1890.

(I) ANNA ROBERTSON, eldest daughter of William and Mary (Livingston) Robertson, was born December 8, 1776, in the town of Salem, Washington County, New York, and died February 9, 1853, in South Argyle, Washington County, New York.

John McNeil, Jr., and Anna Robertson were married January 12, 1804, in Argyle, Washington County, New York.

John McNeil, Jr., son of John and Jane (Whorry) McNeil, was born December 4, 1773, in Argyle, Washington County, New

York, and died April 14, 1813, in Argyle, Washington County, New York.

John McNeil, Sr., was a son of Archibald and Catherine (McArthur) McNeil. Archibald McNeil came from Argyleshire, Scotland, to America in 1739, and died January 14, 1815, in Argyle, Washington County, New York.

John and Anna (Robertson) McNeil had:

(I) William McNeil, died young.

(II) John R. McNeil, born March 20, 1808; died June 14, 1877.

(III) Moses Livingston McNeil, born December 7, 1809; died April 6, 1889.

(IV) James McNeil, born May 3, 1812; died April 7, 1886.

(II) John R. McNeil, son of John and Anna (Robertson) McNeil, was born March 20, 1808, in Argyle, New York, and died June 14, 1877, in Argyle, New York.

John R. McNeil and Ellen Ann Clark were married November 11, 1835, in Argyle, Washington County, New York.

Ellen Ann Clark, daughter of Ralph and Martha (Savage) Clark, was born October 28, 1810, in Argyle, New York, and died April 29, 1888, in Fort Edward, New York. She was a sister of the wife of Schuyler Colfax.

John R. and Ellen Ann (Clark) McNeil had:

(1) Elizabeth McNeil, born February 20, 1838; died July 25, 1842.

(2) Martha McNeil, born March 11, 1840; died April 1, 1840.

(3) Thomas McNeil, born April 13, 1842; died May 10, 1860.

(4) Mary McNeil, born April 21, 1844.

(5) Anna McNeil, born March 7, 1847.

(6) Susie McNeil, born October 21, 1849.

(7) Evelyn Colfax McNeil, born December 28, 1855; died September 6, 1880.

(4) Mary McNeil, daughter of John R. and Ellen Ann (Clark) McNeil, was born April 21, 1844, in Argyle, New York, and lives in Fort Edward, New York.

George McMurray and Mary McNeil were married Septemreb 12, 1865.

George McMurray, son of Robert and Elizabeth (McFadden) McMurray, was born April 17, 1841, in Fort Edward, New York.

George and Mary (McNeil) McMurray had:

(A) George H. McMurray, born September 28, 1866; died July 12, 1901.

(B) John R. McMurray, born December 17, 1868.

(C) Alfred S. McMurray, born January 26, 1870.

(D) Nellie McMurray, born March 27, 1874; died June 29, 1875.

(E) Adella McMurray, born May 17, 1876; died August 11, 1884.

(F) Harold McMurray, born January 1, 1881; died March 13, 1882.

(G) Howard McMurray, born April 10, 1884; died March 11, 1888.

(A) Dr. George H. McMurray, son of George and Mary (McNeil) McMurray, was born September 28, 1866, in Argyle, New York, and died July 12, 1901, in Glens Falls, New York.

Dr. George H. McMurray and Ida May Haviland were married November 5, 1894, in Glens Falls, New York.

Ida May Haviland, daughter of Ransford B. and Frances Marian (Colvin) Haviland, was born June 29, 1867, in Glens Falls, New York.

(B) John R. Murray, son of George and Mary (McNeil) McMurray, was born December 17, 1868, in Fort Edward, New York.

John R. McMurray and Anna Mary Mory were married May 10, 1903, in Fort Edward, New York.

Anna Mary Mory, daughter of Michel Vale and Rosalina (Alwell) Mory, was born December 18, 1868, in Fort Edward, New York.

(C) Alfred S. McMurray, son of George and Mary (McNeil) McMurray, was born January 26, 1870, in Fort Edward, New York.

Alfred S. McMurray and Laura Anna Martin were married July 7, 1897, in Red Hook, New York.

Laura Anna Martin, daughter of Joseph Fielding and Laura Anna (Brown) Martin, was born November 26, 1877, in Springfield, Illinois.

Alfred S. and Laura Anna (Martin) McMurray had:

(a) Edith Martin McMurray, born April 26, 1898; died January 15, 1902.

(b) Mary Laura McMurray, born July 14, 1900.

(5) Anna McNeil, daughter of John R. and Ellen Ann (Clark) McNeil, was born March 7, 1847, in Argyle, New York.

Daniel Liddle and Anna McNeil were married December 20, 1865, in Argyle, New York.

Daniel Liddle, son of John and Margaret (Stevenson) Liddle, was born November 3, 1838; died October 27, 1895. He was a merchant in Tustin, Michigan.

Daniel and Anna (McNeil) Liddle had:

(A) Ransom G. Liddle, born September 29, 1866, in North Argyle, N. Y.

(B) Nellie Liddle, born January 19, 1869; died February 15, 1892.

(C) William Liddle, born July 31, 1872; died December 10, 1874.

(D) Ralph Clark Liddle, born December 11, 1875, in New York City.

(E) May Edith Liddle, born March 24, 1878, in New York City.

(F) Anna Evelyn Liddle, born March 22, 1880, in New York City.

(G) Bessie Brown Liddle, born November 12, 1882, in New York City.

(H) Margaret Irene Liddle, born December 3, 1884, in Tustin, Michigan.

(I) Mary Sterling Liddle, born September 19, 1887, in Tustin, Michigan.

(D) Ralph Clark Liddle, son of Daniel and Anna (McNeil) Liddle, was born December 11, 1875, in New York City.

Ralph Clark Liddle and Edna Bradford were married December 22, 1903.

Edna Bradford was born March 24, 1880.

(E) May Edith Liddle, daughter of Daniel and Anna (McNeil) Liddle, was born March 24, 1878, in New York City.

Thadeus Sidney Conover and May Edith Liddle were married September 2, 1896.

Thadeus Sidney Conover, son of Albert and Jean (Selkirk) Conover, was born September 10, 1873. Lives in Flint, Mich.

Thadeus Sidney and May Edith (Liddle) Conover had:

(a) Anna Jean Conover, born October 31, 1899, in Tustin, Michigan.

(b) George Van Amber Conover, born July 7, 1902, in Flint, Michigan.

(c) Thadeus Sidney Conover, born April 12, 1904, in Flint, Michigan.

(6) Susie H. McNeil, daughter of John R. and Ellen Ann (Clark) McNeil, was born October 21, 1849, in Argyle, New York.

Chalmers McClaughry and Susie H. McNeil were married March 12, 1884, in Glens Falls, New York.

Chalmers McClaughry, son of Ebenezer and Mary S. (Clark) McClaughry, was born September 23, 1847, in Argyle, New York, and died June, 1887.

Chalmers and Susie H. (McNeil) McClaughry had:

(A) Blanche McClaughry, born December 27, 1884, in Tustin, Michigan.

Albert Nicholson and Mrs. Susie H. (McNeil) McClaughry were married February 14, 1895, at Whitehall, New York, and live at Fort Ann, New York.

Albert Nicholson, son of John Livingston and Mary (Swift) Nicholson, was born February 5, 1840, at Fort Edward, New York. He served nearly four years in the civil war; was a member of the One-Hundred-Twenty-third New York Infantry; was in Andersonville and Florence prisons for almost six months.

(III) Moses Livingston McNeil, son of John and Anna (Robertson) McNeil, was born December 7, 1809, in Argyle, New York, and died April 6, 1889.

Moses Livingston McNeil and Margaret Brennan were mar-married November 1, 1855, in Argyle, New York.

Margaret Brennan, daughter of John and Mary (Nash) Brennan, was born July 23, 1838, in Carrick, or Suir, Ireland, and died May 8, 1878.

Moses Livingston and Margaret (Brennan) McNeil had:

(1) James B. McNeil, born May 21, 1857. Unmarried.

(2) Elizabeth McNeil, born August 29, 1859.

(3) Phebe McNeil, born July 23, 1861.

(4) John McNeil, born November 23, 1869; died August 11, 1892.

(5) William T. McNeil, born May 17, 1872; died July 23, 1900.

(6) Mary Ellen McNeil, born February 4, 1875. Unmarried.

(2) Elizabeth McNeil, daughter of Moses Livingston and

Margaret (Brennan) McNeil, was born August 29, 1859, and died November, 1906.

Frederick Emerson White and Elizabeth McNeil were married June 10, 1896, and lived at Florence, Arizona.

Frederick Emerson and Elizabeth (McNeil) White had:

(A) Nell Robertson White, born October 22, 1897; died January 22, 1899.

(B) Neil Emerson White, born February 11, 1900.

(C) Inez Elizabeth White, born November 16, 1901.

(3) Phebe McNeil, daughter of Moses Livingston and Margaret (Brennan) McNeil, was born July 23, 1861.

Augustine Gray Williams and Phebe McNeil were married June 18, 1891.

Augustine Gray Williams, son of John Thomas and Augusta (Moore) Williams, was born November 24, 1855, at Palmyra, Missouri.

Augustine Gray and Phebe (McNeil) Williams had:

(A) Floy McNeil Williams, born December 12, 1893.

(B) Clyde Livingston Williams, born December 27, 1896; died May 24, 1897.

(IV) James McNeil son of John and Anna (Robertson) McNeil, was born May 3, 1812, in Argyle, New York, and died April 7, 1886, in San Francisco, California. He arrived at San Francisco, California, October 10, 1849, on the bark Sir Walter Scott, from New York.

James McNeil and Susan Bowen Hathaway were married May 6, 1841, in New York City.

Susan Bowen Hathaway, daughter of Stephen and Lydia (Swain) Hathaway, was born in 1817, in New Bedford, Massachusetts, and died October 31, 1854, in Napa, California. She, with her two children, William Hathaway McNeil and Anna McNeil, arrived at San Francisco, California, October 10, 1852. on ship "John Quincy Adams" from New York. The lineage of Mrs. McNeil is quite interesting, as several of her ancestors came over in the "Mayflower."

James and Susan (Hathaway) McNeil had:

(A) William Hathaway McNeil, born February 10, 1842.

(B) Anna McNeil, born December 31, 1848; died December 13, 1862.

James McNeil and Ellen K. Thrall were married July 1, 1858, in San Francisco, California.

Ellen K. Thrall, adopted daughter of Reuben R. Thrall, was

born October 10, 1830, in Rutland, Vermont, and died October 30, 1890, in San Francisco, California.

James and Ellen K. (Thrall) McNeil had:

(C) Allan McNeil, born June 4, 1859; died November 8, 1859.

(A) William Hathaway McNeil, son of James and Susan Bowen (Hathaway) McNeil, was born February 10, 1842, in Schuylerville, New York, and now lives at 1022 North Nineteenth street, St. Joseph, Missouri. He enlisted November 4, 1862, at San Francisco, California, in the "California 100," afterwards assigned as Company "A," Second Massachusetts Cavalry; discharged as corporal by special order No. 326, paragraph 4, Adjutant General's office, at Washington, D. C., June 25, 1865. "A. G. O."

Sailed From San Francisco December 11, 1862; arrived at Camp Readeville, Mass., January 4, 1863. First Battalion, Second Massachusetts Cavalry, Companies "A," "B," "D" and "H," to Yorktown, February 12, 1863. First battle South Anna Bridge, captured General Fitzhugh Lee.

May, 1863, at Williamsburg, Va., with Twelfth Pennsylvania Cavalry, Colonel Spear.

July, 1863, special duty defences of Washington at the Chain Bridge. During this time the remainder of the regiment was at Gettysburg, and other duty.

August, 1863, regiment assembled for first time at Centerville, Va. (Bull Run battlefield.) During summer and fall scouting in country between the Potomac River and the Blue Ridge, Virginia. (Mosby's Guerillas keeping the regiment busy.)

October, 1863, to Vienna Court House, Virginia, (seventeen miles from Washington) for winter quarters. May, 1864, to Falls Church, Virginia; then, after Battle of the Wilderness, to the battlefield to bring the wounded to hospitals at Washington. July, 1864, in provisional brigade to repel Early's attack on Washington. August, 1864, placed in Third Brigade, First Division, Cavalry Corps, General Merritt, Sheridan's Army, Shenandoah Valley. In all the battles of that campaign from Halltown to Cedar Creek.

November, 1864, winter quarters near Winchester, Virginia, till February 27, 1865, at which time began Sheridan's Cavalry raid from Winchester to Petersburg. Destruction of the James River Canal, and Early's entire army, reaching Petersburg March 26, 1865. In the brilliant operations on the left of Grant's Army to April 9, 1865, and the surrender of Lee; then to relief of General Sherman, returning to Petersburg May 10, 1865; and mustered out, at close of the war, at Fairfax Court House, July 20, 1865.

William Hathaway McNeil and Alice Lea were married February 19, 1879, in Atchison, Kansas.

Alice Lea, daughter of James Henry and Ellen (Campbell) Lea, was born February 26, 1845, in Alton, Illinois, and died October 28, 1883, in Atchison, Kansas.

James Henry Lea was born December 19, 1808, in Philadelphia, Pa., and died June 4, 1890, in Atchison, Kansas.

Ellen (Campbell) Lea was born February 26, 1820, in Shippenburg, Pa., and died March 25, 1874, in Atchison, Kansas.

William Hathaway McNeil and Mary G. Sherwood were married July 15, 1886, at St. Joseph, Missouri.

Mary G. Sherwood, daughter of William Marshall and Charlotte C. (Hall) Sherwood, was born April 18, 1854, in Wilmington, North Carolina.

(B) Anna McNeil, daughter of James and Susan Bowen (Hathaway) McNeil, was born December 31, 1848, in Windsor, Vermont, and died December 13, 1862, in San Francisco, California.

(C) Allan McNeil, son of James and Ellen K. (Thrall) McNeil, was born June 4, 1859, at Napa, California, and died November 8, 1859, at Napa, California.

(II) GILBERT ROBERTSON, eldest son of William and Mary (Livingston) Robertson, was born August 24, 1778, in the town of Greenwich, Washington County, New York, and died February 10, 1865, at his home in Argyle, New York. He got the homestead of his father, William Robertson.

Gilbert Robertson and Elizabeth Dow were married October 1, 1804, in Argyle, New York.

Elizabeth Dow was born February 15, 1781, near the River Dee, in Aberdeenshire, Scotland; came to America in 1802; and died February 13, 1852, in Argyle, New York.

Gilbert and Elizabeth (Dow) Robertson had:

(I) Mary L. Robertson, born July 24, 1805; died February 15, 1828.

(II) Jeannette Robertson, born April 24, 1807; died February 28, 1855.

(III) William D. Robertson, born January 31, 1810; died July 6, 1897.

(IV) Margaret Ann Robertson, born April 4, 1812; died July 20, 1844.

(V) Gilbert Robertson, Jr., born February 8, 1815; died April 23, 1896.

(VI) Eliza Robertson, born January 1, 1817; died May 1, 1851.

(I) Mary L. Robertson, eldest daughter of Gilbert and Elizabeth (Dow) Robertson, was born July 24, 1805, and died February 15, 1828.

James Small and Mary L. Robertson were married October 19, 1826, in Argyle, New York. The descendants of this family may be found under the Small genealogy.

(II) Jeannette Robertson, second daughter of Gilbert and Elizabeth (Dow) Robertson, was born April 24, 1807, and died February 28, 1855.

Thomas Reid and Jeannette Robertson were married August 23, 1831, in Argyle, New York.

Thomas Reid, son of John and Margaret (McArthur) Reid, was born August 28, 1800, in Greenwich, New York, and died December 10, 1898.

Thomas and Jeannette (Robertson) Reid had:

(1) Mary L. Reid, born May 31, 1832, in Greenwich, New York.

(2) John Reid, born September 10, 1834; died August 7, 1839.

(3) Elizabeth Reid, born September 7, 1839; died March 20, 1902.

(4) James Reid, born July 12, 1841. Unmarried.

(1) Mary L. Reid, eldest daughter of Thomas and Jeannette (Robertson) Reid, was born May 31, 1832, in the town of Greenwich, Washington County, New York.

Archibald Armstrong, Jr., and Mary L. Reid were married February 22, 1855, in Greenwich, New York.

Archibald Armstrong, Jr., son of Archibald and Nancy (Donaldson) Armstrong, was born June 17, 1828, in Argyle, New York, and died September 7, 1903.

Archibald and Mary L. (Reid) Armstrong, Jr., had:

(A) Thomas Reid Armstrong, born November 3, 1857; died September 22, 1859.

(B) Jeannette Armstrong, born July 9, 1862, in Argyle, New York.

Fred W. Kenyon and Jeannette Armstrong were married January 10, 1883, in Argyle, New York.

(III) Hon. William D. Robertson, eldest son of Gilbert and Elizabeth (Dow) Robertson, was born January 10, 1810, in the town of Argyle, Washington County, New York, on the old homestead of his grandfather, William Robertson, and died July 6, 1897, on the same place, where he had lived all his life. He was a man of large and beneficent influence in his community and his good works gave him an exalted name throughout all Washington county. He had served his district in the state legislature and was president of the Greenwich & Johnsville Railroad and president of the bank of Greenwich.

Hon. William D. Robertson and Jeannette Shaw were married May 16, 1848, in Argyle, New York.

Jeannette Shaw, daughter of Alexander and Marianne (Livingston) Shaw, was born January 4, 1814, in the town of Greenwich, Washington County, New York, and died March 13, 1892.

Hon. William D. and Jeannette (Shaw) Robertson had:

(1) Gilbert A. Robertson, born February 10, 1850; died October 22, 1871.

(2) Mary Eliza Robertson, born August 27, 1851; died August 30, 1851.

(IV) Margaret Ann Robertson, third daughter of Gilbert and Elizabeth (Dow) Robertson, was born April 4, 1812, and died July 20, 1844.

David Law and Margaret Ann Robertson were married February 7, 1843, in Argyle, New York.

David Law, son of Robert I. and Anna (Small) Law, was born March 29, 1813, and died February 20, 1889, in Shushan, Washington County, New York.

David and Margaret Ann (Robertson) Law had,

(I) Anna Mary Law, born July 20, 1844; died September 9, 1866.

(V) Hon. Gilbert Robertson, Jr., second son of Gilbert and Elizabeth (Dow) Robertson, was born February 8, 1815, in Argyle, New York, and died April 23, 1896, in Troy, New York. After attending the common school he prepared for college at the academy in Cambridge, Washington County, and at the Herkimer academy, then in charge of Dr. Chanel, a celebrated teacher of the time. He was ambitious and industrious, and in 1833, when only 18 years of age, entered Union College at Schenectady from which he was graduated in 1837. Subsequently he taught school in Columbia County for two years. In 1839 he entered the law office of Cady & Fairchild at Salem, remaining until 1840, when he came to Troy and entered the office of Hayner & Gould.

In 1843 he was admitted to the bar and commenced the practice of law, which he continued until the time of his death. He was elected a school trustee in 1843 and continued as such three years. Previous to the adoption of the present system he brought about many reforms and succeeded in having the amount of money appropriated to the schools doubled. This greatly enhanced interest in the schools of the city and was instrumental in leading the way to the adoption of the existing system. He also manifested much interest in the Young Men's Association and as far back as 1847 was its president, after having been its corresponding secretary. In 1847 he was appointed by the Governor of the state a justice of the justices' court of Troy and in 1848, the office having become elective he was chosen to the same position, which he held until 1853. During four years of that time he was also a police justice. In 1851 he was elected to the office of recorder, which was abolished in 1867, and served until 1856. By virtue of that office he was presiding officer of the common council and took an active interest in all important matters brought before that body. While engaged in that capacity, on account of the heavy expense with which the city was burdened by the ownership of the Troy and Schenectady railroad a number of citizens in 1852 petitioned the common council to sell the road as a means of relief. He was one of the committee appointed by the common council to consider the proposition. Russell Sage, who was also a director of the company, was another. The committee recommended that a committee be appointed to sell the road for not less than $200,000. Judge Robertson was also placed on that committee. An agreement was presented by Mayor Gould, executed with Edwin D. Morgan for the sale of the road at the price named, $200,000, and the deal was consummated.

In 1859 he was elected county judge and he was re-elected in 1863. During his incumbency he was distinguished for his fair judicial rulings and strict impartiality. He was even then active in politics, but never allowed his partisanship to influence his judicial action. December 29, 1869, Judge Robertson was appointed United States assessor of internal revenue of New York state by President Grant.

In 1873 he was appointed postmaster of Troy by President Grant, and assumed the duties of the office February 9, 1874. He was reappointed February 18, 1878, and again April 4, 1882, the last time by President Arthur. His term expired March 16, 1886. The change in the national administration resulted April 28, 1886, in the appointment of Edward Dolan by President Cleveland to succeed him as postmaster. Judge Robertson was the eighteenth postmaster of Troy. During his incumbency he spared no pains to make the service acceptable. He introduced many improvements giving increased facilities, and so satisfactory was his administration that almost every business firm and prominent citizen, irrespective of political bias, signed the petition for his reappointment. It was during his postmastership that Judge Robertson was at the height of his political power. He was a born leader and organizer, and was at the head of a Republican organization which has never had an equal since in this city or county. There were no breaks in those days, for the astuteness and diplomacy of Judge Robertson kept all in line. He knew when to make concessions and when to be aggressive, and used his power to the best advantage in every case.

He was originally a Whig, but when the Republican party was formed he became one of its most active workers. In 1856 he was elected chairman of the Republican county committee, and with the exception of one year held the office twenty years. He was a member of the Republican State committee and also of its executive committee for three years. He was the leader in all Republican conventions and was an adept at "pouring oil on the troubled waters" when stormy scenes were enacted.

Judge Robertson was appointed a member of the State Board of Mediation and Arbitration by Governor Hill in 1886, and served in that capacity until a few weeks before his death. He was a member of the committee of one hundred appointed to arrange for the celebration of Troy's centennial and was one of the committee of the Troy bar having in charge the Thursday evening "Lawyers' Night."

During his long term of practice as a lawyer, Judge Robertson was associated with several partners. He was senior member of the firm of Robertson, Foster & North; Robertson, Foster & Kelley, and Robertson & Batchelder. Of recent years he had been alone in his practice, but a few weeks before his death his old partner, Samuel Foster, returned to Troy and they became associated again under the firm name of Robertson & Foster.

Gilbert Robertson, Jr., was an honest man. His integrity was never questioned and never assailed, either in political, social or business life. He was loyal to friends, and his genial, big-hearted manner made him a most magnetic man. His unvarying integrity and his strong personality conjured friendship and retained it. He was loved by his friends and respected by those opposed to him. Wherever he went to conventions he was consulted by the leaders and was recognized as a power. Judge Robertson was good and kind and possessed the best endowments of manhood. As a citizen, lawyer, official and politician he was eminent in all, and as a father, husband and friend, affectionate, tender, thoughtful and steadfast. The public had confidence in him, and in the many responsible trusts conferred upon him there was never a betrayal. His contemporaries included the men who made Troy, and he stood high among them. As a lawyer, Judge Robertson was astute and logical. Most of his legal work was confined to the office, and his advice was regarded as sound and reliable.

Judge Robertson discharged the duties of every position he held with such fidelity, intelligence and impartiality that even the suspicion of wrong-doing was never for a moment entertained against him. He held a high position for the acuteness and accuracy of his legal opinions. But as a social, genial companion, he exercised a power amongst his associates which has been rarely equaled, and which can never be forgotten by the Rensselaer county bar.

Until within a few years Judge Robertson was an enthusiastic equestrian, and the residents of all parts of Rensselaer county will remember the magnificent appearance of horse and rider. He frequently took long horseback rides, going out into the country and enjoying the beauties of nature days at a time. He was a man of magnificent physique and would attract attention in any assembly. By his death Troy loses a figure which has been among the most prominent in its history.—From the Troy Papers. April 24, 1896.

Hon. Gilbert Robertson, Jr., and Angeline Daggett were married June 10, 1852, in Troy, New York.

Angeline Daggett, daughter of Dr. Joseph and Rachel (Mitchel) Daggett, was born March 22, 1832, in Troy, New York, where she still lives.

Hon. Gilbert and Angeline (Daggett) Robertson had:

(1) Gilbert Daggett Robertson, born March 14, 1853.

(2) Mary Elizabeth Robertson, born September 5, 1854. Unmarried.

(3) William Robertson, born November 13, 1857; died November 21, 1857.

(4) John Livingston Robertson, born March 27, 1869. Unmarried.

(1) Gilbert Daggett Robertson and Annie Louise Eames were married May 18, 1880, in Worcester, Massachusetts. They live at 320 Boylston street, Boston, Massachusetts. No issue.

(VI) Eliza Robertson, fourth daughter of Gilbert and Elizabeth (Dow) Robertson, was born January 1, 1817, and died May 1, 1851.

William Lendrum and Eliza Robertson were married September 2, 1845, in Argyle, New York.

William Lendrum, son of George and Mary (Robinson) Lendrum, was born December 16, 1816, in Argyle, New York, and died July 8, 1880, in Argyle.

Mary (Robinson) Lendrum was a sister of Ann Robinson, wife of Archibald Robertson, Sr., of Argyle.

William and Eliza (Robertson) Lendrum had:

(1) Mary E. Lendrum, born July 7, 1846; died August 31, 1868.

(2) Anna I. Lendrum, born July 27, 1848.

John McArthur Reid and Anna I. Lendrum were married December 15, 1868, in Argyle, New York, where Mrs. Reid still resides, R. F. D. No. 2.

John McArthur Reid, son of John and Elizabeth (McInarie) Reid, was born February 12, 1844, in Argyle, New York, and died March 16, 1904, in Argyle, New York.

John McArthur and Anna I. (Lendrum) Reid had:

(A) Mary Elizabeth Reid, born October 1, 1870; died September 28, 1874.

(B) William J. Reid, born October 9, 1872.

(C) Archibald L. Reid, born January 19, 1876.

(D) Anna Jeannette Reid, born May 4, 1887; died May 7, 1887.

(B) William J. Reid, eldest son of John McArthur and Anna I. (Lendrum) Reid, was born October 9, 1872, in Argyle, New York, and now owns and lives on the old William D. Robertson homestead, in Argyle, New York, postoffice, North Greenwich, New York.

William J. Reid and Mary Alice Robertson were married October 31, 1900.

Mary Alice Robertson, second daughter of Captain Duncan and Alice (Armstrong) Robertson, was born July 23, 1870, in Argyle, New York, and died April 16, 1903, in Argyle, New York.

(C) Archibald L. Reid, second son of John McArthur and Anna I. (Lendrum) Reid, was born January 19, 1876, in Argyle, New York. He is unmarried and lives in Argyle, New York, R. F. D. No. 2.

(III) ARCHIBALD ROBERTSON, second son of William and Mary (Livingston) Robertson, was born March 1, 1780, in the town of Greenwich, Washington County New York, and died December 31, 1849, in Argyle, Washington County, New York. He got that part of his father's homestead which lies west of the road, and has, since his death, been owned and occupied by his son, Captain Duncan Robertson, and his grandson, Archibald William Robertson.

Archibald Robertson and Mary Ann Cook were married July 10, 1808.

Mary Ann Cook, daughter of Thomas and Mary Ann (Mahan) Cook, was born September 13, 1783, in Argyle, New York, and died July 2, or 15, 1814, in Argyle, New York.

Archibald and Mary Ann (Cook) Robertson had:

(I) William A. Robertson, born December 5, 1809; died May 10, 1883.

(II) Thomas Robertson, born August 27, 1811; died September 9, 1899.

(III) Archibald Robertson, Jr., born June 20, 1813: died September 19, 1879.

(I) William A. Robertson, eldest son of Archibald and Mary Ann (Cook) Robertson, was born December 5, 1809, in Argyle, New York, and died May 10, 1883, at the home of Rev. Gilbert H. Robertson, in Sandwich, Illinois. He was known to the family by the familiar name of "Bill A."

(II) Thomas Robertson, second son of Archibald and Mary Ann (Cook) Robertson, was born August 27, 1811, on the farm near South Argyle, Washington County, New York, and died September 9, 1899, at the home of his son, Alexander Shaw Robertson, in Chicago, Illinois.

When he was little more than three years old his mother

died, but the boy retained a vivid recollection of her, which continued throughout a long life. At fourteen he was apprenticed to his uncle, John Robertson, who, with William Robertson, his brother, was operating a tannery at Coila, New York. He remained "learning his trade" until he was twenty-one years old. His compensation was his board and clothes and a very limited allowance of spending money. During the last two years of this period he did the work of a "journeyman," but received no wages. As he used to say afterwards, it never occurred to him that he could do anything else but serve out his apprenticeship to the last day. Conscientiously keeping his engagements became the habit of his life. After working as a "journeyman" for several years and becoming foreman of the shop he concluded that he needed more education and he spent a year in school. He afterwards, with his brother, William A. Robertson, embarked in the grocery business in Troy, New York. In 1840 he married Mary Shaw, daughter of Alexander Shaw, of Greenwich. Mary Shaw and her sister, Jeannette, wife of William D. Robertson, were twins, and like the twins in the ballad, "each looked more like the other than herself, folks used to say." It has come down among the family traditions that during the period of courtship the unsuspecting lover was made the victim of numerous substitutions and he afterwards blushingly admitted that he never felt quite sure which was Mary until after the wedding. In 1848 he gave up the grocery business and bought a tannery, and shortly after a grist mill at Lakeville, (now Cossayuna) in Washington County, New York. Here he lived and carried on the tanning and milling business for thirty years. He was one of the most active and public spirited citizens of the county, and was regarded as a man of superior intelligence and unblemished honor. He and his wife were devout members of the United Presbyterian Church and their five children were brought up with all strictness in that rigid faith. The Shorter Catechism was recited every Sabbath afternoon and all work and play were strictly forbidden on that day. Father, mother and five children occupied the family pew every Lord's Day and the children regularly attended Sabbath school and bible class. It was a Scotch Presbyterian family with some of the austerity worn off, for Thomas Robertson was a kind and affectionate husband and father, and a most desirable neighbor and citizen. In 1872 he sold his property at Lakeville and came to Chicago, where he continued to reside most of the time until his death, September 9, 1899, being then eighty-eight years and eight days old. Until a few months before he died it was his habit to walk several miles each day. He walked and moved about with firm and easy step until taken with his last illness., Although for several years he had not been engaged in any business he was constantly employed in reading, writing or walking, his active mind requiring constant employment. In person he bore so striking a resemblance to the poet Longfellow, that the photographs of the two can hardly be distinguished.—Alexander Shaw Robertson.

Thomas Robertson and Mary Shaw were married May 19, 1840, in the town of Greenwich, Washington County, New York.

Mary Shaw, daughter of Alexander and Marianne (Livingston) Shaw, was born January 4, 1814, in the town of Greenwich, Washington County, New York, and died May 24, 1867, at Lakeville, in the same county.

Thomas and Mary (Shaw) Robertson had:

(1) Archibald Robertson, born June 27, 1844; died November 7, 1867.

(2) Alexander Shaw Robertson, born June 12, 1846.

(3) Mary Anna Robertson, born June 24, 1848.

(4) John Robertson, born February 11, 1851; died May 26, 1865.

(5) William Thomas Robertson, born January 5, 1854: died May 20, 1885.

(1) Archibald Robertson, eldest son of Thomas and Mary (Shaw) Robertson, was born June 27, 1844, at Lakeville, New York, and died November 7, 1867, in the same place. He served all through the civil war and came home and died of lockjaw from a wound in his hand received in his father's mill. He was lieutenant in Company "D," Ninety-third Regiment, N. Y. Volunteers, Infantry.

(2) Alexander Shaw Robertson, second son of Thomas and Mary (Shaw) Robertson, was born June 12, 1846, in Lakeville, New York, and is a lawyer in Chicago.

Alexander Shaw Robertson and Lucretia M. Wallbridge were married April 22, 1870, in Cairo, Illinois.

Lucretia M. Walbridge, daughter of Egbert and Ann Eliza (Tuthill) Walbridge, was born March 19, 1852, in Thebes, Illinois.

Alexander Shaw and Lucretia M. (Walbridge) Robertson had:

(A) Jeannette Louise Robertson, born February 20, 1880; died March 26, 1880.

(B) Egbert Thomas Robertson, born December 8, 1881, in Cairo, Illinois.

(C) Hattie Lucretia Robertson, born December 6, 1883, in Chicago.

(D) Ella Margaret Robertson, born May 17, 1885, in Chicago.

(3) Mary Anna Robertson, only daughter of Thomas and Mary (Shaw) Robertson, was born June 24, 1848, in Lakeville, New York, and now lives at 76 Prospect street, Cambridgeport, in Boston, Massachusetts.

Edwin David Lowe and Mary Anna Robertson were married May 23, 1876, in Sandwich, Illinois.

Edwin David Lowe, son of John and Sarah (Fuller) Lowe, was born March 7, 1851, at Cambridge, Massachusetts.

Edwin David and Mary Anna (Robertson) Lowe had:

(A) Emma Shaw Lowe, born April 8, 1879, in Cambridge, Massachusetts.

(B) Mora Hilton Lowe, born March 26, 1883, in Philadelphia, Pa.

(5) William Thomas Robertson, fourth son of Thomas and Mary (Shaw) Robertson, was born January 5, 1854, in Lakeville, New York, and died May 20, 1885, in Woodlawn, Nebraska, where he was engaged in farming.

William Thomas Robertson and Anna Skinner were married October 17, 1876, in Argyle, New York, and had:

(A) Gilbert H. Robertson, born August 2, 1877.

(B) Archibald J. Robertson, born October 2, 1879.

(C) Mary Robertson, born March 31, 1882; died March 7, 1893.

Mrs. Anna (Skinner) Robertson was married, secondly, to Emil Dahl, and they live at 1430 P street, Lincoln, Nebraska.

(A) Gilbert H. Robertson, eldest son of William Thomas and Anna (Skinner) Robertson, was born August 2, 1877, in Woodlawn, Nebraska.

Gilbert H. Robertson and Jessie M. Waugh were married April 4, 1900, and had:

(a) Margaret Robertson, born April 5, 1901.

(b) Mary Robertson, born January 10, 1903.

(B) Archibald J. Robertson, second son of William Thomas and Anna (Skinner) Robertson, was born October 2, 1879, in Woodlawn, Nebraska.

Archibald J. Robertson and Della Felwock were married January 16, 1900.

(III) Archibald Robertson, Jr., third son of Archibald and Mary Ann (Cook) Robertson, was born June 20, 1813, in Argyle, New York, and died September 19, 1879, in Salem, New York. He was for many years postmaster at Salem.

Archibald Robertson, Jr., and Julia Frances King were married September 16, 1838.

Julia Frances King, daughter of Henry and Huldah (Cook) King, was born May 21, 1818, and died December 2, 1862, aged forty-four years.

Archibald and Julia Frances (King) Robertson, Jr., had:

(1) Mary A. C. Robertson, born August 9, 1839, at Bennington, Vermont.

(2) Julia Frances Robertson, born August 31, 1841; died June 5, 1902.

(3) Sarah H. Robertson, born August 13, 1844.

The three sisters have been living for several years at Seattle, Washington, where Julia Frances Robertson died.

(III) ARCHIBALD ROBERTSON, SR., married, secondly, Anne Robinson, June 20, 1816.

Anne Robinson, daughter of Duncan and Jeannette (Robeson) Robinson, was born February 21, 1794, near Edinburgh, Scotland, and died August 21, 1849, in Argyle, New York. She, with her father's family, came to America in 1801, and settled in Argyle, near what is called "The Lick," or Reid's Springs. Her father died there and was buried in an old burying ground about a mile west of South Argyle. Her mother afterward moved to Duanesburg, Schenectady County, and died there. The only son of Duncan and Jeannette (Robeson) Robinson lived near the tollgate between Argyle and Fort Edward; moved from there to Ohio and was killed by a tree falling on him.

ARCHIBALD and ANNE (ROBINSON) ROBERTSON had:

(I) Mary Livingston Robertson, born April 3, 1820; died December 2, 1843.

(II) Jeannette Robertson, born December 4, 1821.

(III) Ann Eliza Robertson, born November 20, 1823; died November 6, 1893.

(IV) Duncan Robertson, born November 15, 1824; died August 4, 1899.

(V) John Robertson, born December 4, 1825; died April 20, 1850.

(VI) Catherine Eleanor Robertson, born February 4, 1828.

(VII) Gilbert Hamilton Robertson, born November 28, 1831.

(I) Mary Livingston Robertson, eldest daughter of Archibald and Anne (Robinson) Robertson, was born April 3, 1820, in Argyle, Washington County, New York, and died December 2, 1843, in Argyle, New York.

William Henry and Mary Livingston Robertson were married May 4, 1841, in Argyle, New York.

William Henry, son of John and Pamelia (Johnson) Henry, was born January 1, 1817, in Greenwich, Washington County, New York, and died April 17, 1877, in Trenton, Missouri.

William and Mary Livingston (Robertson) Henry had:

(1) Mary Livingston Henry, born May 4, 1843; died December 19, 1843.

(II) Jeannette Robertson, second daughter of Archibald and Anne (Robinson) Robertson, was born December 4, 1821, in Argyle, New York, and now lives in Moberly, Missouri.

Edward Law and Jeannette Robertson were married September 12, 1843, in Argyle, New York.

Edward Law, son of Robert I. and Anne Rector (Small) Law, was born September 15, 1817, in the town of Salem, Washington County, New York, and died June 17, 1892, in Fountain Green, Illinois.

The descendants of Edward and Jeannette (Robertson) Law may be found under the head of the Laws, in succeeding pages.

(III) Ann Eliza Robertson, third daughter of Archibald and Anne (Robinson) Robertson, was born November 20, 1823, in Argyle, Washington County, New York, and died November 6, 1893, at her home near Norwood, Mercer County, Illinois.

George Small, Jr., and Ann Eliza Robertson were married September 23, 1846, in Argyle, New York.

George Small, Jr., youngest child of George and Jeannette (Lourie) Small, was born August 5, 1823, in the town of Jackson, Washington County, New York, and died March 25, 1898, at his home near Norwood, Mercer County, Illinois.

The descendants of George and Ann Eliza (Robertson) Small may be found under the head of Smalls in succeeding pages.

(IV) Duncan Robertson, eldest son of Archibald and Anne (Robinson) Robertson, was born November 15, 1824, in Argyle, Washington County, New York, and died August 4, 1899, in the same place.

Captain Duncan Robertson was Captain of Company "F," One-Hundred-Twenty-third New York Infantry. The company was organized at Argyle, New York, August 22, 1862, and mustered into service at Salem, New York, September 4, 1862; and discharged June 29, 1865. Captain Duncan Robertson went out as a captain and served until his regiment was discharged. He was in the following engagements: Chancellorsville, Resaca, Dallas, Lost Mountain, Pine Mountain, Culp's Farm, Chattahoochie, Peach Tree Creek, Siege of Atlanta, Savannah, Averysboro, Bentonville, Kenesaw Mountain and Raleigh.

He was a farmer and lived all his life on the farm where he was born and where his father had lived before him.

Duncan Robertson and Alice Armstrong were married February 27, 1851, in Argyle, New York.

Alice Armstrong, daughter of Archibald and Nancy (Donaldson) Armstrong, was born February 8, 1830, in Argyle, New York, and died January 29, 1905, in Argyle, New York, on the Robertson homestead.

Duncan and Alice (Armstrong) Robertson had:

(1) Anna F. Robertson, born October 1, 1852. Unmarried.

(2) Archibald William Robertson, born November 11, 1858.

(3) Mary Alice Robertson, born July 23, 1870; died April 16, 1903.

(4) John A. Robertson, born April 20, 1873; died March 29, 1875.

(2) Archibald William Robertson, eldest son of Duncan and Alice (Armstrong) Robertson, was born November 11, 1858, on the farm owned and occupied by his father and grandfather before him, where he still resides.

Archibald William Robertson and Jenevieve Alicia Johnson were married September 28, 1904, in South Argyle, Washington County, New York.

Jenevieve Alicia Johnson, daughter of William Martin and

Jane Alice (McBeth) Johnson, was born September 30, 1879, in Napa County, California.

Archibald William and Jenevieve Alicia (Johnson) Robertson had:

(A) Geraldine Alice Robertson, born February 12, 1906.

(3) Mary Alice Robertson, second daughter of Captain Duncan and Alice (Armstrong) Robertson, was born July 23, 1870, in Argyle, New York, and died April 16, 1903, in Argyle, New York.

William J. Reid and Mary Alice Robertson were married October 31, 1900, in Argyle, New York.

William J. Reid, eldest son of John McArthur and Anna I. (Lendrum) Reid, was born October 9, 1872, in Argyle, New York. He bought the old homestead of William D. Robertson, where he lives.

(V) John Robertson, second son of Archibald and Anne (Robinson) Robertson, was born December 4, 1824, in Argyle, New York, and died April 20, 1850, near Sacramento, California, whither he had gone with the "Forty-niners." He was buried near Sacramento.

(VI) Catherine Eleanor Robertson, fourth daughter of Archibald and Anne (Robinson) Robertson, was born February 4, 1828, in Argyle, New York, and now lives in Keokuk, Iowa, where she has lived since 1856.

Alexander Lourie and Catherine Eleanor Robertson were married December 15, 1855, at the residence of George Small, at Wheatland, Will County, Illinois.

Alexander Lourie, son of George and Mary (Irvine) Lourie, was born April 6, 1823, in the town of Jackson, Washington County, New York, and died March 7, 1878, in Keokuk, Iowa. He was a prominent architect in that city.

Alexander Lourie married, first, Mary Sophia Bigelow, September 5, 1849.

Mary Sophia Bigelow, daughter of Anson and Eliza (Moores) Bigelow, was born November 9, 1827, and died February 4, 1854.

Alexander and Mary Sophia (Bigelow) Lourie had:

(1) Herbert Mattoon Lourie, born September 15, 1850.

(2) Eliza Moores Lourie, born September 11, 1852.

(1) Herbert Mattoon Lourie, son of Alexander and Mary Sophia (Bigelow) Lourie, was born September 15, 1850, in Jackson, Washington County, New York, and has lived most of his life in Keokuk, Iowa, where he continues to reside.

Herbert Mattoon Lourie and Elizabeth Jane Steele were married October 5, 1875, in Keokuk, Iowa.

Elizabeth Jane Steele, daughter of William and Margaret Steele, was born September 26, 1852, and died December 18, 1886.

Herbert Mattoon and Elizabeth Jane (Steele) Lourie had:

(A) Ralph Bigelow Lourie, born July 22, 1876.

(B) Lloyd Steele Lourie, born September 3, 1877.

(C) Grace Elizabeth Lourie, born March 22, 1879.

(D) Herbert Shaw Lourie, born January 23, 1881.

(E) Arthur William Lourie, born December 11, 1882; died January 30, 1896.

Herbert Mattoon Lourie and Laura Alice Hamill were married May 22, 1889.

Laura Alice Hamill, daughter of Smith and Nancy Hamill, was born April 11, 1856, and died September 1, 1905.

(A) Ralph Bigelow Lourie, eldest son of Herbert Mattoon and Elizabeth Jane (Steele) Lourie, was born July 22, 1876.

Ralph Bigelow Lourie and Margaret Isabel Bruce were married November 11, 1902, at Montgomery, Alabama.

(B) Lloyd Steele Lourie, second son of Herbert Mattoon and Elizabeth Jane (Steele) Lourie, was born September 3, 1877, in Keokuk, Iowa, and now lives in Chicago, where he has established a fine business in dentistry.

Dr. Lloyd Steele Lourie and Flora McDonald Carpenter were married September 4, 1905,. at Grand Tracedie, Prince Edward's Island.

Flora McDonald Carpenter, daughter of Amos and Helen (Fraser) Carpenter, was born September 26, 1879.

(2) Eliza Moores Lourie, daughter of Alexander and Mary Sophia (Bigelow) Lourie, was born September 11, 1852, in Jackson, Washington County, New York, and now lives in Los Angeles, California.

Rev. Edward Brown Graham and Eliza Moores Lourie were married June 1, 1876, in Keokuk, Iowa.

Rev. Edward Brown Graham, son of James Harvey and

Mary Jane Graham, was born January 25, 1851, and died September 7, 1898.

Rev. Edward Brown and Eliza Moores (Lourie) Graham had:

(A) Mary Clara Graham, born March 4, 1877.

(B) Laura Graham, born January 19, 1879.

(C) Lois Graham, born November 2, 1892.

James S. Campbell, of Tarkio, Missouri, and Laura Graham were married March 1, 1906.

Alexander and Catherine Eleanor (Robertson) Lourie had:

(1) Hamilton Alexander Lourie, born June 16, 1859; died October 10, 1862.

(2) Irvine Robertson Lourie, born June 7, 1862; died June 21, 1864.

(3) George Brown Lourie, born October 24, 1864.

(4) Mary Jeannette Lourie, born May 13, 1867.

(5) Anna Eurella Lourie, born January 19, 1871.

(3) George Brown Lourie, third son of Alexander and Catherine Eleanor (Robertson) Lourie, was born October 24, 1864, in Keokuk, Iowa, and lives in Racine, Wisconsin.

George Brown Lourie and Anna Stanley Crocker were married January 30, 1889, in Omaha, Nebraska.

Anna Stanley Crocker was born January 2, 1869, at Petrolium, Pa.

George Brown and Anna Stanley (Crocker) Lourie had:

(A) Catherine Lourie, born July 3, 1893, in Omaha, Neb.

(B) Donald Bradford Lourie, born August 22, 1898, in Decatur, Ala.

(VII) Gilbert Hamilton Robertson, third and youngest son of Archibald and Anne (Robinson) Robertson, was born November 28, 1831, in South Argyle, Washington County, New York, and now lives in Sandwich, Illinois.

After a preparatory course at the Argyle Academy he was graduated from Union College, at Schenectady, New York, in 1849. After spending two or three years in the South he went to the Associate Presbyterian Theological Seminary, at Canonsburg, Pa., from which he was graduated in 1855. Was licensed in 1855 by the Associate Presbyterian Presbytery of Cambridge, at East Greenwich, New York.

Settled in North Hebron, New York, in 1858. This church was one of the Associate Reformed Churches before the union which occurred the same year between the Associate and Associate Reformed Presbyterian Churches forming the United Presbyterian Church. Was the first minister ordained in the United Presbyterian Church.

Accepted a call from the Park Presbyterian Church, Troy, New York, in 1860. This was an Old School Presbyterian Church.

Accepted a call from the New School Presbyterian Church at Sandwich, Illinois, in 1865.

Accepted a call from the New School Presbyterian Church at Springfield, Illinois, in 1867. During this pastorate was the union of the Old and New School Churches. Preached the opening sermon at the consolidation of the Presbyteries of Central Illinois at their joint meeting at Bloomington, Illinois.

Accepted a call to Fourth-street Presbyterian Church at Louisville, Kentucky, in 1870.

In 1872 was editor of the Louisville Daily Commercial; and in 1874 took charge of the Sandwich Gazette at Sandwich, Ills.

From 1882 to 1886 was postmaster at Sandwich, Illinois.

From 1890 to 1894 was Deputy Collector of Internal Revenue at Chicago.

From 1899 to 1901 was mayor of Sandwich, Illinois.

In 1877 became a minister in the Methodist Protestant Church and continues in same connection.

Rev. Gilbert Hamilton Robertson and Mary Beveridge were married May 31, 1859, in Xenia, Ohio.

Mary Beveridge, daughter of Rev. Thomas and Eliza (Armitage) Beveridge, D. D., was born March 31, 1837, in Xenia, Ohio.

Rev. Gilbert Hamilton and Mary (Beveridge) Robertson had:

(1) William Hamilton Robertson, born July 10, 1860.
(2) Alma Elizabeth Robertson, born April 26, 1862.
(3) Henry Knight Robertson, born October 15, 1866.

(1) William Hamilton Robertson, eldest son of Rev. Gilbert Hamilton and Mary (Beveridge) Robertson, was born July 10, 1860, in Troy, New York, and now lives in Austin, Cook County, Illinois. He is secretary to James A. Patten, of the firm of Bartlett, Frazier & Carrington, Western Union Building, Chicago, which position he has occupied for more than ten years. In 1891 Mr. Robertson was a commissioner to the

General Assembly of the Presbyterian Church, in session that year at Detroit.

William Hamilton Robertson and Fannie Schnebly were married May 19, 1887, in Peoria, Illinois.

William Hamilton and Fannie (Schnebly) Robertson had:

(A) Dorothy Virginia Robertson, born February 20, 1892, in Sandwich, Illinois.

(2) Alma Elizabeth Robertson, daughter of Rev. Gilbert Hamilton and Mary (Beveridge) Robertson, was born April 26, 1862, in Troy, New York, and lives in Sandwich, Illinois.

S. P. Sedgwick and Alma Elizabeth Robertson were married September 6, 1883, in Sandwich, Illinois.

S. P. Sedgwick, son of Hon. W. W. and Sarah (Toombs) Sedgwick, was born March 1, 1860, in Sandwich, Illinois.

S. P. and Alma Elizabeth (Robertson) Sedgwick had:

(A) Ray Hamilton Sedgwick, born August 9, 1884, in Sandwich, Illinois.

(B) Westel Willoughby Sedgwick, born October 18, 1886, in Sandwich, Illinois.

(C) Marjorie Sedgwick, born November 9, 1888, in Sandwich, Illinois.

(3) Henry Knight Robertson, second son of Rev. Gilbert Hamilton and Mary (Beveridge) Robertson, was born October 15, 1866, in Sandwich, Illinois.

Henry Knight Robertson and Zillah Dubrock were married October 3, 1889, in Somonauk, Illinois.

(IV) JEANNETTE ROBERTSON, second daughter of William and Mary (Livingston) Robertson, was born January 26, 1782, in Greenwich, New York, and died February 23, 1856, at Fort Edward, New York.

James McDougall and Jeannette Robertson were married in Argyle, Washington County, New York.

LINEAGE OF JAMES M'DOUGALL.

(I) Sir John MacDougall of Dunolly, joined the rising in 1715 and suffered forfeiture in consequence. He married, in 1712, Mary, daughter of Sir Donald MacDonald, fourth Baronet of Slate, by his wife, Mary, daughter of Donald MacDonald of Castletown. He left two daughters, the elder of whom was married to John Maclean of Lachbuy, and a son and successor,

(II) Sir Alexander MacDougall of Dunolly, who was restored to his father's forfeited estates by charter from the Duke of Argyle in 1745. He married Mary, daughter of Sir Alexander Campbell of Barcaldine, County Argyle, and had issue:

(III) Alexander MacDougall, fourth son, who came to America with the Argyle colonists; settled in Orange County, New York, and married a lady from Holland. In 1765 he drew lot 129 of the Argyle Patent, in Washington County, New York. He took an active part in the French and Revolutionary wars and is said to have commanded a brigade at the battle of Saratoga. He had:

(IV) John MacDougall, born April 4, 1753, in Orange County, New York; married Elizabeth, daughter of Captain John and Catherine Beaty of Argyle, Washington County, New York, and had:

(V) James MacDougall, born January 10, 1783, at Fort Edward, Washington County, New York, and died in September, 1862, at Fort Edward, Washington County, New York.

James and Jeannette (Robertson) McDougall had:

(I) William McDougall, born November 16, 1806; died in 1875.

(II) Elizabeth Beaty McDougall, born June 23, 1808; died December 8, 1871.

(III) Mary McDougall, born November 10, 1810; died September 1, 1886.

(IV) John McDougall, born October 13, 1813; died June 10, 1877.

(V) Alexander McDougall, born July 25, 1815; died July 17, 1874.

(VI) Jane Ann McDougall, born December 19, 1819; died in April, 1905.

(VII) Margaret McDougall, born December 27, 1821; died January 11, 1858.

(VIII) Gilbert Robertson McDougall, born August 28, 1824; died September 12, 1892.

(I) William McDougall, eldest son of James and Jeannette (Robertson) McDougall, was born November 16, 1806, at the home of his grandfather, William Robertson, and died in 1875, in Tennessee. He married, first, Rebecca Hamilton, and had:

(1) Wellington McDougall.

(2) William McDougall.

(3) James McDougall.

He married, secondly, Jane ————, and had:

(1) John McDougall, born in 1854, in Tennessee.

(2) Alexander McDougall, born in 1856, in Tennessee.

(3) Jeannette McDougall, born in 1858, in Tennessee.

(II) Elizabeth Beaty McDougall, eldest daughter of James and Jeannette (Robertson) McDougall, was born June 23, 1808, and died December 8, 1871.

Hiram Crawford and Elizabeth Beaty McDougall were mareird April 28, 1836.

Hiram Crawford, son of John and Margaret (Simpson) Crawford, was born April 9, 1808, in Argyle, New York, and died June 24, 1888.

Hiram and Elizabeth Beaty (McDougall) Crawford had:

(1) James Edward Crawford, born February 22, 1837.

(2) Jeannette M. Crawford, born May 18, 1844; died March 15, 1866.

(3) John M. Crawford, born February 22, 1846; died May 12, 1893.

(3) John M. Crawford and Sarah E. Smith were married September 24, 1873, and had:

(A) Minnie E. Crawford, born November 26, 1875.

(B) Albert S. Crawford, born November 27, 1877.

(C) Frank A. Crawford, born November 4, 1884.

(B) Albert S. Crawford and Mary Clough were married February 9, 1905, at the home of James C. Clough, near Cossayuna, New York.

(III) Mary McDougall, second daughter of James and Jeannette (Robertson) McDougall, was born November 10, 1810, and died, unmarried, September 1, 1886.

(IV) John McDougall, second son of James and Jeannette (Robertson) McDougall, was born October 13, 1813, at Fort Edward, New York, and died June 10, 1877, at Danforth, Illinois.

John McDougall and Mary Epperson were married April 12, 1849, in Columbia, Adair County, Kentucky.

Mary Epperson, daughter of Colonel William and Elizabeth (Montgomery) Epperson, was born March 20, 1820, in Columbia, Adair County, Kentucky.

John and Mary (Epperson) McDougall had:

(1) William James McDougall, born January 11, 1850.

(2) Charles Gilbert McDougall, born September 12, 1852.

(3) Margaret Ann McDougall, born January 13, 1855; died January 30, 1882.

(4) Sarah Elizabeth McDougall, born June 10, 1858.

(3) Emma Jeannette McDougall, born April 30, 1862.

(1) William James McDougall, eldest son of John and Mary (Epperson) McDougall, was born January 11, 1850, in Rowena, Russell County, Kentucky, and now lives at Danforth, Illinois.

(2) Charles Gilbert McDougall, second son of John and Mary (Epperson) McDougall, was born September 12, 1852, in Rowena, Russell County, Kentucky, and now lives in Longwood, a suburb of Chicago.

Charles Gilbert McDougall and Mary Ruckrigel were married June 6, 1893, in Ashkum, Illinois.

Mary Ruckrigel, daughter of John and Mary Ruckrigel, was born November 20, 1862, in Louisville, Kentucky, and died April 15, 1902, in Stuttgart, Arkansas.

Charles Gilbert and Mary (Ruckrigel) McDougall had:

(A) Mabel Irene McDougall, born June 3, 1894, in Danforth, Illinois.

(B) Charles William McDougall, born June 20, 1895, in Danforth, Illinois.

(C) Gilbert Henry McDougall, born September 26, 1898, in Danforth, Illinois.

Charles Gilbert McDougall and Anna Mary Patten were married August 3, 1905, at the home of Charles J. Patten, in Sandwich, Ilinois, by the Rev. Gilbert Hamilton Robertson, D. D.

Anna Mary Patten, daughter of Hon. William and Jane (Somes) Patten, was born July 17, 1860, near Sandwich, Illinois.

(3) Margaret Ann McDougall, eldest daughter of John and Mary (Epperson) McDougall, was born January 13, 1855, Russell Springs, in Russell, County, Kentucky, and died, unmarried, January 30, 1882, in Danforth, Illinois.

(4) Sarah Elizabeth McDougall, second daughter of John and Mary (Epperson) McDougall, was born June 10, 1858, near Jamestown, Russell County, Kentucky.

Ernest Severy and Sarah Elizabeth McDougall were married March 14, 1888, in Kankakee, Illinois.

Ernest Severy, son of Cyrus Morrell and Deland (Eastman) Severy, was born November 26, 1861, in East Dixfield, Oxford County, Maine. He was educated at the State Normal School at Normal, Illinois, and was graduated from the law department of the Northwestern University, at Chicago, Illinois. He lives in Longwood and practices law in Chicago.

(5) Emma Jeannette McDougall, third daughter of John and Mary (Epperson) McDougall, was born April 30, 1862, near Jamestown, Russell County, Kentucky.

Dr. Charles Frank Smith and Emma Jeannette McDougall were married February 10, 1881, at Danforth, Illinois. They live at Kankakee, Illinois.

Dr. Charles Frank Smith, son of Morris G. and Orissa (Lake) Smith, was born June 6, 1857, in Gouveneur, St. Lawrence County, New York.

Dr. Charles Frank and Emma Jeannette (McDougall) Smith had:

(A) Charles Kenneth Smith, born May 9, 1883, in Danforth. Illinois.

(V) Alexander McDougall, third son of James and Jeannette (Robertson) McDougall, was born July 25, 1815, at Fort Edward, New York, and died July 17, 1874, at Fort Edward, New York.

Alexander McDougall and Martha Jane Nelson were married February 12, 1846.

Martha Jane Nelson, daughter of Samuel and Jane (Crawford) Nelson, was born February 12, 1826, in Hebron, New York. and died April 17, 1894, in Fort Edward, New York.

Alexander and Martha Jane (Nelson) McDougall had:

(1) Jennie C. McDougall, born January 9, 1848, in Fort Edward, New York.

(2) Mary L. McDougall, born August 18, 1851, in Fort Edward, New York.

(3) Hattie McDougall, born February 9, 1854; died September 5, 1887.

(4) Wellington McDougall, born October 12, 1855.

(5) John McDougall, born April 13, 1860.

(6) Margaret McDougall, born April 26, 1863; died February 16, 1885.

(1) Jennie C. McDougall, eldest daughter of Alexander and Martha Jane (Nelson) McDougall, was born January 9, 1848, at Fort Edward, N. Y.

Rev. A. E. Smith and Jennie C. McDougall were married January 2, 1868, at the home of Alexander McDougall, in Fort Edward, New York.

Rev. A. E. Smith was born October 19, 1836, in Jefferson County, Ohio.

Rev. A. E. and Jennie C. (McDougall) Smith had,

(A) William Alexander Smith, born April 15, 1874.

(4) Wellington McDougall, eldest son of Alexander and Martha Jane (Nelson) McDougall, was born October 12, 1855, in Fort Edward, New York.

Wellington McDougall and Nellie Conklin were married December 22, 1886, in Sandy Hill, New York, and had:

(A) Grace Cameron McDougall, born November 2, 1892, in Fort Edward.

(B) Jeannette E. McDougall, born October 22, 1899; died January 14, 1903.

(C) Wellington Cameron McDougall, born August 11, 1902.

(5) John McDougall, second son of Alexander and Martha Jane (Nelson) McDougall, was born April 13, 1860, in Fort Edward, New York.

John McDougall and Anna Wilder were married November 30, 1887, in Sandy Hill, New York, and had,

(A) Charles Howard McDougall, born May 2, 1890, in Sandy Hill, New York.

(VI) Jane Ann McDougall, third daughter of James and Jeannette (Robertson) McDougall, was born December 19, 1819, and died April 1, 1905.

Samuel Cameron and Jane Ann McDougall were married December 14, 1843.

Samuel Cameron, son of John and Julia Ann (Hudson) Cameron, was born April 27, 1817, in Warrensburg, New York, and died February 13, 1878, in Sioux City, Iowa. Samuel Cameron and family moved from Fort Edward, New York, to Sioux City, Iowa, in 1857, and Mrs. Cameron and her son, James, moved to Williston, Tennessee, in 1899.

Samuel and Jane Ann (McDougall) Cameron had:

(1) Wellington Cameron, born November 12, 1844; died June, 1847.

(2) James Cameron, born March 23, 1847.

(VII) Margaret McDougall, fourth daughter of James and Jeannette (Robertson) McDougall, was born December 27, 1821, and died January 11, 1858.

John M. Reaves and Margaret McDougall were married in 1848.

John M. Reaves, son of Henry and Maria Reaves, was born in 1819 and died in 1859.

John M. and Margaret (McDougall) Reaves had:

(1) Mary Elizabeth Reaves, born June 1, 1853; died January 27, 1904.

(2) Margaret Reaves, born February 8, 1856.

(3) Jeannette Reaves, born February 8, 1858; died July 24, 1892.

(1) Mary Elizabeth Reaves, eldest daughter of John M. and Margaret (McDougall) Reaves, was born June 1, 1853, in Fort Edward, New York, and died January 27, 1904, in New York City.

Andrew J. Millard and Mary Elizabeth Reaves were married October, 1865, in Sioux City, Iowa.

Andrew J. Millard, son of M. J. Millard, was born in May, 1837, and died in September, 1895.

Andrew J. and Mary Elizabeth (Reaves) Millard had:

(a) Anna Millard, born August 1, 1876, in Sioux City, Iowa.

William H. Harris and Anna Millard were married October, 1892, in Sioux City, Iowa.

William H. Harris, son of William Harris, was born January, 1867, in New York.

William H. and Anna (Millard) Harris had:

(a) Lorraine Harris, born May 11, 1894, in Sioux City, Iowa.

(2) Margaret L. Reaves, second daughter of John M. and Margaret (McDougall) Reaves, was born February 8, 1856.

Lorenzo Benson Atwood and Margaret L. Reaves were married June 29, 1872, in Sioux City, Iowa.

Lorenzo Benson Atwood, son of Henry Atwood, was born

December 31, 1838, in Livermore, Maine, and died June 29, 1898, in Sioux City, Iowa.

Lorenzo Benson and Margaret L. (Reaves) Atwood had:

(a) Flora Atwood, born June 29, 1873; died April 1, 1877.

(b) Charles G. Atwood, born April 11, 1876, died December 28, 1902.

(c) Marguerite Atwood, born December 9, 1879.

Louis A. Hall and Marguerite Atwood were married November 17, 1892, in Sioux City, Iowa.

Louis A. Hall, son of Jacob A. Hall, was born in Greenfield, Indiana.

John William Turtle and Mrs. Margaret L. (Reaves) Atwood were married September 26, 1903, in New York City.

John William Turtle, son of William and Fannie Turtle, was born June 27, 1858, in Sheffield, England, and resides at 1444 Sixth avenue, Des Moines, Iowa, where he is general passenger agent for several railroads.

(VIII) Gilbert Robertson McDougall, fourth son of James and Jeannette (Robertson) McDougall, was born August 28, 1824, and died September 12, 1892, in Seattle, Washington.

Gilbert Robertson McDougall and Margaret Macready were married September, 1875, in Sioux City, Iowa, and had:

(1) Jeannette Isabella McDougall, born in 1876, in Sioux City, Iowa.

(V) WILLIAM ROBERTSON, JR., third son of William and Mary (Livingston) Robertson, was born December 15, 1783, in the town of Greenwich, Washington county, New York, and died November 1, 1857, in Coila, New York.

William Robertson, Jr., and Mary McDoual were married May 13, 1824, in the town of Jackson, Washington county, New York.

Mary McDoual, daughter of John (born in Scotland) and Sarah (Thomas) McDoual, was born September 5, 1803, in the town of Cambridge, Washington county, New York, and died April 8, 1900.

Sarah (Thomas) McDoual was the second daughter of Captain Alexander Thomas of Rhode Island, who was a captain in the Revolutionary army.

William and Mary (McDoual) Robertson had:

(I) Sarah Mary Robertson, born May 15, 1825; died September 25, 1845.

(II) Alexander Livingston Robertson, born June 29, 1827; died November 25, 1869, in Texas, unmarried.

(III) William John Robertson, born May 29, 1830; died August 31, 1904.

(IV) Jane Ann Robertson, born June 13, 1832, died November 17, 1834.

(V) Henry Gilbert Robertson, born May 11, 1837. Unmarried. Coila, N. Y.

(VI) Anna Eliza Robertson, born May 11, 1839; died November 19, 1884.

(III) William John Robertson, second son of William and Mary (McDoual) Robertson, was born May 29, 1830, in Coila, Washington county, New York, and died August 31, 1904, in Washington county, New York.

William John Robertson and Mary Louise Colwell were married September 10, 1874, in Richmond, Texas.

(VI) Anna Eliza Robertson, third daughter of William and Mary (McDoual) Robertson, was born May 11, 1839, in Coila, New York, and died November 19, 1884, in Philadelphia, Pa.

Dr. Alphonso Cannon and Anna Eliza Robertson were married January 15, 1861, in Richmond, Texas.

Dr. Alphonso Cannon died in July, 1865, in Hempstead, Texas.

Dr. Alphonso and Anna Eliza (Robertson) Cannon had:

(1) Stanley Cannon, born May 12, 1862; died October 12, 1863.

Rev. James Price and Mrs. Anna Eliza (Robertson) Cannon were married September 7, 1872, in Coila, New York.

(VI) JOHN ROBERTSON, fourth son of William and Mary (Livingston) Robertson, was born May 2, 1786, in the town of Greenwich, Washington county, New York, and died September 2, 1873, in Coila, New York.

John Robertson and Ann Small were married July 8, 1824, in Cambridge, Washington county, New York.

Ann Small, eldest daughter of Edward and Phebe (Thomas) Small, was born December 24, 1803, in Cambridge, New York, and died September, 15, 1850, in Coila, New York.

Phebe Thomas was the youngest daughter of Captain Alexander Thomas of Rhode Island, who was a captain in the Revolutionary army.

John and Ann (Small) Robertson had:

(I) Mary Jane Robertson, born May 25, 1825; died September 26, 1850.

(II) James Edward Robertson, born March 23, 1827; died May 1, 1887.

(III) Phebe Ann Robertson, born September 25, 1829; died February 22, 1870.

(IV) Sarah Small Robertson, born January 26, 1832; died February 8, 1873.

(V) William Hamilton Robertson, born April 19, 1834; died December 8, 1872.

(VI) Jeannette Small Robertson, born April 18, 1836; died May 26, 1862.

(VII) Eliza Robertson, born July 14, 1838; died March 15, 1878.

(I) Mary Jane Robertson, eldest daughter of John and Ann (Small) Robertson, was born May 25, 1825, in Coila, New York, and died September 26, 1850, in Wheatland, Will county, Illinois.

Alexander White and Mary Jane Robertson were married April 5, 1849, in Coila, New York.

Alexander White, son of Robert and Elizabeth (Hung) White, was born January 17, 1817, in Argyle, New York, and came to Somonauk, Illinois, in May, 1849. where he resided until his death, January 12, 1899.

Alexander and Mary Jane (Robertson) White had:

(1) John Robertson White, born September 18, 1850, in Wheatland, Illinois.

John Robertson White and Jennie Williams were married September 5, 1877, at Waterloo, Iowa, but have since removed to Gordon Grove, California. They had:

(a) Ella J. White, born June 25, 1878; died January 3, 1888.

(b) Effie D. White, born June 26, 1881.

(c) Fred M. White, born October 30, 1886.

(II) James Edward Robertson, eldest son of John and Ann (Small) Robertson, was born March 23, 1827, in Coila, New York, and died May 1, 1887, in Glens Falls, New York.

James Edward Robertson and Mary J. Reid were married December 29, 1865, in North Greenwich, Washington county, New York.

Mary J. Reid, daughter of William and Ann (King) Reid,

was born November 20, 1832, in North Greenwich, Washington county, New York, and still lives at Coila, New York.

James Edward and Mary J. (Reid) Robertson had:

(1) Anna Eliza Robertson, born November 19, 1866.

(2) Mary Tilford Robertson, born July 4, 1867.

(3) Fanny Robertson, born February 14, 1869.

(4) William D. Robertson, born November 20, 1872.

(1) Anna Eliza Robertson, eldest daughter of James Edward and Mary J. (Reid) Robertson, was born November 19, 1866, in Coila, New York.

Rev. Howard Shriver MacAyeal and Anna Eliza Robertson were married April 24, 1889, in Coila, New York.

Rev. Howard Shriver MacAyeal, son of Rev. Robert and Mary Ellen (Sharpe) MacAyeal, was born November 8, 1865, in Oskaloosa, Iowa. He was graduated from Lawrence, Massachusetts, High School; from Geneva College, Beaver Falls, Pennsylvania; took postgraduate course in Edinburgh, Scotland; was graduated from Xenia Theological Seminary, Xenia, Ohio; preached in Cambridge, Nebraska, First Congregational church; Omaha, Nebraska, Plymouth Congregational church; St. Louis, Missouri, Central Congregational church; now at Akron, Ohio, First Congregational church. His father was a United Presbyterian minister.

Rev. Howard Shriver and Anna Eliza (Robertson) MacAyeal had:

(a) Robert Archie MacAyeal, born March 18, 1896.

(2) Mary Tilford Robertson, second daughter of James Edward and Mary J. (Reid) Robertson, was born July 4, 1867, in Coila, New York.

Dr. Porter Robert McMaster and Mary Tilford Robertson were married February 6, 1896, and live at 1201 South Salina street, Syracuse, New York.

Porter Robert McMaster, A. M., M. D., son of William S. and Mary (Reynolds) McMaster, was born September 5, 1865, at Lockport, New York, and now lives at 1201 Salina street, Syracuse, New York. He was graduated from Princeton University; from the College of Physicians and Surgeons, in the city of New York (medical department of Columbia University, New York City), in 1892; former house physician Presbyterian Hospital, New York City; former resident physician Midwifery Hospital, Broome street, New York; lecturer in surgery, Syracuse University College of Medicine; visiting physician to the

Hospital of the Good Shepherd; member Syracuse Academy of Medicine and Onodaga County Medical Society; medical examiner Manhattan Life Insurance Company of New York, and Penn Mutual Life Insurance Company of Philadelphia.

(3) Fannie Robertson, third daughter of James Edward and Mary J. (Reid) Robertson, was born February 14, 1869, in Coila, New York.

Alfred George Hill and Fannie Robertson were married August 30, 1899.

Alfred George Hill, son of James and Electa (Hoyt) Hill, was born August 24, 1867. He is a lawyer in Coila, New York.

(4) Dr. William D. Robertson, only son of James Edward and Mary J. (Reid) Robertson, was born November 20, 1872, in Coila, New York. He was graduated from Princeton University, Princeton, New Jersey, in class of 1895, and from Bellevue Medical College, New York City, in 1898, receiving second honor in class and an appointment in Bellevue Hospital, where he served two years. He is unmarried and practicing his profession in Mt. Vernon, New York.

(III) Phebe Ann Robertson, second daughter of John and Ann (Small) Robertson, was born September 25, 1829, in Coila, New York, and died February 22, 1870, in Washington, Iowa.

Samuel Black Glasgow and Phebe Ann Robertson were married April 8, 1857, in Birmingham, Iowa.

Samuel Black Glasgow, son of Joseph and Margaret (Black) Glasgow, was born March 9, 1830, in Adams County, Ohio.

Samuel Black and Phebe Ann (Robertson) Glasgow had:

(1) Joseph Montgomery Glasgow, born July 22, 1861.
(2) Anna Mary Small Glasgow, born October 15, 1863.

(1) Hon. Joseph Montgomery Glasgow was graduated from the law department of Michigan University in the class of 1887, and in 1892 was elected Municipal Judge in Seattle, Washington.

(2) David F. Wilson and Anna Mary Small Glasgow were married April 30, 1890, near Augusta, Montana.

David F. Wilson was born December 4, 1852, in St. Joseph, Missouri.

(IV) Sarah Small Robertson, third daughter of John and Ann (Small) Robertson, was born January 26, 1832, in Coila,

New York, and died February 8, 1873, in Lebanon, Kentucky.

Albert Edmonds and Sarah Small Robertson were married January 29, 1863.

Albert Edmonds, son of Benjamin and Sarah (Merriweather) Edmonds, was born July 11, 1831, in Lebanon, Kentucky, and died September 5, 1887, in Lebanon, Kentucky.

Albert and Sarah Small (Robertson) Edmonds had:

(1) Clelland Jackson Edmonds, born December 23, 1863.

(2) James Edward Edmonds, born August 13, 1865.

(3) John Robertson Edmonds, born January 9, 1873; died August 10, 1873.

(V) Dr. William Hamilton Robertson, second son of John and Ann (Small) Robertson, was born April 19, 1834, in Coila, New York, and died December 8, 1872, in San Francisco, California.

Dr. William Robertson married and had:

(1) Willetta H. Robertson, who was married to William Hendrickson, Jr., attorney-at-law, San Francisco, Cal., and had:

(a) Alfred Davis Hendrickson, born March 4, 1897.

(b) William Hendrickson, III., born March 17, 1901.

(VII) Eliza Robertson, fifth daughter of John and Ann (Small) Robertson, was born July 14, 1838, in Coila, New York, and died March 15, 1878.

James Maxwell and Eliza Robertson were married March 14, 1866, in Coila, New York.

James Maxwell, son of George and Margaret (McDoual) Maxwell, was born February 28, 1824. He still lives in Cambridge, New York, and has been married again.

Margaret McDoual was a sister of John McDoual, father of Mrs. William Robertson, Jr.

(VII) HON. ALEXANDER ROBERTSON, fifth son of William and Mary (Livingston) Robertson, was born October 30, 1788, in Argyle, Washington county, New York, and died January 27, 1852, in Salem, New York. He settled in Salem and was Surrogate of the County of Washington, succeeding Judge Willard in that office.

Hon. Alexander Robertson and Jane Savage McDougall were married June 20, 1837, in East Greenwich, Washington county, New York.

Jane Savage McDougall, daughter of William and Eleanor (Livingston) McDougall, was born August 13, 1804, in East

Greenwich, New York, and died November 22, 1883, in East Greenwich, New York.

Jane Savage McDougall's father, William McDougall, Jr., son of William and Sarah (Gilleband) McDougall, was born September 23, 1770, in New York City, and died January 17, 1819, at his home near East Greenwich, New York.

Eleanor (Livingston) McDougall was the daughter of Archibald and Eleanor (McNaughton) Livingston.

Hon. Alexander and Jane Savage (McDougall) Robertson had:

(I) William Robertson, born April 30, 1838; died March 15, 1869.

(II) Alexander Livingston Robertson, born September 22, 1840.

(III) Ellen Mary Robertson, born February 2, 1846.

(I) William Robertson, eldest son of Hon. Alexander and Jane Savage (McDougall) Robertson, was born April 30, 1838, and died March 15, 1869. He was a justice of the peace in Salem. He volunteered in the Black Horse Cavalry in the Civil War and served until discharged. He was a second lieutenant.

William Robertson and Mary Bartlett, daughter of Mathias Bartlett, were married June 11, 1864, in Salem, New York.

William and Mary (Bartlett) Robertson had:

(1) Eleanor Livingston Robertson, born July 29, 1865. Unmarried.

(2) William M. Robertson, born April 7, 1868. Unmarried.

(II) Alexander L. Robertson, second son of Hon. Alexander and Jane Savage (McDougall) Robertson, was born September 22, 1840, in Salem, New York.

Alexander L. Robertson and Anna Beechlin were married December 31, 1879, in Black River Falls, Wisconsin, and had:

(1) Alexander Beechlin Robertson, born November 29, 1882, in Bradford, Pennsylvania.

(2) Gertrude Eleanor Robertson, born May 17, 1889, in Wellsville, Alleghany County, New York.

(III) Ellen Mary Robertson, only daughter of Hon. Alexander and Jane Savage (McDougall) Robertson, was born February 2, 1846, in Salem, New York.

J. M. Snyder and Ellen Mary Robertson were married October 7, 1884, in Salem, New York, where they still live.

(VIII) MOSES ROBERTSON, sixth son of William and Mary (Livingston) Robertson, was born April 25, 1791, in Argyle, New York, and died February 17, 1869, at the home of his nephew, Hon. William Patten, near Sandwich, Illinois. He was for many years a merchant in East Greenwich, New York. He never married. After the death of his brother-in-law, James Patten of Salem, he was very kind to his sister, Mary, and her children, and when he became old they wrote inviting him to come and make his home with them. He came to Illinois in May, 1855, and the closing years of his life were spent with his nephew, Hon. William Patten, and family.

(IX) MARY ROBERTSON, youngest child of William and Mary (Livingston) Robertson, was born August 7, 1793, in Argyle, Washington County, New York, and died April 6, 1890, at the home of her son, Hon. William Patten, near Sandwich, DeKalb County, Illinois.

James Patten and Mary Robertson were married April 18, 1816, by the Rev. Alexander Bullions, D. D., at the home of William Robertson, Jr., in East Greenwich, Washington County, New York.

James Patten, son of William and Martha Nesbit Patten, was born July 4, 1793, near the city of Monaghan, Ireland, and came to America with his father's family in June, 1794, and settled in Argyle, Washington County, New York, and, with the exception of one year spent in Montreal, Canada, lived in Salem, Washington county, New York, until his death, December 21, 1827.

James and Mary (Robertson) Patten had:

(I) William Patten, born January 21, 1817; died February 1, 1897.

(II) Eleanor Livingston Patten, born December 8, 1818; died July 1, 1835.

(III) Robert Patten, born April 13, 1820; died June 1, 1876.

(IV) Alexander Robertson Patten, born August 14, 1823; died June 23, 1863.

(V) Martha Nesbit Patten, born May 5, 1826; died March 21, 1847.

(I) Hon. William Patten, eldest son of James and Mary (Robertson) Patten, was born January 21, 1817, in East Greenwich, Washington County, New York, and died February 1, 1897, in Yuma, Colorado. He came West in May, 1843, and reached Somonauk, DeKalb County, Illinois, May 17, 1843, near the present city of Sandwich, Illinois. He served eight years in the Illinois Legislature and was a member of the Legislature at the time of the Lincoln-Douglass contest for Senatorship, and voted for Abraham Lincoln. He was for forty years a ruling elder in the United Presbyterian Church near Sandwich. He was captain of Company "H," One-Hundred-Fifty-sixth Regiment, Illinois Volunteers.

William Patten and Elizabeth N. Pratt were married October 11, 1843, in the town of Greenwich, Washington County, New York.

Elizabeth N. Pratt, daughter of Simon Newcomb and Deborah (Nelson) Pratt, was born December 8, 1819, at Lake, in the town of Greenwich, Washington County, New York, and died at her home near Sandwich, Illinois, January 8, 1856.

Hon. William and Elizabeth N. (Pratt) Patten had:

(1) James Miller Patten, born April 16, 1845; died September 29, 1849.

(2) Simon Newcomb Patten, born May 3, 1847; died May 22, 1848.

(3) Edward Moses Patten, born August 6, 1849.

(4) Simon Nelson Patten, born May 1, 1852.

(5) Jennie Maria Patten, born November 27, 1854.

(3) Edward Moses Patten, third son of Hon. William and Elizabeth N. (Pratt) Patten, was born August 6, 1849, near Sandwich, Illinois. After his marriage he went to Collins, Iowa, and, in 1888, removed to Yuma, Colorado, where he still resides.

Edward Moses Patten and Harriet J. Marselus were married January 22, 1879, near Sandwich, Illinois.

Harriet J. Marselus, daughter of David and Sarah (Knights) Marselus, of Sandwich, Illinois, was born September 4, 1856, at Amsterdam, New York, and died May 3, 1896, in Yuma, Colorado.

Edward Moses and Harriet J. (Marselus) Patten had:

(A) William David Patten, born November 18, 1879; died November 20, 1879.

(B) Mary Louise Patten, born April 6, 1881; died July 6, 1901.

(C) Sarah Elizabeth Patten, born March 31, 1883.

(D) Ethel Abigail Patten, born May 7, 1885.

(E) Albert Edward Patten, born June 19, 1887.

(F) Jennie Grace Patten, born April 17, 1890.

(B) Mary Louise Patten, eldest daughter of Edward Moses and Harriet J. (Marselus) Patten, was born April 6, 1881, near Collins, Iowa; was graduated from the Brush High School, Colorado; taught the following year in the Brush High School; died July 6, 1901, at St. Luke's Hospital in Denver, Colorado, after an operation for appendicitis.

(C) Sarah Elizabeth Patten, second daughter of Edward Moses and Harriet J. (Marselus) Patten, was born March 31, 1883, near Collins, Iowa, and was graduated from the Northern Illinois Normal School, at DeKalb, Illinois, June 15, 1905.

(D) Ethel Abigail Patten, third daughter of Edward Moses and Harriet J. (Marselus) Patten, was born May 7, 1885, near Collins, Iowa, and was graduated from the Sandwich, Illinois, High School, June 9, 1905.

Ethel Abigail Patten married Clare Lett, son of Samuel Lett, and grandson of Hon. Thomas Lett, one of the prominent pioneers of LaSalle County, Illinois. Mr. Samuel Lett owns the farm formerly owned by Hon. William Patten, near Sandwich, Illinois.

(E) Albert Edward Patten, second son of Edward Moses and Harriet J. (Marselus) Patten, was born June 19, 1887, near Collins, Iowa, and is attending school at Lake Winona, Indiana.

(F) Jennie Grace Patten, fourth daughter of Edward Moses and Harriet J. (Marselus) Patten, was born April 17, 1890, at Yuma, Colorado, and is attending the Northwestern University, at Evanston, Illinois.

(4) Simon Nelson Patten, fourth son of Hon. William and Elizabeth N. (Pratt) Patten, was born May 1, 1852, near Sandwich, Illinois. In 1879 he received the degree of Ph. D. from the University of Halle, Germany. Since 1888 he has been professor of political economy in the Wharton School of Finance and Commerce, in the University of Pennsylvania.

Simon Nelson Patten and Charlotte Kimball were married September 2, 1903, in Canton, New York.

Charlotte Kimball, daughter of Solon Dexter and Jennie (Greene) Kimball, was born September 2, 1873, in Adams, Jefferson County, New York.

(5) Jennie Maria Patten, only daughter of Hon. William and Elizabeth N. (Pratt) Patten, was born November 27, 1854, near Sandwich, Illinois, and now lives with her brother, Edward Moses Patten, at Yuma, Colorado. She has devoted a great deal of attention to the genealogy of the McNaughton, Livingston, Robertson and Patten families, and it is through her assistance that I have been able to learn much of the early history of these families in this country.

(I) Hon. William Patten and Jane Somes were married August 12, 1856, in the town of Greenwich, Washington County, New York.

Jane Somes, daughter of Jonas and Lois (Hanks) Somes, was born April 17, 1829, in the town of Argyle, Washington County, New York, and now lives at Edmond, Oklahoma.

Hon. William and Jane (Somes)Patten had:

(1) Charles J. Patten, born September 7, 1857.
(2) Anna Mary Patten, born July 17, 1860.
(3) Alexander Robertson Patten, born July 18, 1864.
(4) William Somes Patten, born May 21, 1869.
(5) Frederick Livingston Patten, born July 20, 1872.

(1) Charles J. Patten, eldest son of Hon. William and Jane (Somes) Patten, was born September 7, 1857, near Sandwich, Illinois; he succeeded his father in the ownership of the homestead near Sandwich, Illinois, and lived there nearly twenty years. In 1902 he sold his farm and moved into Sandwich, Illinois.

Charles J. Patten and Harriet C. Field were married March 28, 1884, in West Alden, New York.

Harriet C. Field, daughter of Oliver and Harriet (Coleman) Field, was born January 18, 1856, at West Alden, New York.

(2) Anna Mary Patten, only daughter of Hon. William and Jane (Somes) Patten, was born July 17, 1860, near Sandwich, Illinois.

Charles Gilbert McDougall and Anna Mary Patten were married August 3, 1905, at the home of Charles J. Patten, in Sandwich, Illinois, by the Rev. Gilbert Hamilton Robertson, D. D.

Charles Gilbert McDougall, second son of John and Mary (Epperson) McDougall, was born September 12, 1852, in Adair County, Kentucky, and now lives in Longwood, a suburb of Chicago.

(4) William Somes Patten, third son of Hon. William and Jane (Somes) Patten, was born May 21, 1869, near Sandwich, Illinois. January 18, 1904, he was elected president of the First National Bank, in Edmond, Oklahoma Territory.

William Somes Patten and Erma May Howard were married April 6, 1898, in Edmond, Oklahoma, where they now reside.

Erma May Howard, daughter of Addison A. and Adeline (Herreld) Howard, was born August 30, 1877, in Morgantown, Kentucky.

William Somes and Erma May (Howard) Patten had:

(A) William Howard Patten, born December 20, 1898.

(B) Mabel Erma Patten, born July 24, 1903.

(5) Frederick Livingston Patten, fourth son of Hon. William and Jane (Somes) Patten, was born July 20, 1872, near Sandwich, Illinois.

Frederick Livingston Patten and Clara May McNew were married September 13, 1899. at the home of her grandfather, W. R. Heath, near Collins, Iowa.

Clara May McNew, daughter of Rev. Frederick and Clara (Heath) McNew, was born March 3, 1881, in Middletown, Henry County, Indiana.

Frederick Livingston and Clara May (McNew) Patten had:

(A) Charles Heath Patten, born January 29, 1893; died February 3, 1893.

(II) Eleanor Livingston Patten, eldest daughter of James and Mary (Robertson) Patten, was born December 8, 1818, in Granville, Washington County, New York, and died July 1, 1835, at her home in the town of Greenwich, Washington County, New York.

(III) Robert Patten, second son of James and Mary (Robertson) Patten, was born April 13, 1820, in Granville, Washington County, New York, and died June 1, 1876, in Hillsdale, Kansas. At the age of twenty-two he was commissioned captain of a company of Vermont militia. He was first made a first lieutenant, and the captain being ill he trained his company so well as to win a prize at an encampment of the Vermont State militia, and at that time they made him captain.

He came to Illinois in 1844. He drilled the first company from Sandwich (April, 1861) and would have gone to the front as their captain had he not been prevented by his ill health.

He was the first station agent at Sandwich and served two years. He was one of the founders of Sandwich and removed from his farm to Sandwich in the spring of 1854. He erected the first dwelling house and grist mill in Sandwich and owned the first lumber yard. He was the first to ship pork from Sandwich; then they only shipped dressed hogs.

Robert Patten and Catherine M. Sibley were married March 4, 1846, in Bennington, Vermont.

Catherine M. Sibley, daughter of John and Lovica (Clinch) Sibley, was born January 5, 1826, in Bennington, Vermont, and now lives with her daughter, Mrs. J. M. Mannen, near Paola, Kansas.

Robert and Catherine M. (Sibley) Patten had:

(1) Mary Catherine Patten, born December 6, 1846; died April 12, 1871.

(2) Helen Martha Patten, born December 29, 1849.

(3) Alice Lovica Patten, born May 14, 1853; died April 1, 1881.

(4) Gilbert Robertson Patten, born June 9, 1857; died April 1, 1858.

(5) Julia Frances Patten, born February 5, 1859; died December 28, 1863.

(1) Mary Catherine Patten, eldest daughter of Robert and Catherine M. (Sibley) Patten, was born December 6, 1846, near Sandwich, Illinois, and died April 12, 1871, in Hillsdale, Kansas.

Owen Lindsay Post and Mary Catherine Patten were married August 13, 1867, in Sandwich, Illinois.

Owen Lindsay Post, son of Captain Joseph and Mary Post, of Deep River, Connecticut, was born February 17, 1840, in Saybrook, Connecticut, and now lives in New London, Connecticut.

Owen Lindsay and Mary Catherine (Patten) Post had:

(A) Robert Patten Post, born June 2, 1868; died July 31, 1870.

(B) Catherine Mary Post, born March 29, 1871; died August 12, 1871.

(2) Helen Martha Patten, second daughter of Robert and Catherine M. (Sibley) Patten, was born December 29, 1849, near Sandwich, Illinois.

John Melvin Mannen and Helen Martha Patten were married March 12, 1884, in Hillsdale, Kansas.

John Melvin Mannen, son of William R. and Maria (Hall)

Mannen, was born June 1, 1848, in Downs, McLean County, Illinois, and came to Kansas May 4, 1859, with his father's family and settled near Paola, Kansas, and now owns the farm formerly owned by his father, where he has lived forty-five years.

(3) Alice Lovica Patten, third daughter of Robert and Catherine M. (Sibley) Patten, was born May 14, 1853, near Sandwich, Illinois, and died April 1, 1881, near Lane, Franklin County, Kansas.

Robert Dale Protzman and Alice Lovica Patten were married September 29, 1875, in Hillsdale, Kansas.

Robert Dale Protzman, son of Ezra and Catherine (Weaver) Protzman, was born September 17, 1851, in Marion County, Indiana, and died October 19, 1883, near Lane, Kansas.

Robert Dale and Alice Lovica (Patten) Protzman had:

(A) Gilbert Irving Protzman, born December 17, 1877.

Gilbert Irving Protzman and Ethel Kershner were married November 8, 1900, in Stanton township, Miami County, Kansas.

Ethel Kershner, daughter of Andrew and Mary (Barrett) Kershner, was born April 8, 1880.

Gilbert Irving and Ethel (Kershner) Protzman had:

(a) Mary Alice Protzman, born January 26, 1902.

(b) Catherine Agnes Protzman, born January 16, 1906.

(IV) Alexander Robertson Patten, third son of James and Mary (Robertson) Patten was born August 14, 1823, in the town of Greenwich, Washington County, New York, and died June 23, 1863, in Sandwich, Illinois.

Alexander Robertson Patten came to Illinois in 1844 accompanied by his mother and sister, and was for several years a merchant in Freeland, Illinois, and was afterwards one of the prominent business men of Sandwich, Illinois, where he died.

Alexander Robertson Patten and Agnes Beveridge were married February 18, 1851, in the town of Somonauk, DeKalb County, Illinois.

Agnes Beveridge, daughter of George and Ann (Hoy) Beveridge, was born June 17, 1829, in the town of Greenwich, Washington County, New York, and now lives with her son, James A. Patten, in Evanston, Illinois.

Alexander Robertson and Agnes (Beveridge) Patten had:

(1) James A. Patten, born May 8, 1852.

(2) George W. Patten, born February 7, 1854.

(3) William Livingston Patten, born October 28, 1856; died May 20, 1860.

(4) Thomas Beveridge Patten, born April 30, 1859; died October 19, 1883.

(5) Henry Jay Patten, born June 30, 1862.

(1) James A. Patten, eldest son of Alexander Robertson and Agnes (Beveridge) Patten, was born May 8, 1852, near Sandwich, Illinois. He completed the course in the Academy of the Northwestern University in 1869 ready for the freshman year, but never returned. He and his brother, George, went into the grain business and he has continued in that ever since. He was elected mayor of Evanston in April, 1901, and served a term of two years. He lives in Evanston; is a prominent member of the Board of Trade in Chicago, and has made a large fortune.

James A. Patten and Amanda Buchanan were married April 9, 1885, in Chicago, Illinois.

Amanda Buchanan, daughter of James and Sophronia Foster (Ballou) Buchanan, was born December 20, 1858, in Cumberland, Ohio.

James A. and Amanda (Buchanan) Patten had:

(A) Agnes Patten, born September 3, 1891, in Chicago, Illinois.

(B) Thomas Beveridge Patten, born July 23, 1893, in Chicago, Illinois.

(C) John Lourie Patten, born February 19, 1896, in Chicago, Illinois.

(2) George W. Patten, second son of Alexander Robertson and Agnes (Beveridge) Patten, was born February 7, 1854, near Sandwich, Ilinois. He was graduated from Monmouth College in June, 1876. He taught school the first year after his graduation in the public schools of Sandwich, Illinois, and then secured employment in Chicago with the old firm of G. P. Comstock & Company, and remained with them for a period of about three years, when, upon their failure, he and his brother, James, started in business for themselves, and have been in the grain trade ever since. He has been very successful; has accumulated a fortune; and is not married. He lives with his brother, James, in Evanston.

(5) Henry Jay Patten, fifth son of Alexander Robertson and Agnes (Beveridge) Patten, was born June 30, 1862, near Sandwich, Illinois. He was graduated from Cornell University in June, 1884. After leaving college he went into the employ

of his brothers, James and George, and after a period of five or six years he was taken in as a partner. He lives in Evanston.

Henry Jay Patten and Emma Therese Herpin were married December 18, 1893, in Pasadena, California.

Emma Therese Herpin, daughter of Auguste and Laura (Martin) Herpin, was born December 14, 1869, in Jordoigne, Belgium.

Henry Jay and Emma Therese (Herpin) Patten had:

(A) Rhoda Violet Patten, born December 22, 1894.

(V) Martha Nesbit Patten, second daughter of James and Mary (Robertson) Patten, was born May 5, 1826, in the town of Greenwich, Washington County, New York, and came to Illinois in 1844 with her mother and brother, Alexander. She was married to Dr. W. M. Sweetland of Newark, Illinois. They resided in Chicago, Illinois, but a short time before her death they returned to her brother, Robert Patten, in Somonauk township, DeKalb County, Illinois, where she died March 21, 1847.

Dr. W. M. Sweetland, son of Colonel Bowen and Elizabeth (Durkee) Sweetland, was born November 18, 1819, in Dryden, Tompkins County, New York, and died January 22, 1902, in Highland Park, Illinois. He was for many years a prominent citizen of Newark, Illinois, and afterwards of Highland Park, Illinois. He was at one time mayor of Highland Park.

WILLIAM ROBERTSON, SR., of Argyle, Washington County, New York, married, secondly, Mrs. Agnes Mitchell.

Mrs. Agnes Mitchell was the widow of John Mitchell of Argyle, by whom she had a son, John Mitchell, but no children by William Robertson.

LOURIE-BEVERIDGE.

Parish Register, County Fife, Auctermuchty, Scotland.

"1718, August 22, JOHN LOURIE, in this parish, and ANN GILMORE, in Abernathy, being duly proclaimed, were married."

CHILDREN.

(1) Margaret Lourie, born in 1720.
(2) Janet Lourie, born in 1721.
(3) Ann Lourie, born in 1723.
(4) Mary Lourie, born in 1725.
(5) Alexander Lourie, born in 1728.
(6) Margaret Lourie, born in 1730.
(7) Christian Lourie, born in 1732.
(8) John Lourie, born in 1737.

GEORGE BEVERIDGE.

Parish Register, County Fife, Strathmiglo, Scotland.

"1745, March 2, GEORGE BEVERIDGE, weaver in this parish, and JANET LOURIE, daughter to John Lourie, tenant in Galoway, in the Parish of Abernathy, were proclaimed in marriage."

CHILDREN.

(1) Matthew Beveridge.
(2) Jeannette Beveridge.
(3) Andrew Beveridge.
(4) Ann Beveridge.

George Beveridge lived in Strathmiglo. His old home is still standing; over one door are inscribed the letters, "G. B."; over another, "M. B."

Matthew had sons, George and Matthew; grandson, Matthew; and great-grandson, William, grandfather of Miss Mary Jane Beveridge Miller, 258 North Twentieth street, Columbus, Ohio, who now owns the old homestead.

Jeannette Beveridge was married to a man named Thompson

Andrew Beveridge married Isabel Cummings, grandparents of Ex-Governor John Lourie Beveridge.

Ann Beveridge was married to James Small.

GEORGE FOTHERINGHAM.

Parish Register, County Fife, Auctermuchty, Scotland.

"1762, October 23, George Fotheringham, in this parish, and Janet Lourie, in the Parish of Abernathy, gave up their names for proclamation in order to marriage."

George Beveridge having died George Fotheringham married his widow, Janet (Lourie) Beveridge. They had one child, Janet Fotheringham.

George Fotheringham died and his widow in 1774, with her children, Andrew and Ann, by her first husband, and Janet, by her second husband, emigrated to America; settled in Cambridge, Washington County, New York; died there and was buried in Cambridge cemetery.

Inscription on her tomb: "In memory of Mrs. Janet Fotheringham, who came from Fifeshire, Scotland, in 1774, and departed this life, October 18, 1802, in the eighty-third year of her age."

Dr. Thomas Beveridge married Janet Fotheringham in Cambridge, Washington County, New York, and had:

(1) John Beveridge.

(2) Jennette Beveridge, married to George Lourie, his second wife.

(3) George Beveridge.

(4) Ann Beveridge, married to Isaac Ashton.

(5) Thomas Beveridge, married Elizabeth Armitage, parents of Mrs. Gilbert Hamilton Robertson.

Dr. Thomas Beveridge, born 1749, Eastside, Parish of Fossoway, Fifeshire, Scotland; bred under ministry of Brother William Moir of Muckart; entered Divinity Hall under Rev. William Moncrief of Alloa; after license assisted Rev. Adam Gib in Edinburgh; ordained by the Associate Presbytery of Edinburgh, September 23, 1783; arrived in America in spring of 1784—sixteen weeks' voyage—went to Cambridge, New York, in fall of 1784; settled in Cambridge, September 10, 1789; died July 23, 1798, in Barnet, Vermont, and buried there in his forty-ninth year.

Jennet Beveridge, his wife, was buried in Cambridge cemetery.

Inscription on her tomb: "To the memory of Mrs. Jennet Beveridge, relict of the Rev. Thomas Beveridge, pastor of the Associate Congregation of Cambridge, and daughter of George and Jennet Fotheringham. She was born in Autermuchty, in Fifeshire, Scotland. She departed this life in November 8, 1820, in the fifty-seventh year of her age."

The following little story is a clipping from a newspaper, but I do not know the author's name:

"One of the most remarkable instances of a heroine pioneer was the case of Mrs. Featheringame (Fotheringham), a widow with three children, who sailed from the North of Ireland [she came from Fifeshire, Scotland.—Ed.] to this, then wilderness, region that she might be near the ministrations of Dr. Thomas Clarke, who had previously brought a portion of his colony from Ballibay to a new settlement in Salem. The children of Mrs. Featheringame, by her first husband, a Mr. George Beveridge, were Andrew and Ann, and by her second husband, a daughter named Jennette.

"In the year 1774, after a tedious voyage of eleven weeks, this lone woman with her children came within sight of Boston. But the greatest excitement then prevailed in consequence of the tyrannical measures of Great Britain, and John Hancock and other patriots were boldly coming forward to defend the rights of freemen. Not permitted to land at Boston, the vessel disembarked at Marblehead, and surprising to relate, Mrs. Featheringame and her children, walked all the way from the shores of Massachusetts to the wilderness scenes of old Cambridge, N. Y.

"As Sidney Smith once said: 'We talk of human life as a journey; but how variously is that journey performed. There are those who come forth girt, and shod and mantled, to walk on velvet lawns and smooth terraces, where every gale is arrested and every beam is tempered. There are others who walk on the Alpine paths of life, against driving misery, and through stormy sorrows, over sharp afflictions; walk with bare feet and naked breast, jaded, mangled and chilled.'

"Andrew Beveridge, the son of Mrs. Featheringame by her first husband, settled on a farm near Coila, known in our times as the Small farm. Ann, the daughter, married James Small, the father of Edward and George Small, prominent citizens of Jackson. Jennette Featheringame married the Rev. Thomas Beveridge, the pioneer minister and first settled pastor of the U. P. Church, of Coila; and the father of the late Rev. Thomas Beveridge, D. D., of Xenia, Ohio; and of Mrs. George Lourie and Mrs. Isaac Ashton. What untold influence for good has the family of Mrs. Featheringame exerted in a wide community. Could John Bunyan have chosen a better original for his Christiana and her children? Of this old mother in Israel we may well say: 'Many daughters have done virtuously, but thou excellest them all.'

"Alexander Lourie, a Scotchman, came to America in 'Ye olden times,' and after living some time in Orange County, N. Y., removed to Jackson, settling on lands since owned and occupied by his grandson, Thomas Beveridge Lourie. George Lourie, a son of the pioneer, was the father of the present Thomas B. and also of the scholarly and venerable Judge James Lourie, of Greenwich, N. Y. The pioneer's daughters were: Jeannette, who married George Small; Margaret, who became Mrs. Robert Armstrong; and Mary, who married John Shiland, of Cambridge.

"The Lourie family with their relatives, the Beveridges, some of whose descendants are still living in this and other towns in old Washington County, as well as in other States of the Union, have exhibited in a marked degree the leading traits which belong to the character of the best citizens of that 'bonny Isle'—the land of Burns, with its inestimable attractions and cherished memories.

"Thomas B. Lourie, the grandson of the pioneer, married a daughter of the Hon. John Stevenson, of Cambridge, and devoted himself chiefly to farming and to the duties of a good citizen, not unmindful of 'the unfeigned faith' which 'dwelt in his grandmother,' the saintly Mrs. Thomas Beveridge, whose maiden name was Jennette Featheringame, the little girl who walked from Boston to Cambridge, N. Y."

Andrew Beveridge, son of George and Jannet (Lourie) Beveridge, was born in 1752, in Strathmiglo, Fifeshire, Scotland; came to America in 1774; died March 27, 1835, in North Hebron, Washington County, New York. He was a brother of Ann (Beveridge) Small, our great-grandmother.

Andrew Beveridge and Isabelle Cummings were married January 23, 1784.

Isabelle Cummings was born in 1760, and died October 30, 1836.

They were both buried in the Hebron cemetery.

Andrew and Isabelle (Cummings) Beveridge had:

(1) George Beveridge, born March 16, 1785; died May 10, 1870.

(2) Thomas Beveridge, born February 15, 1787; died February 11, 1869.

(3) Jennet Beveridge, born January 6, 1789; died March 15, 1813.

(4) James Beveridge, born February 28, 1791; died —— 1881.

(5) Alexander Beveridge, born May 4, 1793; died June 2, 1874.

(6) John Beveridge, born May 31, 1795; died July 30, 1878.

(7) Ann Beveridge, born October 16, 1797; died February 16, 1858.

(8) Matthew Beveridge, born February 2, 1800; died May 25, 1875.

(9) Andrew Beveridge, born May 26, 1802; died July 3, 1883.

(10) David Beveridge, born July 23, 1805; died September 12, 1879.

(1) George Beveridge, son of Andrew and Isabelle (Cummings) Beveridge, was born March 16, 1785; married Ann Hoy; lived in Greenwich, Washington County, New York; moved to Illinois in May, 1842; settled in south part of DeKalb county; died there, May 10, 1870, and was buried in Somonauk cemetery.

George and Ann (Hoy) Beveridge had:

(1) Jennet Beveridge, married to James Henry.
(2) Isabel Beveridge, married to William French.
(3) James Hoy Beveridge, married Elizabeth Disbrow.
(4) Andrew M. Beveridge, married to Sarah Loomis.
(5) Thomas Beveridge, married Elizabeth Irwin.
(6) John Lourie Beveridge, married Helen M. Judson.
(7) Agnes Beveridge, married to Alexander R. Patten.

John L. and his wife, Helen M. (Judson) Beveridge and Agnes (Beveridge) Patten are the only survivors.

John L. Beveridge and Helen M. Judson were married January 26, 1848, in Chicago, and had:

Alla May Beveridge, who was married to Samuel B. Raymond, and had: Lourie, William, and Helen who was married to Shirly High, all of Chicago.

Philo Judson Beveridge, who married Ella Reutzger of Poughkeepsie, New York, and had: Kuhne and Ray Beveridge. He married, secondly, Daedda Wilcox, and had: Marion, Daedda and Phyllis. He and his second family live in Hollywood, California; Kuhne and Ray live in Europe.

Kuhne Beveridge, the celebrated sculptor, daughter of Philo and Ella (Reutzger) Beveridge, was born October 31, 1874. The exquisite character of her work has made her name one of the most famous in the modern world of art. She now (1907) resides in London.

James Hoy Beveridge, eldest son of George Beveridge, was born December 3, 1817; came west in 1842; was a delegate to the first Republican Illinois State convention held at Bloomington in 1856; was circuit clerk of DeKalb County for eight years; State treasurer of Illinois 1865-7; a member and secretary of the commission which built the present Illinois State House 1867-77; treasurer of the Lincoln Monument (Springfield, Ill.) Association. Died January 26, 1896. Mrs. Beveridge died October 22, 1905. The surviving children are Merritt Hoy Beveridge, living near Sandwich, Ill., and Mrs. Gertrude (Beveridge) Thompson, of Chicago.

Rev. Andrew M. Beveridge, D. D., was born January 20, 1820; died January 6, 1889. He was graduated from Jefferson College, Canonsburg, Pa., in 1884; member of the class of '49, Princeton Theological Seminary. Dr. Beveridge was pastor of the Presbyterian church at Hoosic Falls, New York, 1851-1858; First Presbyterian church, Lansingburg, New York, 1858-1882. He married, December 22, 1848, Sarah Loomis, daughter of Rev. Aretas Loomis, D. D., of Bennington, Vt.

Henry Loomis Beveridge, president of the Beveridge Paper Company, Indianapolis, Indiana, is a son of above.

EX-GOVERNOR JOHN L. BEVERIDGE was born in the town of Greenwich, Washington County, New York, July 6, 1824, a son of George and Ann Beveridge. He was reared upon a farm; in the winter attending the district school, where he mastered the common branches, and obtained a taste of the higher studies. In the spring of 1842, when in his eighteenth year, his father's family moved to DeKalb County, Illinois. During the next three years, by great persistency, he managed to obtain a year and a half of solid schooling—his academic education—at Granville (Putnam county) Academy and at Rock River Seminary, located at Mt. Morris, Ogle county. In the fall of 1845 he started out to make a place for himself in the world. His first experience was in teaching school in various counties in Tennessee. Next, he commenced to read law, and was admitted to the bar. In the fall of 1849, through the mismanagement of his associate, he lost what little he had accumulated, and was left in debt. Two years later, having paid his creditors, he, with his wife and two children, went back to his father's house in DeKalb county, and soon afterward made arrangements to enter a law office in Sycamore. In the spring of 1854, he removed to Evanston, then just planted. Dr. Judson, his father-in-law, was the financial agent of the Northwestern University, and during Mr. Beveridge's first year's residence in Evanston, he occupied himself with business connected with that institution. In the spring of 1855, he opened a law office in Chicago, and continued his profession until the summer of 1861, slowly improving his condition, and laying the foundation for a successful and remunerative practice.

The war record of Governor Beveridge commenced with his enlistment, August 27, 1861. He recruited Company "F," Eighth Illinois Cavalry, which several citizens of Evanston joined, and in September was unanimously chosen captain of the company. The next day he was selected by the line officers as one of the majors of the regiment. In October, the regiment was ordered to Washington, participating afterward in all the battles fought by the Army of the Potomac. Under General Stoneman he was in the advance upon Richmond. Upon the retreat of the army from the James River, his regiment was in the rear of the retreating forces, and his battalion the extreme rear. The Eighth Regiment was the only cavalry force which crossed the river at Fredericksburg, and Major Beveridge led his regiment at Gettysburg, Williamsport, Boonboro, Funkstown, Falling Waters, and between Rappahannock and Culpepper.

General Farnsworth having obtained permission from the War Department to organize another regiment of cavalry, at his invitation, and by the consent of Governor Yates, Major Beveridge undertook the recruiting and organization of the Seventeenth Illinois Cavalry, having resigned his commission for this purpose, November 3, 1863. He was mustered and commissioned colonel of the Seventeenth, January 28, 1864, and was in command of it until October, 1865, when he was ordered to St. Louis to preside over a military commission for the trial of military offenders, and was finally mustered out of service February 6, 1866. Colonel Beveridge was breveted brigadier-general for gallant and meritorious conduct March 7, 1865.

On his return to civil life he resumed the practice of his profession, and in the summer of 1866 he was elected by the Republicans to the office of sheriff of Cook county. He served the two years' term, then resumed the practice of law, and in November, 1870, was elected State Senator from the Twenty-fifth District. He served during the winter of 1871 and at the special sessions of May and October. Receiving the nomination of his party for Congressman-at-Large, he resigned his Senatorship and was elected to Congress in November, 1871. In November, 1872, he was elected Lieutenant-Governor, and in January, 1873, resigned as Congressman to enter upon the duties of his new position. On the 10th of January, 1873, he took the oath of office, and upon the resignation of General Oglesby as Governor, who had been elected United States Senator, General Beveridge become Governor of the State.

On October 27, 1881, General John L. Beveridge succeeded Frank Gilbert as sub-treasurer, and was succeeded by James G. Healy on October 1, 1885.—History of Chicago, by A. T. Andreas; Patriotism of Illinois. By T. M. Eddy.

Ann Beveridge was sister of Andrew Beveridge; Andrew Beveridge was father of George Beveridge; George Beveridge was father of Ex-Governor John L. Beveridge, Ex-State Treasurer James H. Beveridge, and Agnes (Beveridge) Patten.

Ex-Governor John L. Beveridge's grandfather, Andrew Beveridge, was, therefore, brother of our great-grandmother, Ann (Beveridge) Small.

Dr. George Beveridge of Reinbeck, Iowa, historian of the Beveridge family, to whom I am indebted for data of the Beveridge family, was a grandson of Alexander Beveridge, fifth son of Andrew Beveridge. Dr. Beveridge died at his home in Reinbeck, Iowa, October 3, 1907. The Beveridge data collected by him is now in the possession of his brother, Dr. J. M. Beveridge, of Oregon, Illinois.

I am also indebted to Ex.-Governor John L. Beveridge for data of the Beveridge family.

The Beveridges are believed to have been originally Flemish.

Dr. George Beveridge visited Scotland a few years ago and secured the parish registers before given, and also photographs of the early homes of the Beveridges. One is "Beveridge House in 'Cash Feus' (street), Strathmiglo, Fifeshire, Scotland, in which Matthew Beveridge, brother of Ann (Beveridge) Small, lived from 1798 to 1833;" the other is "Cash Feus" (street), in Strathmiglo, Fifeshire, Scotland.—Street in which George Beveridge lived (1745) and where his daughter, Ann (Beveridge) Small was probably born."

The Hon. John L. Beveridge, writing from Hollywood, Cal., says: "It is supposed Senator Beveridge's great-grandfather was a cousin of my grandfather."

In answer to a query regarding the above, Senator Beveridge wrote: "I am sorry to say that I can give you no information on this matter. I did have the 'family tree' running back a good many years, but I was so busy at the time it was given to me that I paid no attention to it. I have not the remotest idea where it is. The truth is, the immediate duties before me every day have been such that I have not paid the attention to this matter that I should have."

Albert J. Beveridge, of Indianapolis, was born on a farm in Highland county, Ohio, October 6, 1862; his father and brothers were soldiers in the Union army. He was graduated at DePauw University, Greencastle, Indiana, in 1885; was admitted to the bar in 1886, and has since then devoted himself to his profession; was married to Katherine Maude Langsdale November 24. 1887, who died June 19, 1900; was elected to the Senate of the United

States by the Sixty-first General Assembly of Indiana January 17, 1899, for the term beginning March 4 following: was re-elected in 1905. Senator Beveridge married, secondly, Catherine Eddy of Chicago, August 7, 1907.

SMALL.

William Small, Esq., of Kindrogan, County Perth, who married Isabel, daughter of Donald Farquharson, Esq., of Woodfield, was father of

William Small, Esq., of Kindrogan, who married Agnes, (Anne) daughter of James Stewart, Esq., of Urrard, County Perth, and was succeeded, at his decease, by his son,

William Small, Esq., of Kindrogan, who married in 1776, Margaret, daughter of Walter Keir, Esq., of Balcairie, County Perth, and by her had, with a daughter, who died unmarried, and two sons, who both died young, another son, the present

Patrick Small-Keir, Esq., of Kindrogan.

(I believe that our great-grandfather, James Small, was a younger son of William and Anne (Stewart) Small, and brother of William Small, who married Margaret Keir in 1776.—Ed.)

Small Coat of Arms—Per fesse, wavy, gu. and arg., a lion passant, sa., pierced through with a dagger, in bend, ppr., entering at the shoulder, hilted, or.

Crest—A branch of palm, ppr., erect.

Motto—Ratione non ira. (By reason; not by rage.)

Seat—Kindrogan, County Perth.—Burke's Landed Gentry. Vol. 1, p. 665. 1852.

WILLIAM SMALL OF KINDROGAN, married ANNE STEWART.

LINEAGE OF ANNE STEWART.

This is a branch of the Royal House of Stewart.

John Stewart, the first of Urrard, was lineally descended from John Stewart, progenitor of the Athol Stewarts, who was fourth son of Alexander Lord Badenoch, Earl of Buchan, a younger son of King Robert II. He married a daughter of M'Grigor, and was father of

Robert Stewart of Urrard, who married a daughter of Robertson of Fascally, and had, with other issue:

Alexander Stewart, his heir, and George Stewart of Baloan.

Tradition affirms that this Robert, being in a foray with the Marquis of Athol, and returning home on *verbal leave,* his lands of Urrard were seized as those of a vassal, who had deserted his lord superior. Craig Urrard is situated behind Blair Castle, and the site of the old mansion of the family is still pointed out in the park of Blair.

The son and successor,

Alexander Stewart, wedded Christian, daughter of Leslie of Renrory, (now called Urrard) Governor of the Castle of Blair, and was succeeded by his son,

Robert Stewart of Urrard, who married Margaret, daughter of the celebrated Charles Robertson of Auchleeks, commonly called Fearlach n'n T'ed, and had two sons,

John Stewart, his heir;

William Stewart.

The elder son,

John Stewart of Urrard, married, first, a daughter of Menzies of Rotmills, by whom he had five sons, viz.:

(I) James Stewart, his heir.

(II) Charles Stewart, merchant and baillie in Perth, whose only daughter was married to Robert Craigie, advocate, afterwards lord president.

(III) Samuel Stewart, a surgeon in Dundee.

(IV) Alexander Stewart, clerk to the Regality in Athol.

(V) Another son, who died in early youth, of fright during the battle of Killicrankie, fought near the mansion house of Urrard, in 1689.

John Stewart of Urrard wedded, secondly, Jean, daughter of

James Stewart of Fincastle. He was succeeded, at his decease, by his eldest son,

James Stewart of Urrard, who married, first, Anne, daughter of Campbell of Balgershoe, and had, by her, two sons and six daughters, viz.:

(I) John Stewart, his heir.

(II) Samuel Stewart, merchant in Perth, whose son, Samuel, also a merchant in the same city, purchased the lands of Coltenchar, and others, but died unmarried.

(III) Christian, married to Mungo Campbell of Clunimore, afterwards of Monzie.

(IV) Jean Stewart, called "Minay n', lean," married to Niel Glasham of Clune. This lady acted a remarkable part in Stirling Castle after the battle in 1715.

(V) Barbara Stewart, married to Hamilton, minister of Blair.

(VI) Margaret Stewart, married to Alexander Stewart of Clochfoldich.

(VII) ANNE STEWART, married to WILLIAM SMALL of Kindrogan.

(VIII) Another daughter.—History of the Commoners. By John Burke. Vol. 4, p. 40. 1838.

(1) JAMES SMALL, supposed to be a son of William and Anne (Stewart) Small, ancestor of our branch of the Small family in America, was born in 1749, in Scotland; came from Glasgow, Scotland, to America in 1774; settled in Cambridge, Washington County, New York, and died August 13, 1827, and is buried in the Cambridge cemetery. He was a soldier in the Revolutionary war; enlisted in the Albany County Militia, Sixteenth Regiment.

"I remember my father telling me that his grandmother at one time had to retreat to the cellar because she feared being attacked by a party of Indians that demanded food. When General Burgoyne and his troops went from Saratoga to Bennington, they captured my great-grandfather and took him with them for the purpose of having him show them the way. He escaped from them at a place called Oak Hill, and returned home. The British army passed very near the old homestead, and a portion of their military road is now a part of the present road from Cambridge to Greenwich. The road that passes the old homestead to-day is on the old military road.

"After the battle of Bennington a detachment of Hessians

returning to Saratoga encamped for the night on the old homestead, on a little stream about fifty rods west of my great-grandfather's cabin. We had a number of shoe-buckles and bayonets that were found on the site of the camp by my brother and myself. His son, Edward Small, was an officer in the militia, being appointed an ensign April 14, 1800, by Governor John Jay; and a lieutenant the 26th of March, 1804, by Governor Dewitt Clinton."—Dr. Charles B. Small.

James Small and Ann Beveridge were married in Cambridge, Washington County, New York.

Ann Beveridge, daughter of George and Janet (Lourie) Beveridge, was born in 1755, in Strathmiglo, Fifeshire, Scotland; came to America in 1774; and died June 10, 1830, in Cambridge, New York, and is buried in the Cambridge cemetery.

Inscription on tomb: "In memory of James Small, who departed this life August 13, 1827, in the seventy-ninth year of his age."

"Depart my friends, dry up your tears,
Here I must lie till Christ appears."

"In memory of Ann Small, consort of James Small, who departed this life on the 10th day of June, 1830, in the seventy-sixth year of her age."

James and Ann (Beveridge) Small had:

(I) EDWARD SMALL, born December 12, 1777; died October 28, 1855.

(II) GEORGE SMALL, born March 3, 1782; died July 14, 1855.

(III) JEANNETTE SMALL, born June 20, 1784; died March 4, 1848.

(IV) ANN RECTOR SMALL, born in 1786; died November 7, 1845.

(I) EDWARD SMALL, eldest son of James and Ann (Beveridge) Small, was born December 12, 1777, at Cambridge, Washington County, New York, and died October 28, 1855, at Cambridge, New York. He was an officer in the militia, being appointed an ensign April 14, 1800, by Governor John Jay; and a lieutenant March 26, 1804, by Governor DeWitt Clinton. His grandson, Dr. Charles B. Small of Saratoga Springs, New York, has the original commissions and his silver-mounted dress sword.

"I lived with my grandfather, Edward Small, in the winter of 1847. I always thought he was a grand old man, of good common sense. He was what I would call to-day a model farmer—a place for everything and everything in its place; six feet, two inches in height, broad shouldered; weighed over 200 pounds; no extra flesh; honest and upright in all his dealings with his neighbors.

"He was a captain in the war of 1812; was at the battle of Plattsburg; had soldier's land warrant, but did not use it. He had a family of twelve children; eight lived to manhood."—John L. Richardson, Wyoming, Iowa.

Edward Small and Phebe Thomas were married December 11, 1802.

Phebe Thomas, youngest child of Captain Alexander and Ursilla (Oldridge) Thomas, was born July 24, 1784, in Rhode Island, and died June 8, 1855.

Captain Alexander Thomas was a captain in the Revolutionary Army.

LINEAGE OF PHEBE THOMAS.

When William Bradford was elected Governor in the years 1641 to 1644, William Thomas was elected assistant in 1642 and 1643, supplying the place of Miles Standish.

Joseph Thomas, supposed to be the son of the above William Thomas, married Ruth Fish, daughter of Daniel and Abigail (Mumford) Fish, and had:

(1) Ruth Thomas, born November 15, 1726.
(2) Mary Thomas, born April 21, 1732.
(3) Joseph Thomas.

No records of this Joseph's birth, death or marriage, but Daniel Fish in his will speaks of his daughter, Ruth Thomas, and the record of the two children of Joseph Thomas and Ruth Fish, given above, are taken from the vital records of Portsmouth, R. I., as are all the immediately following records of births and marriages.

(3) Joseph Thomas, son of Joseph and Ruth (Fish) Thomas, married Sarah Estes, daughter of Robert and Ann (Durfee) Estes, March 15, 1737.

Have no record of the date of birth or death of this Joseph. His will, dated August 27, 1777, was recorded July 10, 1788.

Joseph and Sarah (Estes) Thomas had:

(1) Anne Thomas, born August 4, 1739.

(2) Joseph Thomas, born January 3, 1741-2. Married Ruth Tabor.

(3) ALEXANDER THOMAS, born November 25, 1743.

(4) Ruth Thomas, born August 16, 1745.

(5) Lucianna Thomas, born March 29, 1747; died before 1777.

(6) Elizabeth Thomas, born November 15, 1748.

(7) Daniel Thomas, born November 3, 1750.

(8) Richard Thomas, born November 28, 1752.

(9) Jeremiah Thomas.

(10) Robert Thomas, born January 29, 1757. Married Abigail Thurston.

(11) Seth Thomas.

(12) David Thomas.

(13) Jonathan Thomas.

(3) Captain Alexander Thomas, son of Joseph and Sarah (Estes) Thomas, was born November 25, 1743.

Captain Alexander Thomas was the father of Phebe Thomas. The records of his military service are to be found in the office of the Secretary of State of Rhode Island at Providence, R. I. Captain Thomas was at the February session of the General Assembly of the State of Rhode Island, 1778, elected captain of Colonel Topham's regiment, he having previous to his election as captain served as second lieutenant and lieutenant, respectively. At one time he commanded a company of minute-men and patroled the Hudson River about Albany, New York.

Captain Thomas lent the Continental Government the sum of two thousand and five pounds, which was never repaid. Daniel Webster was endeavoring, when he died, to secure the payment of this money to the heirs of Captain Thomas. His house in Portsmouth, Rhode Island, is still standing. It was occupied by the Hessians when the British were in the possession of Rhode Island, but his wife and children were allowed to remain in one room.

Captain Thomas had six brothers in the service. His brother, Jeremiah, was one of the men chosen by General Barton to accompany him when he captured General Prescott. I have not found the exact date of Captain Thomas' death, but his will was admitted to probate October 5, 1812.

In Marshfield, Massachusetts, is the old Thomas homestead, now owned by heirs of Daniel Webster, and there is the old burying ground of the Thomas family. The William Thomas, spoken of, is of that family, and my uncle, Captain Orrin Hall, who died in 1904, at the age of eighty-nine years, said our line is from this William.

Captain Alexander and Ursilla (Oldridge) Thomas had:

(1) Susanah Thomas, born June 25, 1767.

(2) Sarah Thomas, born April 16, 1769.

(3) Anne Thomas, born January 22, 1771.

(4) Rhody Thomas, born July 13, 1774.

(5) Mary Thomas, born May 18, 1777.

(6) Arnold Thomas, born June 22, 1781.

(7) PHEBE THOMAS, born July 24, 1784.—Lillian Ford Andrews, great-great-granddaughter of Captain Alexander Thomas.

EDWARD and PHEBE (THOMAS) SMALL had:

(I) Ann Small, born December 24, 1803; died September 15, 1850.

(II) Eliza Small, born October 11, 1805; died March 16, 1887.

(III) Jeannette Small, born August 29, 1808; died June 4, 1821.

(IV) Mary Small, born November 17, 1810.

(V) Susanah Small, born June 19, 1813; died January 22, 1880.

(VI) James E. Small (twins), born December 11, 1815; died March 6, 1877.

(VII) Ursula Small (twins), born December 11, 1815; died December 11, 1817.

(VIII) Sarah E. Small, born September 24, 1817; died January 28, 1898.

(IX) Alexander Small, born January 28, 1820; died February 12, 1892.

(X) Thomas Small (twins) born March 24, 1822; died April 24, 1822.

(XI) Jeannette Small (twins), born March 24, 1822; died April 24, 1822.

(XII) Thomas B. Small, born May 26, 1824; died May 7, 1849.

(I) Ann Small, eldest daughter of Edward and Phebe (Thomas) Small, was born December 24, 1803, in Cambridge, New York, and died September 15, 1850, in Coila, New York.

John Robertson and Ann Small were married July 8, 1824, in Cambridge, New York.

John Robertson, fourth son of William and Mary (Livingston) Robertson, was born May 2, 1786, in the town of Greenwich, Washington County, New York, and died September 2, 1873, in Coila, New York.

The descendants of John and Ann (Small) Robertson may be found under the head of John Robertson on preceding pages.

(II) Eliza Small, second daughter of Edward and Phebe (Thomas) Small, was born October 11, 1805, in Cambridge, New York, and died March 16, 1887.

Robert McClellan and Eliza Small were married October 10, 1822.

Robert McClellan, son of John and Sarah (Thomas) McClellan, was born June 16, 1799, and died June 24, 1880.

Robert and Eliza (Small) McClellan had:

(1) Ursula McClellan, born January 11, 1825; died May 22, 1826.

(2) John McClellan, born January 31, 1827; died September 15, 1828.

(3) Edward S. McClellan, born July 14, 1829; died August 12, 1900.

(4) Francis W. McClellan, born October 21, 1831.

(5) Sarah Thompson McClellan, born May 21, 1835; died March 12, 1836.

(6) James Alexander McClellan, born January 22, 1842; died July 7, 1906.

(7) Mary Ellen McClellan, born May 2, 1849.

(3) Edward S. McClellan, second son of Robert and Eliza (Small) McClellan, was born July 14, 1829, and died August 12, 1900.

Edward S. McClellan and Helen Clark were married in 1853.

Edward S. and Helen (Clark) McClellan had:

(A) Albert McClellan, born September 12, 1855.

(B) Edward F. McClellan, born June 18, 1858.

(4) Francis W. McClellan, third son of Robert and Eliza (Small) McClellan, was born October 21, 1831, and resides at Winfield, Kansas. He has in his possession the old family clock, which his great-grandfather, James Small, brought from Scotland. This venerable relic is highly prized in the McClellan family. Remarkable to state, this ancient clock still keeps almost perfect time.

Francis W. McClellan and Sarah Ann Selvey were married April 3, 1856.

Sarah Ann Selvey, daughter of Walter Selvey, was born April, 1832, and died May 31, 1859.

Francis W. and Sarah Ann (Selvey) McClellan had:

(A) Francis Herndon McClellan, born April 31, 1857; died August 1, 1907.

Francis W. McClellan and Sarah Reeves Jackson were marreid June 9, 1870.

Sarah Reeves Jackson, daughter of Peter and Angeline (Hanson) Jackson, was born August 15, 1848.

Francis W. and Sarah Reeves (Jackson) McClellan had:

(A) Ethel Corrine McClellan, born April 17, 1872.

(B) Myrta Lisle McClellan, born March 28, 1875.

(C) Ada Angeline McClellan, born March 18, 1883.

(6) James Alexander McClellan, fourth son of Robert and Eliza (Small) McClellan, was born January 22, 1842; died July 7, 1906, in Manila, Philippine Islands. He served three years in the Fifth Iowa Infantry during the Civil war. After the war taught school several years and was connected with the Seattle Post-Intelligencer for ten or twelve years before going to the Philippines.

James Alexander McClellan and Luella Allyn were married in 1867.

Luella Allyn was born December 24, 1843.

James Alexander and Luella (Allyn) McClellan had:

(A) Fred A. McClellan, born March 2, 1868.

(B) Edward A. McClellan, born September 30, 1869. He is an interpreter for the Government in the Philippine Islands.

(C) Maud A. McClellan, born August 16, 1873.

(7) Mary Ellen McClellan, third daughter of Robert and Eliza (Small) McClellan, was born May 2, 1849, and was married to Frank Wade, and now lives in Russell, Kansas.

(IV) Mary Small, fourth daughter of Edward and Phebe (Thomas) Small, was born November 17, 1810.

Rev. Samuel McArthur and Mary Small were married July 31, 1838, and lived some place in the West.

(V) Susanah Small, fifth daughter of Edward and Phebe (Thomas) Small, was born June 19, 1813, and died February 22, 1880.

James Richardson and Susanah Small were married May 9, 1833.

James Richardson was born in 1797, in Scotland; came to America in 1832; and died September 18, 1880. He was a carpenter.

James and Susanah (Small) Richardson had:

(1) Edward Richardson, born January 24, 1834; died February 22, 1885.

(2) Jeannette Richardson, born January 12, 1836.

(3) John L. Richardson, born January 31, 1838.

(4) Annie E. Richardson, born April 2, 1840.

(5) Mary Richardson, born May 17, 1842.

(6) James A. Richardson, born October 5, 1844.

(7) Phebe Richardson, born January 8, 1847; died March 25, 1879.

(8) Susanah R. Richardson, born September 25, 1854.

(9) Sarah E. Richardson, born December 1, 1857.

(1) Edward Richardson, eldest son of James and Susanah (Small) Richardson, was born January 24, 1834, in Washington County, New York, and died February 22, 1885.

Edward Richardson and Katherine Stevenson were married September 26, 1862.

Katherine Stevenson, daughter of James and Nancy (Moore) Stevenson, was born May 3, 1840.

Edward and Katherine (Stevenson) Richardson had:

(A) Gertrude Richardson, born July 13, 1869; died September 22, 1886.

(B) Frank Ledgewood Richardson, born August 28, 1875.

(C) William Walter Richardson, born March 12, 1880.

(D) Susan Richardson, born November 2, 1882.

(B) Frank Ledgewood Richardson, eldest son of Edward and Katherine (Stevenson) Richardson, was born August 28, 1875, and is a rising young lawyer in Winfield, Kansas.

Mrs. Katherine (Stevenson) Richardson married, secondly, Samuel S. Hurd, January 18, 1886.

(2) Jeannette Richardson, eldest daughter of James and Susanah (Small) Richardson, was born January 12, 1836, in Argyle, Washington County, New York, and lives in Iberia, Ohio.

Robert McClarren and Jeannette Richardson were married March 13, 1855.

Robert McClarren, son of Robert and Sarah (McClenathen)

McClarren, was born January 8, 1826, in Burgettown, Pennsylvania, and died August 20, 1892.

Robert and Jeannette (Richardson) McClarren had:

(A) Arminta McClarren, born February 4, 1856.
(B) Mary Jane McClarren, born April 14, 1858.
(C) Sarah Ann McClarren, born February 29, 1860.
(D) Florence McClarren, born June 18, 1862.
(E) James F. McClaren,
(F) Anna Grace McClarren (twins), born August 7, 1865.
(G) Charles Edward McClarren, born October 1, 1870.

(A) Arminta McClarren, eldest daughter of Robert and Jeannette (Richardson) McClarren, was born February 4, 1856, in Morrow County, Ohio.

John Parker Hale Collins and Arminta McClarren were married November 16, 1875, by Rev. John P. Robb of Iberia, Ohio.

John Parker Hale Collins, son of James Clarkson and Martha (Anderson) Collins, was born October 18, 1852, in Green County, Ohio, and lives at Monmouth, Illinois.

John Parker Hale Collins and Arminta (McClarren) Collins had:

(a) Cornelius Bruce Collins, born September 5, 1876.
(b) Edward LeRoy Collins, born August 27, 1879.
(c) Pauline May Collins, born April 26, 1881.
(d) Robert McClarren Collins, born August 8, 1883.
(e) Ethel Grace Collins, born September 23, 1885.
(f) Martha Eunice Collins, born May 16, 1890.
(g) Jeannette Collins, born September 5, 1893.

(a) Cornelius Bruce Collins, eldest son of John Parker Hale and Arminta (McClarren) Collins, was born September 5, 1876.

Cornelius Bruce Collins and Edith McMullin were married September 12, 1902, in the Philippine Islands, and now live in Buena Vista, Colorado, where he is superintendent of public schools.

Edith McMullin is a daughter of Lee and Mary B. (Phillips) McMullin.

Cornelius Bruce and Edith (McMullin) Collins had:

(a) Helen Collins, born September 27, 1904; died October 2, 1904.

(B) Mary Jane McClarren, second daughter of Robert and Jeannette (Richardson) McClarren, was born April 14, 1858, in Morrow County, Ohio.

Julian A. Day and Mary Jane McClarren were married March 7, 1882, by Rev. J. P. Robb of Iberia, Ohio.

Julian A. Day, son of James Alfred and Sarah (Stephenson) Day, was born November 23, 1860, near Wyoming, Iowa, and lives at Wyoming, Iowa.

Julian A. and Mary Jane (McClarren) Day had:

(a) Sarah Jeannette Day, born August 31, 1884.

(b) Fred A. Day, born June 6, 1886.

(c) Cleo Grace Day, born March 15, 1889.

(d) Robert Howard Day, born November 21, 1896.

(C) Sarah Ann McClarren, third daughter of Robert and Jeannette (Richardson) McClarren, was born February 29, 1860, near Iberia, Ohio.

Stephen Mitchell Jaggers and Sarah Ann McClarren were married June 15, 1896.

Stephen Mitchell Jaggers, son of David and Elizabeth (Williams) Jaggers, was born October 7, 1857, in Licking County, Ohio, and lives in Galion, Ohio.

Stephen Mitchell and Sarah Ann (McClarren) Jaggers had:

(a) Paul Dales Jaggers, born September 30, 1897, near Iberia, Ohio.

(b) John Tompkins Jaggers, born December 28, 1899.

(D) Florence McClarren, fourth daughter of Robert and Jeannette (Richardson) McClarren, was born June 18, 1862.

William Alexander Sherrill and Florence McClarren were married December 27, 1887.

William Alexander Sherrill, son of David Huntington and Lydia Elvira (Howk) Sherrill, was born May 15, 1865, and lives near Julesburg, Colorado.

William Alexander and Florence (McClarren) Sherrill had:

(a) Hattie Sherrill, born January 22, 1889.

(b) Robert Huntington Sherrill, born March 5, 1892.

(c) William Ralph Sherrill, born July 20, 1896.

(d) Charles Edward Sherrill, born February 6, 1899.

(e) Lawrence Raymond Sherrill, born February 14, 1904.

(E) James French McClarren, eldest son of Robert and Jeannette (Richardson) McClarren, was born August 7, 1865, and lives at Iberia, Ohio.

James French McClarren and Jennie Lucretta Moody were married June 25, 1890, by Rev. A. C. Crist.

Jennie Lucretta Moody was born August 1, 1869.

James French and Jennie Lucretta (Moody) McClarren had:
(a) Nellie Moody McClarren, born June 27, 1891.
(b) Robert Mickey McClarren, born April 24, 1893.
(c) Mary Gladys McClarren, born April 15, 1895.
(d) Charles Edward McClarren, born December 19, 1898.
(e) Ella Laura McClarren, born March 6, 1900.
(f) James Donald McClarren, born March 23, 1901.
(g) Edith McClarren, born February 7, 1905.

(F) Anna Grace McClarren, fifth daughter of Robert and Jeannette (Richardson) McClarren, was born August 7, 1865, in Morrow County, Ohio.

Foster Jackson Kyle and Anna Grace McClarren were married October 18, 1893, by Dr. J. P. Robb.

Foster Jackson Kyle was born February 6, 1864, and lives in Springfield, Ohio.

Foster Jackson and Anna Grace (McClarren) Kyle had:

(a) Anna Jeannette Kyle, born September 3, 1894, in Xenia, Ohio.

(b) Florence Louise Kyle, born December 29, 1896.

(c) Helen Kyle, born March 19, 1898; died April 29, 1900.

(d) Roland McClarren Kyle, born September 8, 1899, in Springfield, Ohio.

(e) Mildred Kyle, born February 7, 1902, in Springfield, Ohio.

(f) Mable Ruth Kyle, born December 1, 1903.

(G) Charles Edward McClarren, second son of Robert and Jeannette (Richardson) McClarren, was born October 1, 1870, and lives at St. James, Ohio.

Charles Edward McClarren and Mary Alice Nesbitt were married October 17, 1893.

Mary Alice Nesbitt, daughter of Samuel and Jane Ann (Colmery) Nesbitt, was born November 27, 1871.

Charles Edward and Mary Alice (Nesbitt) McClarren had:

(a) Jennie Irene McClarren, born July 14, 1894.

(b) Mary Lois McClarren, born July 31, 1896; died March 25, 1898.

(c) Samuel Foster McClarren, born November 7, 1898.

(d) Ruth McClarren, born February 4, 1901.

(e) Mildred Belle McClarren, born May 18, 1903.

(3) John L. Richardson, second son of James and Susanah (Small) Richardson, was born January 31, 1873, in Washington

County, New York; came west with his father's family in 1850, and now lives in Wyoming, Iowa.

John L. Richardson enlisted July 18, 1861, in the 26th Ohio Infantry at Camp Chase, Ohio; was discharged November 23, 1865. He was in Wood's Division at the battle of Stone River, Tennessee; in the battle of Chickamauga, Georgia, September 19-20. 1863, Buell's Brigade, Wood's Division; was in siege of Chattanooga, Tennessee; went up the ridge in Wagoner's Brigade, Sheridan's Division; was in the Atlanta Campaign down to Kenesaw Mountain, Georgia.

Mr. Richardson is a retired farmer. He owns a large tract of valuable land near Wyoming, Iowa.

John L. Richardson and Nancy Ellen Stevenson were married July 18, 1868, at Wyoming, Iowa.

Nancy Ellen Stevenson, daughter of James and Nancy (Moore) Stevenson, was born January 21, 1849, in New Castle, Pennsylvania, and died November 23, 1881, at Wyoming, Iowa.

John L. and Nancy Ellen (Stevenson) Richardson had:

(A) Nettie Floy Richardson, born September 3, 1869; died October 9, 1870.

(B) Charles S. Richardson, born October 5, 1871; died August 29, 1873.

(C) Mary J. Richardson, born December 3, 1873; died October 9, 1878.

(D) Florence Richardson, born May 27, 1880; is teaching school at Canon City, Colorado.

John L. Richardson and Almira Iler were married December 28, 1882.

Almira Iler, daughter of David and Bythima (Truax) Iler, was born December 29, 1845.

John L. and Almira (Iler) Richardson had:

(A) Ruby E. Richardson, born November 21, 1883, at Wyoming, Iowa. She attended school at Mt. Vernon, Iowa, and May 2, 1906, was married to Louis Franklin Pealer.

(4) Ann E. Richardson, second daughter of James and Susanah (Small) Richardson, was born April 2, 1840, in Washington County, New York.

Isaac Bender and Ann E. Richardson were married June 15, 1863.

Isaac Bender, son of Jacob and Mary (Pealer) Bender, died in 1869.

Isaac and Ann E. (Richardson) Bender had:

(A) William Richardson Bender, born April 17, 1864.

(B) Lula Bender, born March 12, 1866.
(C) Thomas Bender, born February 6, 1868.

(C) Thomas Bender and Lottie Aarm were married July 4, 1889.

Lottie Aarm was born in London, England, and died in 1890.

Joshua J. Bender and Mrs. Ann E. (Richardson) Bender were married February 22, 1871.

Joshua J. Bender, son of Jacob and Mary (Pealer) Bender, was born June 15, 1844, and lives at 3327 Avenue B, Council Bluffs, Iowa.

Joshua J. Bender served in Company "H," 14th Iowa Infantry, from August 5, 1861, until August 8, 1865. He took part in the following battles: Fort Henry; Fort Donelson; Shiloh; taken prisoner April 6, 1862; was in all the battles and marches of the 1st Brigade, 2d Division, 16th Army Corps. He was captured in the Hornet's Nest, after holding the Old Sunken Road from 8 a. m. until 5:30 p. m. He was mustered out as sergeant.

Joshua J. and Ann E. (Richardson) Bender had:
(A) Laura E. Bender, born February 9, 1876.
(B) Adelbert Bender, born September 5, 1878; died May 10, 1879.

(5) Mary Jane Richardson, third daughter of James and Susanah (Small) Richardson, was born May 17, 1842, in Washington County, New York.

Albert Henry Day and Mary Jane Richardson were married July 4, 1865.

Albert Henry Day was born August 15, 1836, in Pennsylvania, and died in 1881, in Clio, Iowa. He was in the 2d Iowa Cavalry in the civil war.

Albert Henry and Mary Jane (Richardson) Day had:
(A) Charles Ulysses Day, born May 3, 1866.
(B) Albert Burton Day, born October 31, 1867.
(C) George Francis Day, born March 20, 1873.

(A) Charles Ulysses Day, eldest son of Albert Henry and Mary Jane (Richardson) Day, was born May 3, 1866, in Wyoming, Jones County, Iowa, and lives at 838 Moreno Avenue, Colorado Springs. Colorado.

Charles Ulysses Day and Anne F. Eberle were married May 12, 1897, in Cripple Creek, Colorado.

Anne F. Eberle, daughter of Christian and Catherine Eberle, (both born in Germany) was born December 25, 1876.

Charles Ulysses and Anne F. (Eberle) Day had:

(a) Russell George Day, born March 10, 1899, in Colorado Springs, Colorado.

(b) Charles Eberle Day, born September 19, 1904, Colorado Springs, Colorado.

(B) Albert Burton Day, second son of Albert Henry and Mary Jane (Richardson) Day, was born October 31, 1867. He is vice-president and general manager of the Nevada Searchlight Mining Company at Seachlight, Nev., and lives at 511 W. Pico Street, Los Angeles, Cal. Mr. Day was married at Los Angeles September 16, 1906, to Katherine Daifer, who was born September 12, 1871, at Muscatine, Iowa.

(C) George Francis Day, third son of Albert Henry and Mary Jane (Richardson) Day, was born March 20, 1873, in Clio, Wayne County, Iowa, and lives in Franktown, Douglas County, Colorado.

George Francis Day and Edna Pearl Maxwell were married August 24, 1905, in Colorado Springs, Colorado.

Edna Pearl Maxwell, daughter of Martin Absolem and Mary Estelle (Gorsline) Maxwell, was born January 6, 1886, in Waverly. Coffee County, Kansas.

Amos Tryon Harding and Mrs. Mary Jane (Richardson) Day were married September 3, 1883, in Mansfield, Ohio.

Amos Tryon Harding was in Company "C," 15th Ohio Infantry, and was discharged for wounds received in action at Stone River, Tennessee, December 31, 1862.

Amos Tryon and Mary Jane (Richardson) Harding had:

(A) Harriet Robena Harding, born August 28, 1884, in Corsica, Ohio.

John Graham and Harriet Robena Harding were married and had:

(a) Glee Graham.

(6) James A. Richardson, third son of James and Susanah (Small) Richardson, was born October 5, 1844.

James Albert Richardson and Ella Beatrice Johnson were married May 23, 1868.

Ella Beatrice Johnson, daughter of Marcus and Phebe Ann (Tolman) Johnson, was born June 6, 1850.

James Albert and Ella Beatrice (Johnson) Richardson had:

(A) Bertrand E. Richardson, born May 6, 1869.
(B) Josephine A. Richardson, born June 26, 1870.
(C) Charles Porter Richardson, born January 23, 1873.
(D) Clara E. Richardson, born March 2, 1877.
(E) James Edward Richardson, born February 2, 1879.

(A) Bertrand E. Richardson, eldest son of James Albert and Ella Beatrice (Johnson) Richardson, was born May 6, 1869, and lives at Farragut, Iowa, R. R. No. 2, Box 48. He is a farmer.

Bertrand E. Richardson and Emma Belle Fletcher were married August 30, 1891.

Emma Belle Fletcher, daughter of Hiram Daniel and Mary Susan (Kallison) Fletcher, was born July 9, 1873.

Bertrand E. and Emma Belle (Fletcher) Richardson had:

(a) Albert Leland Richardson, born May 22, 1892.
(b) Iva Lorine Richardson, born August 23, 1893.
(c) Bessie Gertrude Richardson, born May 7, 1896.
(d) Eugene Hope Richardson, born March 6, 1898.
(e) Freddie Richardson, born December 23, 1899.
(f) Offa Richardson, born March 11, 1901.
(g) Hiram Fletcher Richardson, born February 14, 1903.

(B) Josephine A. Richardson, eldest daughter of James Albert and Ella Beatrice (Johnson) Richardson, was born June 26, 1870.

Oael Jacob Burt and Josephine A. Richardson were married February 8, 1888. They live at Thayer, Kansas, R. F. D. No. 2.

Oael Jacob Burt, son of Silas and Nancy (Dains) Burt, was born February 7, 1868.

Oael Jacob Burt and Josephine A. (Richardson) Burt had:

(a) Ernest Leaman Burt, born November 30, 1888.
(b) Baby Burt, born December 9, 1890; died January 19, 1891.
(c) Merl Silas Burt, born February 29, 1892.
(d) Ruby Clara Burt, born September 15, 1893.
(e) Lloyd Oael Burt, born November 20, 1894.
(f) Florence Josephine Burt, born January 3, 1897.
(g) George Dewey Burt, born April 17, 1899.
(h) Baby Burt, born July 23, 1900; died July 25, 1900.
(i) Albert Parcus Burt, born August 18, 1902.

(C) Charles Porter Richardson, second son of James Albert and Ella Beatrice (Johnson) Richardson, was born January 23, 1873, in Sidney, Iowa, and lives at 283 Manhattan Avenue, Brooklyn, New York.

Charles Porter Richardson and Rose Anna Jane Sloan were married March 31, 1899.

Rose Anna Jane Sloan, daughter of Craig and Elizabeth (Teeden) Sloan, was born April 29, 1878, in Ontario, Canada. Her parents were both born in Ireland.

Charles Porter and Rose Anna Jane (Sloan) Richardson had:

(a) Charles Edward Richardson, born December 18, 1899, in Brooklyn.

(D) Clara E. Richardson, second daughter of James Albert and Ella Beatrice (Johnson) Richardson, was born March 2, 1877.

John Bernard Feld and Clara E. Richardson were married June 7, 1899, in Marshalltown, Iowa.

John Bernard Feld, son of John and Anna Nora (Flaherty) Feld, was born October 5, 1873.

John Bernard and Clara E. (Richardson) Feld had:

(a) John Walter Feld, born September 9, 1900, in Marshalltown, Iowa.

(b) Eleanor Kathleen Feld, born March 10, 1903; died March 11, 1904.

(c) Edward Leo Feld, born January 18, 1905, in Marshalltown, Iowa.

(d) Mary Clara Feld, born October 7, 1906, in Marshalltown, Iowa.

(E) James Edward Richardson, third son of James Albert and Ella Beatrice (Johnson) Richardson, was born February 2, 1879, at Great Bend, Kansas. Educated in the common schools. Lives at 6621 Union avenue, Chicago.

James Edward Richardson and Matilda Agnes Eckert were married February 7, 1905, in Chicago.

(7) Phebe Richardson, fourth daughter of James and Susanah (Small) Richardson, was born January 8, 1847, and died March 25, 1879.

George Washington James and Phebe Richardson were married October 4, 1866.

George Washington James, son of Walter and Susanah James, was born September 7, 1844. He enlisted in Company "K,"

24th Regiment, Iowa Volunteers, in the civil war. He was in the battles of Champion Hill; siege of Vicksburg, Mississippi; Sabine Cross Roads, Louisiana; Winchester, Virginia, and others. He lives near Wyoming, Iowa.

George Washington and Phebe (Richardson) James had:

(A) Rolla M. James, born July 27, 1867.

(B) Walter G. James, born May 21, 1869.

(C) Edward James, born February 20, 1871; died July 7, 1903.

(D) Fred James, born October 7, 1873; died September or October, 1876.

(A) Rolla M. James, eldest son of George Washington and Phebe (Richardson) James, was born July 27, 1867, at Madison, Jones County, Iowa. He attended school at Wyoming, Iowa, and a short time at Davenport, at the Iowa Commercial College. He was converted in 1887 and united with the M. E. Church and has always been an active worker in that church. Moved from Wyoming to Ledyard, Iowa, in 1899, and to Elmore, Minnesota, in 1903. He owns his own farm and is trying to make the world a little better for having lived in it.

Rolla M. James and Mattie E. Williams were married October 30, 1889.

Mattie E. Williams, daughter of Franklin Scarborough Williams, was born March 30, 1867, in DeWitt, Clinton county, Iowa.

Rolla M. and Mattie E. (Williams) James had:

(a) Alta Maria James, born March 3, 1895, at Wyoming, Iowa.

(b) Clarisa Phœbe James, born May 29, 1896, at Wyoming, Iowa.

(c) Ruth James, born April 27, 1898, at Wyoming, Iowa.

(d) Harriet Irene James, born May 5, 1902, in Ledyard, Iowa.

Alta and Ruth died in infancy.

(B) Walter G. James, second son of George Washington and Phebe (Richardson) James was born May 21, 1869.

Walter G. James and Helda Drake were married July 19, 1896.

Helda Drake was born September 18, 1872.

They have no children and live at 2689 Hamilton Avenue, Chicago.

(C) Edward James, third son of George Washington and

Phebe (Richardson) James, was born February 20, 1871, and died July 7, 1903.

Edward James and Mary Pries were married September 17, 1901.

Mary Pries, daughter of George and Annie (Sozel) Pries, was born September 16, 1880.

Edward and Mary (Pries) James had:

(a) Katherine Helen James, born July 10, 1902.

They live in Spokane, Washington, 121 Marion Block.

(8) Susanah Robenia Richardson, fifth daughter of James and Susanah (Small) Richardson, was born September 25, 1854.

William M. Kilmer and Susanah Robenia Richardson were married September 16, 1875.

William M. Kilmer, son of David and Matilda (Post) Kilmer, was born December 25, 1850, and lives at 2120 Avenue "C," Council Bluffs, Iowa.

William M. and Susanah Robenia (Richardson) Kilmer had:

(A) Eldora Kilmer, born August 7, 1876; died May 18, 1884.

(B) Jessie Kilmer, born September 27, 1879, in Council Bluffs, Iowa.

(C) James Milo Kilmer, born July 28, 1881, in Peoria, Illinois.

(D) Albert L. Kilmer, born February 7, 1886, in Council Bluffs, Iowa.

(E) Mabel M. Kilmer, born March 24, 1888, in Council Bluffs, Iowa.

(F) Florence Ethel Kilmer, born February 2, 1893, Council Bluffs, Iowa.

(9) Sarah E. Richardson, sixth daughter of James and Susanah (Small) Richardson, was born December 1, 1857.

William T. Mills and Sarah E. Richardson were married May 30, 1877.

William T. Mills was born February 1, 1847.

William T. and Sarah E. (Richardson) Mills had:

(A) William Leland Mills, born March 18, 1878.

(B) Georgiana Leona Mills, born August 1, 1879.

(C) Richard Logan Mills, born November 28, 1884.

Mrs. Sarah E. (Richardson) Mills lives at Olive Block, Quincy Street, Cleveland, Ohio.

(VI) James E. Small, eldest son of Edward and Phebe (Thomas) Small, was born December 11, 1815, and died March 6, 1877. He was graduated from Union College at Schenectady, New York; he studied law and was admitted to the bar January 12, 1844, but never practiced his profession, remaining on the old Small homestead, where he died.

James E. Small and Eleanor Stevenson were married June 26, 1849.

Eleanor Stevenson was born July 15, 1809, and died December 31, 1857.

James E. and Eleanor (Stevenson) Small had:

(1) Thomas Edward Small, born August 23, 1852; died May 18, 1861.

James E. Small and Eliza M. Batty were married March 16, 1858.

Eliza M. Batty, daughter of Stephen and Rebecca M. (Mosher) Batty, was born September 29, 1830. She lives at 135 Newbury St., Boston, Mass.

James E. and Eliza M. (Batty) Small had:

(1) Charles B. Small, born April 6, 1860.

(2) William J. Small, born March 11, 1861.

(3) Annie W. Small, born October 7, 1865.

(1) Dr. Charles B. Small, eldest son of James E. and Eliza M. (Batty) Small, was born April 6, 1860, on the old Small homestead and lives at Saratoga Springs, New York. He was educated in the public schools and in the Hudson River Institute, Claverack, New York. His medical education was received at the New York Homeopathic Medical College, class of 1883. He lived in New York City from that time until 1889, when he removed to Saratoga Springs, New York, where he has since lived. He became a practitioner in the regular school in 1897.

Dr. Charles B. Small and Clara Tegner were married May 10, 1883.

Clara Tegner of St. Croix, Danish West Indies, is a great-grand niece of Bishop Elias Tegner, who was poet laureate of Denmark. She is also a descendant on her mother's side of Edward Ford, M. D., who was one of the original members of the Medical Society of London, England, about 1753.

(2) William J. Small, second son of James E. and Eliza M. (Batty) Small, was born March 11, 1861, on the old Small

homestead, at Cambridge, Washington County, New York, and lives at Gem, Idaho.

William J. Small and Annie Beeler were married December 16, 1885.

Annie Beeler, daughter of John and Christiana Beeler, was born June 14, 1867.

William J. and Annie (Beeler) Small had:

(A) William John Small, born November 13, 1889, in Mehama, Oregon.

(B) Charles Edward Small,

(C) James Ellsworth Small,

twins, born January 6, 1903, in Gem, Idaho.

(3) Annie W. Small, only daughter of James E. and Eliza M. (Batty) Small, was born October 7, 1865. She is unmarried and lives with her mother in Boston.

(VIII) Sarah E. Small, seventh daughter of Edward and Phebe (Thomas) Small, was born September 24, 1817, and died January 28, 1898.

J. V. S. Becker and Sarah E. Small were married March 16, 1859.

J. V. S. Becker was born January 8, 1797, and died January 24, 1888, aged 91 years and 16 days.

J. V. S. and Sarah E. (Small) Becker had:

(1) James Edward Becker, born September 8, 1851.

(2) Eleanor Becker, born September 20, 1853.

(3) Charles C. Becker, born August 17, 1855.

(4) Frederick M. Becker, born June 12, 1858.

(5) Henry W. Becker, born January 31, 1861.

(6) John R. Becker, born July 17, 1863.

(1) James Edward Becker, eldest son of J. V. S. and Sarah E. (Small) Becker, was born September 8, 1851. He lives on the old homestead at North Easton, New York.

James Edward Becker and Hannah Brownell were married February 10, 1875.

Hannah Brownell was born March 12, 1852.

James Edward and Hannah (Brownell) Becker had:

(A) Mary Becker, born August 2, 1882; died September 10, 1882.

(B) Lester Becker, born July 4, 1880.

Lester Becker and Alice Sharp were married August 20, 1902.

Alice Sharp was born December 28, 1878.

(2) Eleanor Becker, eldest daughter of J. V. S. and Sarah E. (Small) Becker, was born September 20, 1853, and was married to Edgar Welling, and had:

(A) John Welling.
(B) Annie Welling, born January, 1875.
(C) Frank Welling.
(D) Sarah Welling.

(A) John Welling, son of Edgar and Eleanor (Becker) Welling, married Fannie Stoon.

(3) Charles C. Becker, second son of J. V. S. and Sarah E. (Small) Becker, was born August 17, 1855.

Charles C. Becker and Libbie Brownell were married February 6, 1878.

Libbie Brownell was born July 3, 1858.

Charles C. and Libbie (Brownell) Becker had:

(A) Bessie Becker, born December 22, 1879; died April 6, 1903.

Bessie Becker was married to Frank Nehron.

(4) Frederick M. Becker, third son of J. V. S. and Sarah E. (Small) Becker, was born June 12, 1858. He married Annie Rice and had:

(A) Bertha Becker, born March 15, 1880.
(B) Niles Rice Becker, born June 9, 1882.
(C) Blanche Louise Becker, born September 15, 1889.
(A) Bertha Becker was married to Walter Galbraith.

(5) Henry W. Becker, fourth son of J. V. S. and Sarah E. (Small) Becker, was born January 31, 1861. He married Emma Skiff, who was born June 9, 1859, and had,

(A) Elna Grace Becker, born August 5, 1891.

(6) John R. Becker, fifth son of J. V. S. and Sarah E. (Small) Becker, was born July 17, 1863. He married Martha Hunter, and had:

(A) Annabel R. Becker, born March 19, 1888.
(B) Alfred W. Becker, born September 20, 1891.
(C) Mildred Becker, born September 13, 1899.

(IX) Alexander Small, second son of Edward and Phebe (Thomas) Small, was born January 28, 1820, in Cambridge, New York, and died February 12, 1892, near Yorkville, Kendall County, Illinois. He was reared to agricultural pursuits on his father's farm at Cambridge, New York. August 21, 1838, Alexander Small was commissioned by Colonel Andrew Thompson, Jr., as Corporal in the 114th Regiment, New York Militia; and March 16, 1842, he was commissioned by William H. Seward, then governor of New York, as Lieutenant in the same regiment. These commissions are still preserved by the children of Alexander Small. In 1844 he married Mary Woods, which proved a happy and prosperous union. In 1845 they set out for the West, stopping for two years in Milford, Oakland County, Michigan, where his wife's brother had preceded them, and in 1847 they went still farther west and located in Oswego Township, Kendall County, Illinois. Here he purchased a tract of land, on which he resided until he sold it, in 1890, engaging in farming, stock raising and dairying. His wife, who accompanied him to Illinois and shared his pioneer home for many years, was a noble, Christian woman, a fond mother, good wife and kind neighbor. Mr. Small took no slight part in affairs pertaining to the public good during his long residence in Oswego, and served his township repeatedly in offices of honor and trust, such as supervisor, school director and commissioner of roads. He was also a trustee and deacon in the Congregational Church of Aurora, of which his wife and family were members for many years. His character as a man and citizen was briefly told the writer by one who knew him a lifetime: "To know him is to fully trust him with the certainty of never being deceived."

Alexander Small and Mary Woods were married September 26, 1844, at Cambridge, Washington County, New York.

Mary Woods, daughter of James and Anna (Ketchie) Woods, was born March 1, 1822, in Cambridge, Washington County, New York, and died September 24, 1881, in Oswego Township, Kendall County, Illinois.

Alexander and Mary (Woods) Small had:

(1) Phebe Thomas Small, born November 11,, 1845; died May 11, 1890.

(2) Josephine Small, born September 17, 1848; died June 27, 1904.

(3) James Woods Small, born February 2, 1852.

(4) Edward Small, born February 24, 1854.

(5) Annie Margaret Small, born January 24, 1856.

(6) Thomas Small, born February 10, 1858.

(7) Andrew Small, born September 26, 1861; died March 17, 1882.

(1) Phebe Thomas Small, eldest daughter of Alexander and Mary (Woods) Small, was born November 11, 1845, in Milford, Oakland County, Michigan, and died May 11, 1890, at Cambridge, Washington County, New York.

She lived on the home farm until about eighteen years old and attended the district school, when she attended the Rockford Ladies Seminary (now the Rockford College) during the years of 1863-4 and 1864-5. The following year, 1866, she taught the home school; the next year she spent at her parents' old home in Washington County, New York, visiting relatives. Here she met her future husband, Henry Coulter, and was married January 30, 1868, at her father's home near Aurora, Illinois. She returned with her husband to Cambridge, New York, where she died on their farm five miles east of Cambridge, on May 11, 1890. She attended, with her family, the U. P. Church at Coila, New York, where her father and mother and grandparents had attended before her.

Henry Coulter and Phebe Thomas Small were married January 30, 1868, at her father's home near Aurora, Illinois.

Henry Coulter, son of James and Nancy (Coulter) Coulter, was born May 30, 1834, in Jackson, Washington County, New York, and died November 8, 1894, at White Creek, Washington County, New York.

Henry and Phebe Thomas (Small) Coulter had:

(A) Florence Coulter, born October 31, 1868; died September 14, 1871.

(B) Andrew Woods Coulter, born May 10, 1871.

(C) Edward Small Coulter, born June 17, 1876; died March 30, 1899.

(D) Mary Elizabeth Coulter, born October 10, 1879.

(B) Andrew Woods Coulter, eldest son of Henry and Phebe Thomas (Small) Coulter, was born May 10, 1871, at Cambridge, New York, where he still lives.

Andrew Woods Coulter and Edith May Cornell were married February 21, 1901.

Edith May Cornell, daughter of Flavius Josephus and Mary Elizabeth Cornell, was born October 26, 1877.

Andrew Woods and Edith May (Cornell) Coulter had:

(a) Edward Cornell Coulter, born March 25, 1902.
(b) Blanche Louise Coulter, born December 10, 1903.

(D) Mary Elizabeth Coulter, second daughter of Henry and

Phebe Thomas (Small) Coulter, was born October 10, 1879, at Cambridge, New York.

Walter Willard Herrington and Mary Elizabeth Coulter were married October 2, 1901.

Walter Willard Herrington, son of Russell and Jennie F. (Bosworth) Herrington, was born October 7, 1878.

(2) Josephine Small, second daughter of Alexander and Mary (Woods) Small, was born September 17, 1848, near Aurora, in Oswego Township, Kendall County, Illinois, and died June 27, 1904, near Yorkville, Kendall County, Illinois. She attended the district school until fifteen, when she attended the Rockford Young Ladies' Seminary during the years of 1863-4. She then lived in her father's home until she was married to Henry Hopkins, when she lived on their farm near Yorkville, Illinois, until her death. She was very active in church work and church societies. She, with her husband and family, attended the Presbyterian Church in Kendall County.

Henry McLaen Hopkins and Josephine Small were married October 12, 1876, near Aurora, Illinois, by Rev. N. C. Prentiss.

Henry McLaen Hopkins, son of Archibald and Rachel (McLaen) Hopkins was born August 21, 1845. He owns and lives on a large farm near Yorkville, Kendall County, Illinois.

Henry McLaen and Josephine (Small) Hopkins had:

(A) Mary Alice Hopkins, born January 15, 1878.

(B) James Archibald Hopkins, born August 6, 1880.

(A) Mary Alice Hopkins, only daughter of Henry McLaen and Josephine (Small) Hopkins, was born January 15, 1878, near Yorkville, Illinois. She attended school at Rockford, Illinois, from 1894 to 1898, and was graduated in music in June, 1898; continued collegiate and musical study at Oberlin College and Conservatory, Oberlin, Ohio, 1898-1902; continued musical studies at New England Conservatory of Music, Boston, Massachusetts, 1902-1903, and was graduated in the class of 1903.

(B) James Archibald Hopkins, only son of Henry McLaen and Josephine (Small) Hopkins, was born August 6. 1880. near Yorkville, Illinois. He attended school at Beloit College, Beloit, Wisconsin from 1896 to 1898; took a business course at Gem City Business College. Quincy. Illinois, 1898-1899, and was graduated in 1899.

(3) James Woods Small, eldest son of Alexander and Mary

(Woods) Small, was born February 2, 1852, near Aurora, in Oswego Township, Kendall County, Illinois. He attended the district school until 1873-1874, when he attended Jenning's Seminary, and in 1874-1875 attended Oberlin College, at Oberlin, Ohio. He was then at home until he was married in 1881. He bought a farm adjoining his father's and lived there until 1892, when he removed to Batavia, Kane County, Illinois. After his wife's death, January, 1894, he moved, with his two sons, to Thayer, Mississippi, on account of his health. His wife's sister took his two daughters to live with her at Lostland, Oregon, where they still remain. He and his wife were members of the Congregational Church at Aurora and Batavia, Illinois.

James Woods Small and Ella Glover were married April 20, 1881, at Aurora, Illinois, by Rev. N. A. Prentiss.

Ella Glover, daughter of William W. and Jane Sarah (McKay) Glover, was born September 6, 1852, at Lockport, Illinois, and died January 11, 1894, at Batavia, Illinois.

James Woods and Ella (Glover) Small had:

(A) Alexander Glover Small, born June 22, 1884.

(B) William Bradley Small, born October 22, 1885.

(C) Louise Small, born October 7, 1888.

(D) Ruth Small, born April 29, 1891.

All born near Aurora, in Oswego Township, Kendall County, Illinois.

(4) Edward Small, second son of Alexander and Mary (Woods) Small, was born February 24, 1854, near Aurora, Illinois, on his father's homestead. He attended the district school and Jenning's Seminary. In 1882 he went west to Aberdeen, South Dakota, where he bought a farm, and where he married. In 1902 he moved to Moline, Kansas.

Edward Small and Jessie Swift were married November 16, 1883, at Aberdeen, South Dakota.

Jessie Swift, daughter of Charles Wilmont and Sarah Olive (Douglas) Swift, was born April 9, 1866, and died October 31, 1889, at Aberdeen, Brown County, South Dakota.

Edward and Jessie (Swift) Small had:

(A) Mary Olive Small, born January 5, 1889.

(B) Charles Wilmont Small, born October 7, 1889.

Both born at Aberdeen, South Dakota.

(5) Annie Margaret Small, third daughter of Alexander and Mary (Woods) Small was born January 24, 1856, at her father's home near Aurora, Illinois. She attended the district

school and Jenning's Seminary, at Aurora, Illinois, for several years. After her mother's death in September, 1881, she continued in the care of the home until her father sold his farm in 1890, when she went east to care for her sister, Mrs. Henry Coulter, who was very sick and died in May of that year. She stayed with the family a year, then went west to Aberdeen, South Dakota, to care for her brother Edward's family two years and a half. She then came back to Yorkville, Illinois, to her sister, Mrs. Henry Hopkins, and remained there several years, when she went to Milwaukee, Wisconsin.

William Henry Johnston and Annie Margaret Small were married September 18, 1905, in Milwaukee, Wisconsin.

William Henry Johnston, son of Herbert and Margaret (Brown) Johnston, was born May 17, 1857. They live at Chesterton, Indiana, R. R. No. 2, Box 76.

(6) Thomas Small, third son of Alexander and Mary (Woods) Small, was born February 10, 1858, at his father's home near Aurora, Illinois. He attended the district school and Jenning's Seminary several seasons, and then took charge of his father's home farm until it was sold in 1890, when he went to Bridal Vail, Oregon, and went to work for the Bradley Lumber Company and has continued with them ever since.

(7) Andrew Small, fourth son of Alexander and Mary (Woods) Small, was born September 26, 1861, at his father's home near Aurora, Illinois, and died March 17, 1882 after a lingering illness of several months. He always lived on the home farm with his parents. He attended the district school and Jenning's Seminary. He was a young man of fine character and lovable disposition.

(XII) Thomas B. Small, fourth son and youngest child of Edward and Phebe (Thomas) Small, was born May 26, 1824, and died May 7, 1849.

Dr. Thomas B. Small was graduated from the New York University of Medicine. After graduating he went to Europe and served as interne in hospitals in Paris and Berlin. When he returned to America he located in Schaghticoke, New York; after being there a short time, 1849, he joined a party bound for the California gold fields, as surgeon to the party, and died of dysentery on his way out. He was buried on the banks of the Missouri, about fifty miles above St. Joseph.

(II) GEORGE SMALL, second son of James and Ann (Beveridge) Small, was born March 3, 1782, at Cambridge, Washington County, New York, and died July 14, 1855, at East Greenwich, Washington County, New York, aged 73 years, 4 months and 11 days. His elder brother, Edward, received the original Small homestead at Cambridge from his father, and George received from his father the Small homestead at East Greenwich, and was succeeded by his son, Alexander, and he by his son, James, who still occupies the homestead.

George Small and Jeannette Lourie were married March 31, 1803.

Jeannette Lourie, daughter of Alexander Lourie, who was born in Scotland, was born August 17, 1783, and died August 18, 1865.

George and Jeannette (Lourie) Small had:

(I) James Small, born March 19, 1805; died April 25, 1864.

(II) Elizabeth Small, born May 27, 1807; died March, 1873.

(III) Alexander Small, born September 19, 1809; died May 16, 1855.

(IV) Edward Small, born December 24, 1811; died January 4, 1888.

(V) Ann Small, born April 3, 1819; died July 2, 1881.

(VI) George Small, Jr., born August 5, 1822; died March 25, 1898.

(I) James Small, eldest son of George and Jeannette (Lourie) Small, was born March 19, 1805, in Jackson, Washington County, New York, and died April 25, 1864, in Adams Township, Carroll County, Indiana.

James Small and Mary Livingston Robertson were married October 19, 1826, in Argyle, Washington County, New York.

Mary Livingston Robertson, daughter of Gilbert and Elizabeth (Dow) Robertson, was born July 24, 1805, in Argyle, New York, and died February 15, 1828, in Argyle, Washington County, New York.

James and Mary Livingston (Robertson) Small had,

(1) Gilbert Small, born February 7, 1828; died July 20, 1904.

(1) Rev. Gilbert Small, only son of James and Mary Livingston (Robertson) Small, was born February 7, 1828, in Ar-

gyle, Washington County New York, and died July 20, 1904, in Idaville, Indiana.

Bereaved of his mother when an infant Gilbert was reared by his maternal grandparents. Evincing unusual aptitude for his studies he was sent to the Argyle Academy, where he prepared for college, and in 1849 was graduated from Union College. Later he entered the Associate Theological Seminary at Canonsburg, Pennsylvania, where he remained until 1853, in which year he was licensed to preach by the presbytery of Cambridge, New York. He was ordained by the presbytery of Miami, Ohio, in 1855, and became pastor of a church at North Liberty, same state. At the close of two years of ministerial labors there he went to Indianapolis, where he was pastor of the United Presbyterian church until the fall of 1867. In 1861 he was the chaplain of the Indiana state Legislature, and, during the civil war, in addition to attending to his duties as a minister, he served as clerk of transportation in the quartermaster's department, in the government employ. In 1867 he moved to Idaville, near which place his father had located years before, and where was then the largest numerically organized congregation of United Presbyterians in the state of Indiana. For more than ten years he served as pastor of this church and then securing dismission from the United Presbyterian communion he transferred his connection to the Presbyterian church, and for many years supplied vacancies in pulpits not too remote from his established home in Idaville, his last pastoral relation having been with the Union church in the presbytery of Logansport, which he resigned in April, 1901, and at his own request was placed on the Honorably Retired list of Logansport Presbytery, having been for forty-seven years regularly engaged in ministerial work—to him ever a labor of love.

In this so intimate a relation this honored son of an honorable line exerted an influence for good throughout the region in which his lines were cast, the effect of which is manifest in many ways, and which will remain a lasting monument to his memory. Truly, as a local newspaper said, in referring to the death of this fine Christian gentleman: "In the death of Rev. Gilbert Small, Idaville, and this whole community, loses an influence which had made itself felt in every good way throughout this region for nearly forty years. Christening, marrying, burying, he for years exercised the beneficent office of pastor here, and after that close relation ceased he had fulfilled the office of friend and counsellor, his influence ever being for the right; so that in his death, with the memory of his deeds still fragrant, the community can justly rise up and call him blessed."

Gilbert Small stood high in the councils of the church and his voice and pen were for years recognized as among the authorities in that communion throughout the middle west. He was a widely recognized contributor to the religious press and his writings were ever in demand. For ten years he was clerk of the Wabash Presbytery of the United Presbyterian church; for eight years clerk of the synod of the same church; for eight years member of the board of managers of the Theological Seminary at Xenia, Ohio; for four years member of the board of directors of Monmouth (Illinois) College, and was three times commissioner to the General Assembly of the church. His scholastic attainments were further attested by his membership in Phi Beta Kappa, the most exclusive of the Greek letter societies.

In educational matters Mr. Small likewise took a foremost position, and was one of the early school examiners (county superintendents) of White county, Indiana, his activity and strong personal influence in that capacity contributing very largely to the elevation of educational standards in that part of the state.

In addition to his large religious contributions, Mr. Small was a wide contributor to the secular press, his articles being much sought for by the various newspapers and journals, which he favored. For eight years he was editor of the Idaville Observer; for two years he served on the editorial staff of the Logansport Saturday Night Review; and for seven years previous to his death was chief staff contributor to the Masonic Advocate, a Masonic monthly of wide circulation, his signed articles attracting much attention among Masons all over the country. In this latter service, which he kept up to the very month of his death, Mr. Small took much delight, and his ripe experience and richly stored mind gave to this long series of articles an unusual value. Concerning his work in this connection, an editorial appreciation of his writings published in the Advocate in 1901, said: "Had he become a disciple of this time-honored Institution in his earlier life, he would have been a rival of Mackey, Morris and other celebrities in Masonic literature, whose works, surviving them, have made their names immortal in the annals of Freemasonry."—Albert Garrett Small.

Rev. Gilbert Small and Helen A. Munroe were married February 24, 1857, at North Liberty, Ohio.

Helen A. Munroe was born July 22, 1837, and died April 23, 1858.

Rev. Gilbert Small and Helen A. (Munroe) Small had:

(A) Mary Livingston Small, born December 21, 1857: died

September 30, 1877, the year following her completion of the course in a finishing school for young women at Indianapolis.

Rev. Gilbert Small and Frances A. Garrett were married November 3, 1858, at Indianapolis, Indiana.

Frances A. Garrett, daughter of David and Rosena (Quinn) Garrett, was born February 4, 1837, and died April 27, 1887. She was born in Bellefontaine, Ohio, where her childhood and youth were spent. After graduating at the Bellefontaine High School, she removed with her parents to Indianapolis in 1854, and at once entered the McLean Female Seminary, graduating with the highest honors of her class, after a three-years' course, in June, 1857. Her marriage with Rev. Gilbert Small followed the next year and during a pastorate of nine years in Indianapolis she proved a most faithful and competent helpmeet to him in all his labors in that difficult field. When the field of labor was changed to Idaville she continued to make her presence felt and to the day of her death manifested her zeal in maintaining and extending the cause of her Master, which was ever dear to her heart and always foremost in her thoughts. Hers was a beautiful Christian life and the evidences of her exalted influence upon the social life of that community are many and lasting, her memory being cherished throughout that whole region.—Albert Garrett Small.

Rev. Gilbert and Frances A. (Garrett) Small had:

(A) Harry Ekin Small, born October 28, 1862.
(B) William Robertson Small, and
(C) Albert Garrett Small — Twins, born March 15, 1867.
(D) Stella Rosena Small, born January 25, 1873.

(A) Dr. Harry Ekin Small, eldest son of Rev. Gilbert and Frances A. (Garrett) Small, was born October 28, 1862, in Indianapolis, Indiana. He was reared at Idaville, and after completing the course prescribed in the village schools taught two years in the district schools of White county, devoting his vacations to the study of medicine in the office of a Monticello physician. Thus equipped by preparatory study, he entered the Ohio Eclectic Medical College at Cincinnati, Ohio, from which institution he was graduated in 1883. Locating at Wolcott, Indiana, he entered upon the practice of his chosen profession, later moving to Monticello, where he practiced for a time. In the meantime he had taken a post-graduate course at Rush Medical College, Chicago, and in 1898 moved to Chicago. After a sometime residence and practice there he moved to Sterling, Illinois, later moving to Alpha, Illinois, where he now resides.

Dr. Harry Ekin Small and Anna Lisk were married September 3, 1884, in Wolcott, Indiana.

Anna Lisk, daughter of William and Sarah (Edmunds) Lisk, was born July 4, 1864.

Dr. Harry Ekin and Anna (Lisk) Small had:

(a) Cecile Livingston Small, born June 28, 1885, in Wolcott, Indiana; resides in Chicago.

(BC) William Robertson Small and Albert Garrett Small, twin sons of Rev. Gilbert and Frances A. (Garrett) Small, were born March 15, 1867, in Indianapolis, Indiana, where they now reside. They are selling agent for Barnhart Bros. & Spindler, printers' supplies, Chicago, and editor in the Indianapolis office of the American Press Association, respectively. Reared at Idaville, they taught in the district schools of White county, Indiana, for two years; in June, 1886, founded the Idaville Observer; transferred their services to the Logansport (Indiana) Daily Journal in 1888 as business manager and city editor, respectively, buying into that paper with the organization of a stock company in 1891. Selling their interest in 1894, they established the Logansport Saturday Night Review. Later, in April, 1896, they organized the Jeffersonville (Indiana) Daily World Company. In the fall of that year, W. R. Small became superintendent of the Indiana Newspaper Union (Indianapolis), continuing in that capacity until 1903, when he assumed his present position. A. G. Small returned to Logansport from Jeffersonville, taking the position of associate editor of the Logansport Daily Reporter, later resuming the city editorship of the Logansport Journal, continuing in that position until February, 1900, when he took his present service with the American Press Association. In 1899 Albert G. Small was a commissioner to the General Assembly of the Presbyterian Church from the presbytery of Logansport.

William Robertson Small and Ella Linsday Child were married June 30, 1897, at Kokomo, Indiana.

Ella Linsday Child, daughter of Moses C. and Clementine (Linsday) Child, was born December 29, 1869, at Kokomo, Indiana.

William Robertson and Ella Linsday (Child) Small had:

(a) Gilbert Linsday Small, born May 4, 1899, at Indianapolis, Ind.

Albert Garrett Small and Mary Olive Allen were married September 5, 1888, in Brookston, Indiana.

Mary Olive Allen, daughter of John C. and Nancy Holmes (Steen) Allen, was born September 22, 1865, in Clinton county, Indiana.

Albert Garrett and Mary Olive (Allen) Small had:

(a) Donald Garrett Small, born July 15, 1889, in Logansport, Indiana.

(b) Vivien Allen Small, born July 28, 1893, in Logansport, Indiana.

(D) Stella Rosena Small, only daughter of Rev. Gilbert and Frances A. (Garrett) Small, was born January 25, 1873, in Idaville, Indiana. Following the death of her mother and after a two-years' course at Western Female Seminary, Oxford, Ohio, she made her home with her grand-uncle, Hon. William D. Robertson, at East Greenwich, New York.

John A. MacArthur and Stella Rosena Small were married April 6, 1898, at Greenwich, New York.

John A. MacArthur, son of James and Mary (Alexander) MacArthur, was born May 3, 1868, at Shushan, Washington county, New York, and lives at 2154 Fifth avenue, Troy, New York.

John A. and Stella Rosena (Small) MacArthur had:

(a) William Raymond MacArthur, born September 16, 1899, in Troy, New York.

(b) Frances Garrett MacArthur, born March 12, 1905, in Troy, New York.

Rev. Gilbert Small and Mrs. Emma A. Sanderson were married May 23, 1888, at Lake Cicott, Cass county, Indiana.

Mrs. Emma A. Sanderson, daughter of Blair and Sarah F. (Houk) Buchanan, was born in 1849.

James Small married, secondly, Sarah Nelson in 1832, in Washington county, New York.

Sarah Nelson, daughter of Simon and Lucy (Stockwell) Nelson, was born in 1804, and died May 10, 1886. Her body was interred beside that of her husband in the Idaville cemetery.

Simon Nelson was the son of Joseph and Isabel (Rogers) Nelson.

James and Sarah (Nelson) Small left New York May 1, 1833, proceeded by lake and canal to Peru, Indiana, where they bought a small boat and put all their furniture into it and sailed down the Wabash river until they came to Lockport, Indiana, reaching that point June 1, 1833. They settled in Adams township, Carroll county, Indiana. James Small bought a farm there of 220 acres, where they spent the rest of their lives. That part of the country was heavily timbered. There were no roads and the inhabitants marked their way by making gashes on the trees. The big gray wolves were plentiful.

James Small was among the foremost and most honored pioneer residents of that region. He brought from his eastern home to the then wilderness a practical knowledge of New England farming and experience in life that his pioneer neighbors soon learned to rely on, and it is undoubted that his influence in that community did very much toward bringing about proper conditions of social and economic life in the formative period of the now prosperous and established farming region.

James and Sarah (Nelson) Small had:

(1) George Small, born June 2, 1834.

(2) Mary Ann Small, born January 25, 1836; died August 21, 1879.

(3) Jeannette Small, born March 12, 1839.

(1) George Small, only son of James and Sarah (Nelson) Small, was born June 2, 1834, on the Small homestead in Adams township, Carroll county, Indiana, and now lives on the farm formerly owned by his father. For more than thirty years he has been a deacon in the United Presbyterian Church at Idaville.

George Small and Mary Eldridge were married November 22, 1855.

Mary Eldridge, daughter of Elijah and Elizabeth (Gibson) Eldridge, was born May 7, 1836.

George and Mary (Eldridge) Small had:

(A) Margaret Small, born July 27, 1857.

(B) Jane A. Small, born December 24, 1858; died March 14, 1884.

(C) James Small, born January 5, 1861.

(D) Mary Belle Small, born September 22, 1862; died March 24, 1876.

(E) Frances A. Small, born September 1, 1864.

(F) Ida E. Small, born December 29, 1866.

(G) Elizabeth Small, born February 27, 1869.

(H) John N. Small, born February 25, 1876.

(I) George Thomas Small, born January 12, 1877.

(J) Hugh Edwin Small, born September 2, 1887; died December 31, 1888.

(A) Margaret Small, eldest daughter of George and Mary (Eldridge) Small, was born July 27, 1857, on the Small homestead.

John Campbell and Margaret Small were married July 27, 1893.

John Campbell, son of Robert C. and Elizabeth (Lane) Campbell, was born July 15, 1845, in Jefferson county, Indiana, and lives at Indianapolis, Indiana.

(C) James Small, eldest son of George and Mary (Eldridge) Small, was born January 5, 1861, on the Small homestead, and lives in Idaville, Indiana, where he and his brother, John N. Small, are dealers in hardware and shippers of grain.

James Small and Nancy Barnes were married September 5, 1884.

Nancy Barnes, daughter of Thomas and Prudence (Eldridge) Barnes, was born October 31, 1858.

(E) Frances A. Small, fourth daughter of George and Mary (Eldridge) Small, was born September 1, 1864, and lives in Idaville, Indiana.

Benjamin Ginn and Frances A. Small were married February 20, 1885.

Benjamin Ginn, son of James and Elizabeth Ginn, was born November 21, 1863, and died January 18, 1905.

Benjamin and Frances A. (Small) Ginn had:

(a) Hugh Ginn, born January 13, 1886; died August 24, 1886.

(b) Alma M. Ginn, born November 6, 1887; died December 31, 1887.

(c) Bertha Dean Ginn, born October 9, 1889.

(d) Gertrude Merl Ginn, born August 9, 1894.

(e) Francis Clair Ginn, born November 21, 1902.

(F) Ida E. Small, fifth daughter of George and Mary (Eldridge) Small, was born December 29, 1866.

Charles E. Johnsonbaugh and Ida E. Small were married October 10, 1888.

Charles E. Johnsonbaugh, son of Ira and Angeline (Tam) Johnsonbaugh, was born December 10, 1866, and lives on the original Small farm in Adams township, Carroll county, Indiana.

Charles E. and Ida E. (Small) Johnsonbaugh had:

(a) Jennie Merl Johnsonbaugh, born July 21, 1889.

(b) Goldie Faye Johnsonbaugh, born January 19, 1894.

(c) James Paul Johnsonbaugh, born August 15, 1904; died September 6, 1904.

(G) Elizabeth Small, sixth daughter of George and Mary (Eldridge) Small, was born February 27, 1869.

L. Francis Graham and Elizabeth Small were married July 10, 1890.

L. Francis Graham, son of David and Mary (Pecht) Graham, was born in Pennsylvania and lives on a farm near Burnettscreek, Indiana.

L. Francis and Elizabeth (Small) Graham had:

(a) Ralph Graham, born December 12, 1891.

(b) George Cloyd Graham, born March 31, 1892.

(c) Virdin Graham, born July 5, 1897.

(d) John Wilber Graham, and

(e) James Weldon Graham—twins, born March 29, 1900; the latter died September 6, 1900.

(f) Leona Belle Graham, born November 7, 1902.

(H) John N. Small, second son of George and Mary (Eldridge) Small, was born February 25, 1876. He lives in Idaville, Indiana, where, with his brother James, he is engaged in the hardware business and the shipping of grain.

John N. Small and Margaret H. Davidson were married November 4, 1896.

Margaret H. Davidson, daughter of William and Allie (Barnes) Davidson, was born August 4, 1875.

John N. and Margaret H. (Davidson) Small had:

(a) William Dwight Small, born June 27, 1902.

(2) Mary Ann Small, eldest daughter of James and Sarah (Nelson) Small, was born January 25, 1836, in Carroll county, Indiana, and died August 21, 1879.

Hugh B. Knickerbocker and Mary Ann Small were married April 2, 1855.

Hugh B. Knickerbocker, son of John and Rachel (Bain) Knickerbocker, was born February 7, 1828. He was killed in the battle of Chancellorsville, May 3, 1863. He was a man renowned in the region of his home as a teacher in the Burnettscreek schools; one of the "old school" sort, of whom his pupils, now men of affairs in that village, speak yet with the utmost respect. He was a native of New York and was graduated from Union College, Schenectady, New York, in 1852. In the fall of that year he moved to Indiana and began his work as a teacher in the high school at Burnettscreek. With the beginning of the Civil War he hastened back to New York and aided in the enlistment of the Forty-third Regiment, New York Volunteers, and was made captain of Company "D" of that regiment, at the head of which he served valorously until a soldier's fate overtook him at Chancellorsville.

Hugh B. and Mary Ann (Small) Knickerbocker had:

(A) Sarah Jeannette Knickerbocker, born January 31, 1856.

(B) John H. Knickerbocker, born June 14, 1858.

(A) Sarah Jeannette Knickerbocker, only daughter of Hugh B. and Mary Ann (Small) Knickerbocker, was born January 31, 1856.

Joseph Newton Townsley and Sarah Jeannette Knickerbocker were married March 11, 1896.

Joseph Newton Townsley, son of William and Phebe (Love) Townsley, was born August 13, 1849. They live in Adams township, Carroll county, Indiana.

(B) John H. Knickerbocker, only son of Hugh B. and Mary Ann (Small) Knickerbocker, was born June 14, 1858. He is a fine scholar; was graduated from Monmouth College; given to civil engineering, and is now purchasing agent for a large firm of timber dealers, with headquarters at Logansport, Indiana. He is said to have a rare knowledge of woodcraft.

(3) Jeannette Small, second daughter of James and Sarah (Nelson) Small, was born March 12, 1839, on her father's homestead. She is unmarried. In her earlier years she was a school teacher and had a fine reputation as a disciplinarian in the Burnettscreek schools, which her old pupils have not forgotten to this day, and among whom she is held in the highest regard.

(II) Elizabeth Small, eldest daughter of George and Jeannette (Lourie) Small, was born May 27, 1807, in Jackson, Washington county, New York, and died in March, 1872, in Jackson, Washington county, New York.

George I. Maxwell and Elizabeth Small were married January 19, 1826, in Jackson, Washington county, New York.

George I. Maxwell, son of John and Jeannette (McFarland) Maxwell, was born May 28, 1799, in Jackson, Washington county, New York, and died March 2, 1848, in the same town and county.

George I. and Elizabeth (Small) Maxwell had:

(1) Jeannette Ann Maxwell, born November 18, 1827.

(2) John Maxwell, born October 8, 1829; died April 20, 1901.

(3) George S. Maxwell, born June 28, 1831.

(4) William Maxwell, born May 25, 1833; died April 2, 1900, at Logansport, Indiana.

(5) James A. Maxwell, born April 13, 1835; died July 17, 1862.

(6) Elizabeth Maxwell, born November 19, 1838; died May 5, 1903, at Idavillė, Indiana.

(7) Robert Maxwell, born October 22, 1840; died June 13, 1874.

(8) Mary Agnes Maxwell, born February 23, 1843.

(9) Edward Maxwell, died July 8, 1871.

(10) Thomas Maxwell, died November, 1901.

(Twins, born October 28, 1845.)

(1) Jeannette Ann Maxwell, eldest daughter of George I. and Elizabeth (Small) Maxwell, was born November 18, 1827, in Jackson, Washington County, New York, and now lives in Tarkio, Missouri.

William Harper and Jeannette Ann Maxwell were married October 20, 1856, in Jackson, Washington County, New York.

William Harper, son of William and Jane (Wallace) Harper, was born December 5, 1824, near Antrim, Ireland, and died September 1, 1902, in Tarkio, Missouri.

William and Jeannette Ann (Maxwell) Harper had:

(A) Elizabeth M. Harper, born August 2, 1857; died October 21, 1875.

(B) Jane Wallace Harper, born August 5, 1859.

(C) Anna Mary Harper, born April 13, 1862.

(D) Sarah Isabella Harper, born July 10, 1868.

(A) Elizabeth M. Harper, eldest daughter of William and Jeannette Ann (Maxwell) Harper, was born August 2, 1857, near Iowa City, Iowa, and died October 21, 1875, at Paxton, Illinois.

(B) Jane Wallace Harper, second daughter of William and Jeannette Ann (Maxwell) Harper, was born August 5, 1858, near Iowa City, Iowa.

George L. Fraser and Jane Wallace Harper were married February 7, 1882, at Marshalltown, Iowa.

George L. Fraser, son of William J. and Mary T. (Blanchard) Fraser, was born at Marshalltown, Iowa. Lives at Coal, Henry county, Missouri.

(C) Anna Mary Harper, third daughter of William and Jeannette Ann (Maxwell) Harper, was born April 13, 1862, at Iowa City, Iowa.

James Black and Anna Mary Harper were married September 15, 1892.

James Black, son of William Alexander and Ann (Maltman) Black, was born September 20, 1857, at Ramelton, County Donegal, Ireland.

James and Anna Mary (Harper) Black had:

(a) Anna Jeannette Black, born September 10, 1893.
(b) Martha Elizabeth Black, born May 22, 1896.
(c) Margaret Isabelle Black, born July 1, 1900.

James Black and family live at Waterloo, Iowa.

(2) John Maxwell, eldest son of George I. and Elizabeth (Small) Maxwell, was born October 8, 1829, and died April 20, 1901.

John Maxwell and Sarah Isabella McGeoch were married December 1, 1857.

Sarah Isabella McGeoch, daughter of Alexander and Jeannette (McClellan) McGeoch, was born April 12, 1836, and died June 29, 1866.

John and Sarah Isabella (McGeoch) Maxwell had:

(A) Jeannette E. Maxwell, born November 24, 1858.
(B) Alexander McGeoch Maxwell, born July 16, 1860.
(C) Robert James Maxwell, born November 15, 1862.
(D) George Maxwell, born November 25, 1865; died March 13, 1866.

(A) Jeannette E. Maxwell, eldest daughter of John and Sarah Isabella (McGeoch) Maxwell, was born November 24, 1858, in Jackson, Washington county, New York, and lives at Waterman, Illinois, R. F. D. No. 1.

William Doig McCleery and Jeannette Maxwell were married February 21, 1882, in Jackson, Washington county, New York.

William Doig McCleery, son of James and Jean (Thomson) McCleery, was born June 10, 1848, at Dalton, Ohio, and died April 29, 1903.

William Doig and Jeannette E. (Maxwell) McCleery had:

(a) Ruth McCleery, born January 14, 1883; died June 19, 1884.

(b) Harry McCleery, born December 2, 1884.

(c) Archie McCleery, born September 24, 1888.

(d) John Maxwell McCleery, born August 14, 1890.

(e) Fannie E. McCleery, born June 13, 1892.

(B) Alexander McGeoch Maxwell, eldest son of John and Sarah Isabella (McGeoch) Maxwell, was born July 16, 1860.

Alexander McGeoch Maxwell and Mary McCleery were married December 17, 1884, and had:

(a) Andrew R. Maxwell, born April, 1893.

(C) Robert James Maxwell, second son of John and Sarah Isabella (McGeoch) Maxwell, was born November 15, 1862.

Robert James Maxwell and Ella B. Todd were married January, 1883.

Ella B. (Todd) Maxwell died about 1885.

Robert James Maxwell and Elizabeth Ashton were married August, 1892, and had:

(a) Sarah Jane Maxwell.

(b) Ashton Maxwell.

(2) John Maxwell and Jane Elizabeth McGeoch were married October 20, 1869.

Jane Elizabeth McGeoch, daughter of William and Eleanor (Christie) McGeoch, was born May 15, 1838, and died October 15, 1900.

John and Jane Elizabeth (McGeoch) Maxwell had:

(A) Eleanor Maxwell, born February 14, 1871.

(B) William John Maxwell, born August 27, 1872.

(C) Gilbert Maxwell, born November 1, 1876.

(A) Eleanor Maxwell, eldest daughter of John and Jane Elizabeth (McGeoch) Maxwell, was born February 14, 1871.

Hiram H. Parrish and Eleanor Maxwell were married October 8, 1890.

Hiram H. Parrish, son of Henry H. and Mary (Parrish) Parrish, was born July 3, 1858, and lives at Cambridge, New York, 111 West Main street.

Hiram H. and Eleanor (Maxwell) Parrish had:

(a) Malcomb Maxwell Parrish, born February 26, 1892.

(b) Mary Eleanor Parrish, born November 18, 1895.

(c) Donald McDougall Parrish, born April 15, 1906.

(B) William John Maxwell, eldest son of John and Jane Elizabeth (McGeoch) Maxwell, was born August 27, 1872. He is unmarried and lives at Niagara Falls, New York.

(C) Gilbert Maxwell, second son of John and Jane Elizabeth (McGeoch) Maxwell, was born November 1, 1876, and lives at Cambridge, New York.

Gilbert Maxwell and Helen M. Eldridge were married February 16, 1898.

Helen M. Eldridge, adopted daughter of Harvey R. and Sarah M. Eldridge, was born November 5, 1876, and died August 20, 1898.

Gilbert Maxwell and Bessie Q. Robertson were married May 15, 1901.

Bessie Q. Robertson, daughter of Alvan and Margaret A. (Qua) Robertson, was born June 28, 1879.

(3) George S. Maxwell, second son of George I. and Elizabeth (Small) Maxwell, was born June 28, 1831, in Jackson, Washington county, New York, and lives at East Greenwich, New York.

George S. Maxwell and Margaret Telford were married December 27, 185—.

Margaret (Telford) Maxwell died May 26, 1901.

George S. and Margaret (Telford) Maxwell had:

(A) George I. Maxwell, born March 12, 1856.
(B) Mary Maxwell, born October 5, 1858.
(C) William John Maxwell, born August 5, 1860.
(D) Elizabeth Maxwell, born November 6, 1861.
(E) Anna Belle Maxwell, born January 26, 1869.
(F) Robert Maxwell, born August 14, 1871.
(G) David Maxwell, born September 29, 1873.
(H) Charles M. Maxwell, born December 15, 1875.

(A) George I. Maxwell, eldest son of George S. and Margaret (Telford) Maxwell, was born March 12, 1856.

George I. Maxwell and Annie M. Arnott were married March 10, 1885, and had:

(a) Marion Maxwell, born December 26, 1885.
(b) Elizabeth Maxwell, born May 29, 1887.
(c) Margaret Maxwell, born July 12, 1890.
(d) Alice F. Maxwell, born November 24, 1895.
(e) Ruth Maxwell, born June 17, 1898.

(B) Mary Maxwell, eldest daughter of George S. and Margaret (Telford) Maxwell, was born October 5, 1858.

John Alexander and Mary Maxwell were married December 31, 1879.

John Alexander, son of Maxwell and Ann (Small) Alexander, was born August 21, 1853.

The descendants of the above may be found under Alexanders.

(C) William John Maxwell, second son of George S. and Margaret (Telford) Maxwell, was born August 5, 1860.

William John Maxwell and Ella M. Wilson were married December 31, 1891.

(E) Anna Belle Maxwell, third daughter of George S. and Margaret (Telford) Maxwell, was born January 26, 1869.

Henry P. Murdock and Anna Belle Maxwell were married January 24, 1897, and had:

(a) Margaret L. Murdock, born January 11, 1898.
(b) George J. Murdock, born July 21, 1899.
(c) Robert M. Murdock, born February 6, 1901.

(F) Robert Maxwell, third son of George S. and Margaret (Telford) Maxwell, was born August 14, 1871.

Rev. Robert Maxwell and Maude Pollock were married August 1, 1900. Rev. Robert Maxwell is a missionary to India; address: American Mission, Rawal Pindi, Punjab.

(H) Charles M. Maxwell, fifth son of George S. and Margaret (Telford) Maxwell, was born December 15, 1875.

Charles M. Maxwell and Alice Arnott were married February 3, 1904.

(4) William Maxwell, third son of George I. and Elizabeth (Small) Maxwell, was born May 25, 1833, and died April 2, 1900.

William Maxwell and Martha E. Wilson were married February, 1856, and had:

(A) Wilson H. Maxwell, born May 31, 1859.
(B) Mary B. Maxwell, born February 10, 1864.

(A) Wilson H. Maxwell, only son of William and Martha E. (Wilson) Maxwell, was born May 31, 1859, at West Hebron, New York, and lives in Logansport, Indiana.

Wilson H. Maxwell and Janet M. McNitt were married January 22, 1896, at Reedsville, Pennsylvania.

Janet M. McNitt, daughter of John and Martha (Cummins) McNitt, was born December 6, 1867, in Kishacoquillas Valley, Mifflin county, Pennsylvania.

(B) Mary B. Maxwell, only daughter of William and Martha Elizabeth (Wilson) Maxwell, was born February 10, 1864, at Salem, New York, and lives at Somonauk, Illinois.

Alexander W. Beveridge and Mary B. Maxwell were married December 27, 1899, at Logansport, Indiana.

Alexander W. Beveridge, son of John and Mary (McCleery) Beveridge, was born February 2, 1866, at Victor, DeKalb county, Illinois.

Alexander W. and Mary B. (Maxwell) Beveridge had:

(a) George Maxwell Beveridge, born February 8, 1901, at Kenton, Ohio.

(b) Wilson McNitt Beveridge, born April 18, 1905, at Somonauk, Illinois.

(7) Robert Maxwell, fifth son of George I. and Elizabeth (Small) Maxwell, was born October 22, 1840, and died June 13, 1874.

Robert Maxwell and Barbara Alexander Robertson were married January 8, 1867, at East Greenwich, New York.

Barbara Alexander Robertson, daughter of John and Mary (Alexander) Robertson, was born June 17, 1846.

Robert and Barbara A. Maxwell had:

(a) Margaret Robertson Maxwell, born October 25, 1867.

(b) Charles Maxwell, born August 1, 1870; died June 8, 1871.

(c) Mary Elizabeth Maxwell, born February 18, 1873.

(8) Mary Agnes Maxwell, third daughter of George I. and Elizabeth (Small) Maxwell, was born February 23, 1843, in Jackson, Washington county, New York, and lives at 739 Ann avenue, Kansas City, Kansas.

Alexander Randles and Mary Agnes Maxwell were married February 19, 1867, in Jackson, Washington county, New York.

Alexander Randles, son of Andrew and Margaret Ann (McGeoch) Randles, was born February 13, 1846, at Hebron, Washington county, New York, and lives at 739 Ann avenue, Kansas City, Kansas.

Alexander and Mary Agnes (Maxwell) Randles had:

(A) Herbert Randles, born September 10, 1869.

(B) Anna Elizabeth Randles, born June 20, 1871, at Somonauk, Illinois.

Dr. Herbert Randles, only son of Alexander and Mary Agnes (Maxwell) Randles, was born September 10, 1869, at Somonauk, DeKalb county, Illinois. He was graduated from the Wyandotte Academy, Kansas City, Kansas, in 1887; was graduated from Kansas City College of Pharmacy, Kansas City, Missouri, in 1897; was graduated from the College of Physicians and Surgeons, Medical Department of Kansas City University, Kansas City, Kansas, in 1900. He is practicing medicine in White City, Kansas.

Dr. Herbert Randles and Luella K. Price were married June 27, 1901, in Kansas City, Kansas.

Luella K. Price, daughter of William R. and Elizabeth (Wise) Price, was born September 18, 1874, at Oskaloosa, Kansas.

Dr. Herbert and Luella K. (Price) Randles had:

(a) Marian Elizabeth Randles, born June 2, 1902, in White City, Kansas.

(10) Thomas Maxwell, seventh son of George I. and Elizabeth (Small) Maxwell, was born October 28, 1845, and died November, 1901.

Thomas Maxwell and Mary Anna Bishop were married, and she lives in Shushan, New York.

(III) Alexander Small, second son of George and Jeannette (Lourie) Small, was born September 19, 1809, in Jackson, Washington county, New York, and died May 16, 1855, in the same place. He got the farm formerly owned by his father, at East Greenwich, Washington county, New York. His son, James Small, owns and occupies the same old Small homestead.

Alexander Small and Elizabeth Maxwell were married January 23, 1834, in Jackson, Washington county, New York.

Elizabeth Maxwell, daughter of George Maxwell, was born November 1, 1814, in Jackson, Washington county, New York, and died April 31, 1867.

Alexander and Elizabeth (Maxwell) Small had:

(1) George Edward Small, born February 17, 1836; died November 2, 1845.

(2) Margaret Jane Small, born February 14, 1838; died October 26, 1865.

(3) Jeannette Small, born March 15, 1840; died July 19, 1864.

(4) Thomas Beveridge Small, born March 19, 1842; died October 24, 1881.

(5) James Small, born January 13, 1845.

(6) George Alexander Small, born April 2, 1848.

(7) Joseph McKirahan Small, born April 30, 1851; died April 10, 1874.

(8) Edward Small, born August 31, 1853; died August 22, 1896.

(2) Margaret Jane Small, eldest daughter of Alexander and Elizabeth (Maxwell) Small, was born February 14, 1838, in Jackson, Washington county, New York, and died October 26, 1865, in Selma, Indiana.

William Orr and Margaret Jane Small were married.

Colonel William Orr was a colonel in the late civil war, and died in January, 1867.

Colonel William and Margaret Jane (Small) Orr had:

(A) Julia Elizabeth Orr, born December 15, 1863, at East Greenwich, New York, on the Small homestead.

Charles Perry Campbell and Julia Elizabeth Orr were married April 25, 1889, at Selma, Indiana.

Charles Perry Campbell, son of David C. and Mary A. (Shonts) Campbell, was born October 6, 1867, at Centerville, Iowa, and lives in Chicago.

Charles Perry and Julia Elizabeth (Orr) Campbell had:

(a) Lillie Margaret Campbell, born February 7, 1890, in Centerville, Iowa.

(b) John David Campbell, born August 19, 1891, at Centerville, Iowa.

(c) Marshall Campbell, born December 10, 1895, in Chicago.

(d) Mary Alice Campbell, born November 3, 1897, in Chicago.

(e) Josephine Orr Campbell, born June 14, 1899, in Chicago.

(f) Charles Theodore Campbell, born January 28, 1902, in Chicago.

(g) Ruth Winifred Campbell, born September 4, 1904, in Chicago.

(3) Jeannette Small, second daughter of Alexander and Elizabeth (Maxwell) Small, was born March 15, 1840, at East Greenwich, New York, and died July 19, 1864, in Jackson, Washington county, New York.

John McCandees and Jeannette Small were married in January, 1863.

John McCandees still lives in East Greenwich, New York.

(4) Thomas Beveridge Small, second son of Alexander and Elizabeth (Maxwell) Small, was born March 19, 1842, in Jackson, Washington county, New York, and died October 24, 1881. in Selma, Indiana. He served through the civil war in Company "B," Sixty-first New York Volunteers. At the close of the war he settled in Delaware county, Indiana, near Muncie.

Thomas Beveridge Small and Matilda A. Swanders were married March 11, 1869.

Matilda A. Swanders, daughter of George and Effie Swanders, was born July 20, 1851. Mrs. Thomas B. Small lives R. R. No. 8, Muncie, Indiana.

Thomas Beveridge and Matilda A. (Swanders) Small had:

(A) Jennie E. Small, born January 21, 1870; died November 23, 1903.

(B) Emma F. Small, born August 15, 1871.

(C) Phennie Small, born February 12, 1873; died September 11, 1875.

(D) Margaret Small, born December 20, 1875; died March 14, 1876.

(E) Walter M. Small, born May 11, 1877.

(F) Arthur M. Small, born April 8, 1879.

(G) Roy B. Small, born September 28, 1881.

(E) Walter M. Small, eldest son of Thomas Beveridge and Matilda A. (Swanders) Small, was born May 11, 1877. He lives at Selma, Indiana.

Walter M. Small and Ethel Orr were married April 26, 1905, at Selma, Indiana.

(F) Arthur M. Small, second son of Thomas Beveridge and Matilda A. (Swanders) Small, was born April 8, 1879. He lives in Indianapolis, Indiana.

Arthur M. Small and Lena F. Lee were married May 3, 1905, at Greenville, Ohio.

Lena F. Lee, daughter of Frank and Winona (Eidson) Lee, was born October 26, 1882, in Hamilton county, Indiana.

Arthur M. Small and Lena F. (Lee) Small had:

(a) Alice Virginia Small, born February 26, 1907.

(G) Roy B. Small, third son of Thomas Beveridge and Matilda A. (Swanders) Small, was born September 28, 1881.

Roy B. Small and Jocie Amburn were married November 21, 1903, and had:

(a) Alice Fern Small, born in 1904.

(5) James Small, third son of Alexander and Elizabeth (Maxwell) Small, was born January 13, 1845, at East Greenwich, New York, and lives on the Small homestead at that place.

James Small and Sarah Martha Edie were married May 26, 1868, and had:

(A) Joseph A. Small, born August 16, 1871; died August 19, 1871.

(B) Harriet E. Small, born August 16, 1872.

(C) Alfred Maxwell Small, born May 20, 1879.

(IV) Rev. Edward Small, third son of George and Jeannette (Lourie) Small, was born December 24, 1811, in Jackson, Washington county, New York, and died January 4, 1888, in Mercer, Pennsylvania. He attended the common schools and academies in Salem and Cambridge in his native county. He was graduated at Union College, Schenectady, New York, in 1833. During the four years following he attended the Associate Theological Seminary in Canonsburg, Pennsylvania. In 1837 he was licensed to preach and in June of that year started on a missionary tour through the west on horseback. He held meetings at Mohegan, Mansfield, Bucyrus, Reynoldsburg, Columbus, and Massier's Creek, all in Ohio; Bloomington, Princeton and Burnettscreek, all in Indiana, and on his return trip, at Massier's Creek, Zanesville and Cambridge, in Ohio, and then to Pittsburg, Pennsylvania. He went to Carlisle, Pennsylvania, and subsequently preached at Newark, New Jersey, and various other places in Upper and Lower Canada, and in Philadelphia. In October, 1838, he went to Mercer, Pennsylvania, and in January, 1839, accepted calls to the pastorates of Springfield and Rocky Springs congregations; these he resigned April 3, 1861.

He was a member of the Christian Commission in the war of the rebellion. Since that time he had no fixed charge. He lived in Mercer until the time of his death.

Rev. Edward Small and Mary Ann Hanna were married February 20, 1840, in Cadiz, Harrison county, Ohio.

Mary Ann Hanna, daughter of James Leonard and Mary (Craig) Hanna, was born June 3, 1820, in Cadiz, Ohio, and died March 3, 1889, in Mercer, Pennsylvania.

LINEAGE OF MARY ANN (HANNA) SMALL.

Michael Finley, born in Scotland or Ireland about 1680 or 1690; emigrated from County Armagh, Ireland, to Philadelphia, Pennsylvania, in 1734.

John Finley, son of Michael Finley, married Martha Berkley of Lurgan township, Cumberland county, Pennsylvania. John Finley was killed by the Indians in 1757.

Mary Finley of South Huntington township, Westmoreland county, Pennsylvania, daughter of John and Martha (Berkley) Finley, was married to James Leonard of Enniskillen, County Fermenagh, Ireland; he died in 1791.

Ann Leonard, daughter of James and Mary (Finley) Leonard, was born in 1775, and died in 1818. She was married to John Hanna of Fairfield township, Westmoreland county, Pennsylvania, who was born in 1773, and died in 1847.

James Leonard Hanna, son of John and Ann (Leonard) Hanna, was born in 1797, and died in 1820. He married Mary Craig, born in 1800, and died in 1873.

ANCESTRY OF MARY CRAIG.

John Craig was born in Scotland; emigrated to Ireland and then to Brownsville, Pennsylvania, and married Rebecca Hogg.

Rowland Craig, son of John and Rebecca (Hogg) Craig, was born in 1776 and died in 1824. He married Susanna Rabe, who was born in 1778, and died in 1826.

Mary Craig, daughter of Rowland and Susanna (Rabe) Craig, was born in 1800, and died in 1873. She was married to James Leonard Hanna.

Mary Ann Hanna, daughter of James Leonard and Mary (Craig) Hanna, was born June 3, 1820, in Cadiz, Ohio, and died March 3, 1889, in Mercer, Pennsylvania. She was married to Rev. Edward Small.

Rev. Samuel Finley, D. D., second son of Michael Finley, was president of Princeton College, 1761-66. President Finley's great-grandson was Samuel Finley Breese Morse, the inventor of the telegraph.

John Finley, the present president of the College of the City of New York, belongs to this same family, as also does Martha Finley, the author of the "Elsie" books.

Rev. Edward and Mary Ann (Hanna) Small had:

(1) Mary Hanna Small, born June 26, 1842.

(2) Jeannette Small, born March 23, 1847; died June 16, 1857.

(3) Robert Wilson Small, born July 14, 1850; died May 27, 1857.

(4) Elizabeth Ann Small, born October 27, 1852; died February 19, 1870.

(5) Nellie Small, and

(6) Emma Warren Small—twins, born October 16, 1857; the latter died June 29, 1901.

(7) Edward Hanna Small, born February 22, 1860.

These were all born in Mercer, Pennsylvania.

(1) Mary Hanna Small, eldest daughter of Rev. Edward and Mary Ann (Hanna) Small, was born June 26, 1842, in Mercer, Pennsylvania.

James Alexander Powers Porter and Mary Hanna Small were married January 17, 1861, in Mercer, Pennsylvania.

James Alexander Powers Porter, son of William and Sarah (Custard) Porter, was born July 8, 1835, in Crawford County, Pennsylvania, and died September 21, 1873, in Mercer, Pennsylvania. He was a merchant, having stores in Meadville, Pennsylvania, and Elizabeth, New Jersey. His mother is still living at the age of ninety-six years in Crawford County, Pennsylvania.

James Alexander Powers and Mary Hanna (Small) Porter had:

(A) William Edward Porter, born May 27, 1862; died April 13, 1897.

(B) Jessie Porter, born February 29, 1864.

(A) William Edward Porter, only son of James Alexander Powers and Mary Hanna (Small) Porter, was born May 27, 1862, in Mercer, Pennsylvania, and died April 13, 1897, in Brooklyn, New York. He attended the Hackettstown Seminary in Hackettstown, New Jersey, as did also his sister, Jessie. He was connected with the National Papeterie Company of Springfield, Massachusetts. He had a block of stock in the company, which he represented in traveling to the principal Eastern cities.

(B) Jessie Porter, only daughter of James Alexander Powers and Mary Hanna (Small) Porter, was born February 29, 1864, in New York City.

Joseph Lancaster St. John and Jessie Porter were married December 14, 1881, in Brooklyn, New York.

Joseph Lancaster St. John, son of Chauncey and Sarah Butler St. John, was born in 1852, in New York City. He has offices on Broadway, New York, where he represents a number of paper manufacturing companies. He is a Son of the American Revolution.

Joseph Lancaster and Jessie (Porter) St. John had:
(a) Claire Porter St. John, born December 24, 1882.
(b) Jessie Porter St. John, born December 3, 1888.
(c) Marion Small St. John, born April 20, 1893.
(d) Joseph Lancaster St. John, born October 16, 1895.
(e) Ruth St. John, born August 12, 1898.
All these were born in Brooklyn, New York.

(a) Claire Porter St. John, eldest son of Joseph Lancaster and Jessie (Porter) St. John, was born December 24, 1882, in Brooklyn, New York. He attended Lafayette College, Easton, Pennsylvania, and the State College of Kentucky, at Lexington, at which institution he received the degree of M. E. in 1904.

Claire Porter St. John was drowned August 26, 1905, while canoeing down the Ohio. Late at night his party of three went over a dam, which they mistook for the lock on account of the darkness, and the canoe was upset. Claire could easily have escaped, as he was a strong swimmer, if he had not been swept under two empty coal barges, which were unfortunately being towed up the river just at that time. He was a great athlete in college, having played on the football, baseball and basketball teams as well as having won the mile championship in the college games. He was a most popular fellow and had just begun a very promising career.

(1) Mrs. Mary Hanna (Small) Porter was married, secondly, to William Henry Adams, September 22, 1874, in Brooklyn, New York.

William Henry Adams was born in Ireland. His father was an officer in the British Navy. He is in business in New York City.

William Henry and Mary Hanna (Small) Adams had:

(A) John Henry Adams, born November 10, 1875, in Brooklyn, New York. He is a bank clerk in New York City. In 1906 he accompanied his mother on a trip around the world.

(4) Elizabeth Ann Small third daughter of Rev. Edward and Mary Ann (Hanna) Small, was born October 27, 1852, in Mercer, Pennsylvania, and died February 19, 1870, at Mrs. Carey's school in Philadelphia.

(5) Nellie Small, fourth daughter of Rev. Edward and Mary Ann (Hanna) Small, was born October 16, 1857, in Mercer, Pennsylvania, and still lives there.

John Robinson and Nellie Small were married December 8, 1880, in Pittsburg, Pennsylvania.

John Robinson, son of the Hon. James Harvey and Eliza Mills Robinson, was born June 21, 1853, in Mercer, Pennsylvania, and died November 17, 1888, in Mercer, Pennsylvania. He attended Washington and Jefferson College, Washington, Pennsylvania. He was a lawyer and banker in Mercer, Pennsylvania, and Denver, Colorado.

John and Nellie (Small) Robinson had:

(A) Mary Eliza Robinson, born March 15, 1882, in Denver, Colorado.

(B) Edward Small Robinson, born November 11, 1884, in Mercer, Pennsylvania.

(C) John Harvey Robinson, born December 15, 1887, in Mercer, Pa.

(A) Mary Eliza Robinson, only daughter of John and Nellie (Small) Robinson, was born March 15, 1882, in Denver, Colorado. She was graduated at Wilson College, Chambersburg, Pennsylvania, in 1903.

Lieutenant Wilber E. Blain and Mary Eliza Robinson were married November 15, 1905, in Mercer, Pennsylvania.

Lieutenant Wilber E. Blain, son of Alexander and Sarah Emmeline (Allison) Blain, was born March 29, 1880, in Butler County, Pennsylvania. He was graduated at West Point, June 19, 1904. He is now second lieutenant in the Twenty-third Infantry, U. S. A., stationed at Fort Ontario, Oswego, New York.

Lieutenant Wilber E. and Mary Eliza (Robinson) Blain had:

(a) Edward Small Blain, born October 4, 1906, in Mercer, Pennsylvania.

(B) Edward Small Robinson, eldest son of John and Nellie (Small) Robinson, was born November 11, 1884, in Mercer, Pennsylvania. He was graduated at the United States Naval

Academy, Annapolis, Maryland, January 30, 1905. He is now ensign on the U. S. ship Kentucky.

(C) John Harvey Robinson is studying civil engineering at State College, Pennsylvania.

(6) Emma Warren Small, fifth daughter of Rev. Edward and Mary Ann (Hanna) Small, was born October 16, 1857, in Mercer, Pennsylvania, and died June 29, 1901, in Mercer, Pennsylvania.

John Findley Davitt and Emma Warren Small were married October 15, 1878, in Mercer, Pennsylvania.

John Findley Davitt, son of John C. and Mary (Carothers) Davitt, was born February 2, 1845, in Pittsburg, Pennsylvania, and died January 26, 1901, in McKeesport, Pennsylvania. He was in the iron business in McKeesport, Pennsylvania.

(7) Dr. Edward Hanna Small, second son and youngest child of Rev. Edward and Mary Ann (Hanna) Small, was born February 22, 1860, in Mercer, Pennsylvania. He received the degree of A. B. in 1881, and the degree of A. M. in 1884, from Princeton College, where Rev. Samuel Finley, the brother of his great-great-great-grandfather, John Finley, was president in 1761-6. He received the degree of M. D. from the University of Pennsylvania in 1885. He spent one year as resident physician in a Pittsburg hospital and then was abroad for one year in the hospitals of London, Berlin and Vienna.

For over two years he had offices in Allegheny, but since April, 1890, he has been at the corner of Penn and North Negley avenues, Pittsburg, East End, where he has his residence and offices.

In 1895 he was chairman of the Section of Diseases of Children of the American Medical Association. He is visiting physician to the Pittsburg Hospital for Children and to the South Side Hospital, Pittsburg.

Dr. Edward Hanna Small and Elizabeth McGrew Tindle were married April 21, 1897, in Pittsburg, Pennsylvania.

Elizabeth McGrew Tindle, daughter of Dr. Robert McGrew and Alice Wood Tindle, was born March 4, 1867, in Pittsburg, Pennsylvania.

Mary Hanna, Elizabeth Ann, Nellie and Emma Warren Small all attended the Female Seminary in Washington, Pennsylvania. While the two latter were there, Mrs. Sarah Hanna, of the same family as their mother, was principal and Miss Jeannette Lourie, their father's cousin, was one of the teachers.

(V) Ann Small, second daughter of George and Jeannette (Lourie) Small, was born April 3, 1819, in Jackson, Washington County, New York, and died July 2, 1881.

Maxwell Alexander and Ann Small were married July 4, 1827.

Maxwell Alexander, son of Robert and Mary Alexander, was born June 10, 1810, and died November 11, 1877.

Maxwell and Ann (Small) Alexander had:

(1) Jeannette Alexander, born March 20, 1838; died August 30, 1868.

(2) Robert Alexander, born November 7, 1839.

(3) Mary Alexander, born April 3, 1843.

(4) George Alexander, born July 28, 1845.

(5) Orlando Alexander, born August 26, 1847.

(6) Edward S. Alexander, born September 7, 1849.

(7) Nelson Alexander, born January 11, 1852; died July 8, 1852.

(8) John Alexander, born August 21, 1855.

(9) William James Alexander, born February 6, 1856.

(10) Elizabeth Alexander, born April 24, 1858; died November 17, 1902.

(11) Katherine Alexander, born January 9, 1862; died May 7, 1894.

(1) Jeannette Alexander, eldest daughter of Maxwell and Ann (Small) Alexander, was born March 30, 1838, and died August 30, 1868.

James Alexander Coulter and Jeannette Alexander were married February 22, 1860.

James Alexander Coulter, son of James and Nancy Coulter, was born October 20, 1838, and lives at Cambridge, New York, R. F. D. No. 1.

James Alexander and Jeannette (Alexander) Coulter had:

(A) Anna Coulter, born June 15, 1861.

(B) Henry Coulter, born January 10, 1863.

(C) Fannie Coulter, born August 26, 1864; died August 11, 1867.

(A) Anna Coulter, eldest daughter of James Alexander and Jeannette (Alexander) Coulter, was born June 15, 1861, at Cambridge, New York.

Harvey L. Qua and Anna Coulter were married November 9, 1885.

Harvey L. Qua, son of Joseph and Harriett (Flack) Qua, was born October 16, 1864.

Harvey L. and Anna (Coulter) Qua had:

(a) Henry J. Qua, born January 14, 1888.
(b) Lina Qua, born October 27, 1890.
(c) Fannie Qua, born October 15, 1897.

(B) Henry Coulter, only son of James Alexander and Jeannette (Alexander) Coulter, was born January 10, 1863, at Cambridge, New York.

Henry Coulter and Nancy W. Robertson were married March 2, 1890.

Nancy W. Robertson, daughter of James Woods and Katherine (Rice) Robertson, was born December 1, 1867.

Henry and Nancy W. (Robertson) Coulter had:

(a) Margaret B. Coulter, born December 24, 1890.
(b) Katherine C. Coulter, born October 17, 1892.
(c) Sara M. Coulter, born November 26, 1894.
(d) Blanche Coulter, born April 2, 1896.
(e) Florence Coulter, born February 13, 1899.
(f) James Alexander Coulter, born January 5, 1902.
(g) Harold R. Coulter, born December 16, 1904.

James Alexander Coulter and Cornelia Selfridge were married January 20, 1870.

Cornelia Selfridge, daughter of Oliver and Mary Jane (Maxwell) Selfridge, was born April 7, 1850.

James Alexander and Cornelia (Selfridge) Coulter had:

(A) William S. Coulter, born June 20, 1874.
(B) Louis J. Coulter, born January 19, 1879. Both married.

(2) Robert Alexander, eldest son of Maxwell and Ann (Small) Alexander, was born November 7, 1839, at Cambridge, New York, and lives at Holly Springs, Arkansas.

Robert Alexander and Christiana Sheldon were married December 26, 1866.

Christiana Sheldon, daughter of William and Agnes (McLaury) Sheldon, was born September 23, 1843.

Robert and Christiana (Sheldon) Alexander had:

(A) John Alexander, born June 3, 1863.
(B) William S. Alexander, born September 29, 1872.

(C) Anna A. Alexander, born October 7, 1877.
(D) Maxwell Alexander, born July 28, 1884.

(A) John Alexander, eldest son of Robert and Christiana (Sheldon) Alexander, was born June 3, 1863.

John Alexander and Cora M. Snider were married February 29, 1888.

Cora M. Snider, daughter of Charles and Matilda (Ostein) Snider, was born September 29, 1872.

John and Cora M. (Snider) Alexander had:

(a) Robert Earl Alexander, born in 1895.
(b) Arthur Cleo Alexander, born in 1901.

(B) William S. Alexander, second son of Robert and Christiana (Sheldon) Alexander, was born September 29, 1872.

William S. Alexander and Ella M. Sparks were married September 28, 1897.

Ella M. Sparks, daughter of John and Millie (Jones) Sparks, was born June 12, 1876.

(C) Anna A. Alexander, only daughter of Robert and Christiana (Sheldon) Alexander, was born October 7, 1877.

J. Parker Mizell and Anna A. Alexander were married November 13, 1895.

J. Parker Mizell, son of Robert and Mahala (Rhoe) Mizell, was born September 20, 1869.

J. Parker and Anna A. (Alexander) Mizell had:

(a) Bertha May Mizell, born in 1897.
(b) William Herbert Mizell, born in 1900.

(D) Maxwell Alexander, third son of Robert and Christiana (Sheldon) Alexander, was born July 28, 1884.

Maxwell Alexander and Della Moffitt were married October 2, 1904.

Della Moffitt, daughter of James and Lula (Livingston) Moffitt, was born October 2, 1886.

(3) Mary Alexander, second daughter of Maxwell and Ann (Small) Alexander, was born April 3, 1843, at Cambridge, New York, and lives in Troy, New York.

James MacArthur and Mary Alexander were married December 5, 1865.

James MacArthur, son of John and Jane (McMorris) MacArthur, was born August 3, 1842.

James and Mary (Alexander) MacArthur had:

(A) William MacArthur, born December 17, 1866; died August 25, 1882.

(B) John A. MacArthur, born May 3, 1868.

(C) Anna Belle MacArthur, born December 31, 1872.

(B) John A. MacArthur, second son of James and Mary (Alexander) MacArthur, was born May 3, 1868, at Shushan, New York, and lives at 2154 Fifth avenue, Troy, New York. He is the head of the firm of MacArthur & McBride, dealers in men's furnishings, Troy and Albany.

John MacArthur and Stella Rosena Small were married April 6, 1898, at Greenwich, New York.

Stella Rosena Small, only daughter of Rev. Gilbert and Frances A. (Garrett) Small, was born January 25, 1873, in Idaville, Indiana.

John A. and Stella Rosena (Small) MacArthur had:

(a) William Raymond MacArthur, born September 16, 1890, in Troy, New York.

(b) Frances Garrett MacArthur, born March 12, 1905, in Troy, New York.

(4) George Alexander, second son of Maxwell and Ann (Small) Alexander, was born July 28, 1845, and lives at Lansingburg, New York.

George Alexander and Emma J. Lee were married June 3, 1868, and had:

(A) Eva Alexander.

(B) Anna Alexander.

(C) Maxwell Alexander.

(5) Orlando Alexander, third son of Maxwell and Ann (Small) Alexander was born August 26, 1847, in Washington County, New York, and lives at Canton, South Dakota.

Orlando Alexander and Mary Waters were married December 22, 1869.

Mary Waters, daughter of Barber and Mary Ann (Congdon) Waters, was born March 25, 1849.

Orlando and Mary (Waters) Alexander had:

(A) Charles Alexander, born September 30, 1870.

(B) Anna Mary Alexander, born October 14, 1871.

(C) Ida Alexander, born July 26, 1873.

(D) Frank B. Alexander, born January 3, 1881.

(A) Charles Alexander, eldest son of Orlando and Mary (Waters) Alexander, was born September 30, 1870.

Charles Alexander and Annie Devlin, daughter of Moore and Mary Ann (Duncan) Devlin, were married December 25, 1893.

(B) Anna Mary Alexander, eldest daughter of Orlando and Mary (Waters) Alexander, was born October 14, 1871.

John Munger, son of Dwight and Ann (McKee) Munger, and Anna Mary Alexander were married March 26, 1891.

John and Anna Mary (Alexander) Munger had:

(a) Dwight C. Munger, born November 19, 1894.

(b) Maxie A. Munger, born January 26, 1900.

(c) Ida Munger, born June 10, 1902.

(C) Ida Alexander, second daughter of Orlando and Mary (Waters) Alexander, was born July 26, 1873.

Eugene Goldy, son of Benjamin and Harriet (Stillwell) Goldy, and Ida Alexander were married December 19, 1893.

Eugene and Ida (Alexander) Goldy had:

(a) Frank E. Goldy, born November 6, 1894.

(b) Mary Goldy, born December 2, 1898.

(c) Ward B. Goldy, born October 16, 1901.

(d) Leigh Goldy, born April 6, 1904.

(6) Edward S. Alexander, fourth son of Maxwell and Ann (Small) Alexander, was born September 7, 1849, in Washington County, New York, and lives at Canton, South Dakota. (Lincoln county.)

Edward S. Alexander and Catherine Bailey were married September 30, 1877.

(8) John Alexander, sixth son of Maxwell and Ann (Small) Alexander, was born August 21, 1853, in Washington County, New York, and lives at Cambridge, New York.

John Alexander and Mary Maxwell were married December 31, 1879.

Mary Maxwell, daughter of George S. and Margaret (Telford) Maxwell, was born October 5, 1858.

John and Mary (Maxwell) Alexander had:

(A) Florence Alexander, born August 29, 1883.

(B) Frank B. Alexander, born September 6, 1888; died February 25, 1890.

(C) Emma Belle Alexander, born March 7, 1893.

(D) Mabel Elizabeth Alexander, born July 25, 1895.
(E) Ethel May Alexander, born March 18, 1898.

(9) William James Alexander, seventh son of Maxwell and Ann (Small) Alexander, was born February 6, 1856, in Washington County, New York, and lives at 341 River street, Troy, New York.

William James Alexander and Frances Milks were married September 5, 1878.

Frances Milks, daughter of Matthew and Margaret Milks, was born January 9, 1859.

William James and Frances (Milks) Alexander had:
(A) Fred W. Alexander, born March 20, 1881.
(B) Montgomery Alexander, born September 26, 1888.

(10) Elizabeth Alexander, third daughter of Maxwell and Ann (Small) Alexander, was born April 24, 1858, in Washington County, New York, and died November 17, 1902.

T. E. Baillie and Elizabeth Alexander were married October 1, 1879, and had:
(A) Susie Baillie.
(B) Edward Baillie.

(11) Katherine Alexander, fourth daughter of Maxwell and Ann (Small) Alexander, was born January 9, 1862, in Washington County, New York, and died May 7, 1894.

Burton C. Butler and Katherine Alexander were married.

Burton C. Butler, son of John B. and Mary Jane (Williamson) Butler, was born September 27, 1862, and lives at 121 Twelfth street, Troy, New York.

(VI) George Small, Jr., fourth son and youngest child of George and Jeannette (Lourie) Small, was born August 5, 1822, in the town of Jackson, Washington county, New York, and died March 25, 1898, at his home near Norwood, Mercer County, Illinois. He lived on the Small homestead at East Greenwich, Washington County, New York, until the spring of 1852, when he moved with his family to Wheatland, Will County, Illinois, where he lived until the fall of 1856, when he sold his farm and moved into Aurora, Illinois, and remained there until the spring of 1857, when he removed to Olena, Henderson County, Illinois. In the fall of the same year he removed to North Henderson, Mercer County, Illinois, and in the spring of 1861 bought a farm near Norwood, Mercer County, Illinois, where he lived the remainder of his life. He was a farmer all his life. He was highly respected for his honesty and integrity of character.

George Small, Jr., and Ann Eliza Robertson were married September 23, 1846, in Argyle, Washington County, New York.

Ann Eliza Robertson, third daughter of Archibald and Anne (Robinson) Robertson, was born November 20, 1823, in Argyle, Washington County, New York, and died November 6, 1893, at her home near Norwood, Mercer County, Illinois. She had an unusually bright mind; was very fond of literature and was a great reader, being very well posted in history. She early instilled in the minds of her children a desire for education. She was very ambitious and proud of her children and could not bear the thought of her children falling behind anybody else's children. Her children were carefully reared in the strict faith of the United Presbyterian church, and were expected to go to church and Sabbath school every Sabbath day, rain or shine. The writer remembers that for many years he committed a chapter in the Bible every week and recited it in Sabbath school the following Sabbath. The program for Sabbath day was as follows: Sabbath school at 10 a. m.; sermon from 11 to 1; then a short intermission, followed by another sermon in the afternoon. After the services the family went home and had dinner. After dinner the "Shorter Catechism" was asked and answered, and I might here add that the book was not necessary as we could all ask and answer the questions without the book; if any more time remained before bedtime some of "White's sermons" were read. Mrs. Small was a brilliant conversationalist and a great entertainer, and her power of reading the character of those with whom she came in contact was almost infallible.

George and Ann Eliza (Robertson) Small were buried side by side in the cemetery at Norwood, Mercer County, Illinois.

George and Ann Eliza (Robertson) Small had:

(1) Mary Louise Small, born July 11, 1847.

(2) Archibald Robertson Small, born January 11, 1850; died June 21, 1907.

(3) Jessie Elizabeth Small, born August 11, 1852.

(4) Edward Hamilton Small, born August 31, 1856.

(5) Ella Mattoon Small, born January 24, 1860; died August 27, 1895.

(6) Alice Livingston Small, born July 9, 1864.

(1) Mary Louise Small, eldest daughter of George and Ann Eliza (Robertson) Small, was born July 11, 1847, at East Greenwich, Washington County New York. She was educated

in the common schools and Monmouth College, Monmouth, Illinois, attending the latter from September, 1864, until December, 1866, when she left college to be married. She is now a widow and lives at Gerlaw, Warren County, Illinois, where she has lived ever since her marriage.

John Sutherland Winbigler and Mary Louise Small were married February 20, 1867, at her father's home near Norwood, Mercer County, Illinois.

John Sutherland Winbigler, son of Elias and Anna (Gordon) Winbigler, was born September 3, 1841, at Walnut Ridge, Sullivan County, Indiana, and died at his home at Gerlaw, Illinois, December 30, 1897. His ancestors were German.

He was in the sophomore class in Monmouth College, when he left to enlist in the Civil war. He enlisted in Company "I," Fiftieth Illinois Infantry, at Quincy, Illinois, October 22, 1861; enlistment to date from September 16, 1861.

He was in Chillicothe and St. Joseph, Missouri, until January, 1862, when he joined General Grant at Cairo, Illinois. From there to Smithland, Kentucky, and Fort Henry, Tennessee, February 6, 1862; from there to Fort Donelson, Tennessee, February, 13-14-15, 1862; under fire all the time. Again in battle at Shiloh, Tennessee, April 6-7, 1862, when he had his hat shot from his head; was struck on the arm by a spent ball in the siege of Corinth, Mississippi, in May, 1862. Encamped at Corinth, Mississippi, and vicinity until October 3 and 4, 1862, when he was engaged in the battle of Corinth, Mississippi. Left Corinth October 28, 1863, for middle Tennessee.

Re-enlisted January 1, 1864, for three years or during the war, at Lynnville, Tennessee. Came home on thirty days' furlough, January 25, 1864. Returned February 25, to regiment at Quincy, Illinois. From there went to Lynnville, Tennessee, and on with General Sherman on the Atlanta campaign.

Was in skirmish at Snake Creek Gap and Ostauaula River. Was in battle of Altoona Pass, October 5, 1864. Was with General Sherman from Atlanta to Savannah and from Savannah to Goldsboro, North Carolina; from Goldsboro to Johnston's surrender at Durham, North Carolina; from there to Richmond, Virginia, and the great reunion at Washington, D. C., May, 1865. Discharged at Louisville, Kentucky, and Springfield, Illinois, as first lieutenant, July 14, 1865.

Was in the following engagements: Fort Henry; Fort Donelson; Shiloh; Bears Creek, Mississippi; Siege of Corinth; Battle of Corinth; Snake Creek Gap; Ostauaula River; Altoona Pass and Bentonville, North Carolina.

Enlisted as private; promoted corporal, November 25, 1862; promoted fourth sergeant, February 28, 1863; promoted first sergeant, October 21, 1864; promoted first lieutenant, June 14, 1865. Mustered out of the United States service, July 13, 1865.

When he returned home from the war he engaged in farming and continued in that occupation until his death. He bought part of the farm owned by his father in Spring Grove, Warren County, Ilinois, afterward named Gerlaw, and later another farm west of that. He was a successful farmer and highly respected by all who knew him. He was a good husband and kind father.

John Sutherland and Mary Louise (Small) Winbigler had:

(A) Edward Sutherland Winbigler, born November 24, 1867.

(B) Guy Gordon Winbigler, born June 27, 1869.

(C) Hugh Draper Winbigler, born November 2, 1870.

(D) Roy Winbigler, born January 6, 1873.

(E) John Carl Winbigler, born February 1, 1876; died March 4, 1881.

(F) Bryce Rex Winbigler, born January 19, 1878.

(G) Frank Max Winbigler, born August 5, 1880.

(H) Jessie Winbigler, born April 22, 1883.

(I) Harry Lloyd Winbigler, born May 20, 1889.

(A) Edward Sutherland Winbigler, eldest son of John Sutherland and Mary Louise (Small) Winbigler, was born November 24, 1867, at Spring Grove, Warren County, Illinois. He attended the common schools and later Monmouth College, after which he taught school for a time. He was graduated at Rush Medical College, Chicago, March 38. 1893. He commenced practice in Alexis, Illinois, where he is still located. He has enjoyed a large and lucrative practice.

Dr. Edward Sutherland Winbigler and Anna Gertrude Frantz were married January 30, 1895, at Gerlaw, Warren County, Illinois.

Anna Gertrude Frantz, daughter of John H. and Anna H. (Porter) Frantz, was born August 11, 1867, at Spring Grove, Warren county, Illinois.

Dr. Edward Sutherland and Anna Gertrude (Frantz) Winbigler had:

(a) Chauncey H. Winbigler, born February 1, 1897, at Alexis, Illinois.

(b) Gerald Edward Winbigler, born October 19, 1900, at Alexis, Illinois.

(B) Guy Gordon Winbigler, second son of John Sutherland and Mary Louise (Small) Winbigler, was born June 27, 1869, at Spring Grove, Warren County, Illinois. He attended Monmouth College for some time. He is a successful farmer and lives on the farm that belonged to his father, together with his mother, Jessie and Harry. He is unmarried.

(C) Hugh Draper Winbigler, third son of John Sutherland and Mary Louise (Small) Winbigler, was born November 2, 1870, at Spring Grove, Warren County, Illinois. He attended Monmouth College, also the Normal School at Bushnell, Illinois. He is the chief agent for the Burlington road in Rock Island, Illinois.

Hugh Draper Winbigler and May Loveridge were married October 5, 1899, at Alexis, Illinois.

May Loveridge, daughter of Thomas H. and Margaret (Waddell) Loveridge, was born April 6, 1875, at Alexis, Illinois.

Hugh Draper and May (Loveridge) Winbigler had:

(a) Margaret Louise Winbigler, born October 31, 1900, at Beardstown, Illinois.

(D) Roy Winbigler, fourth son of John Sutherland and Mary Louise (Small) Winbigler, was born January 6, 1873, at Gerlaw, Warren county, Illinois. When the railroad was built through Gerlaw the postoffice was moved from Spring Grove to Gerlaw; the name of the postoffice was changed, but not the residence of the Winbiglers. Their post office is now Monmouth, Illinois, R. F. D. No. 2.

Roy Winbigler attended the Normal School at Bushnell, Illinois. He is a farmer and lives a short distance west of his mother's home.

Roy Winbigler and Ruth Meek were married March 11, 1903, at Monmouth, Illinois.

Ruth Meek, daughter of Samuel L. and Dora May (Patton) Meek, was born July 1, 1877, at Richland, Indiana.

(F) Dr. Bryce Rex Winbigler, sixth son of John Sutherland and Mary Louise (Small) Winbigler, was born January 19, 1878, at Gerlaw, Warren County, Illinois. He was graduated at the Monmouth High School, June 11, 1897. He was graduated at the College of Physicians and Surgeons, Chicago, May 24, 1904. He settled in Seaton, Mercer County, Illinois.

Dr. Bryce Rex Winbigler and Etta Estella Jamison were married April 11, 1907, at Monmouth, Illinois.

Etta Estella Jamison, daughter of Michael Van Tuyl and Velma (Brent) Jamison, was born August 23, 1880, at Ellison, Warren County, Illinois.

(G) Frank Max Winbigler, seventh son of John Sutherland and Mary Louise (Small) Winbigler, was born August 5, 1880, at Gerlaw, Warren County, Illinois. He attended the Monmouth High School; won first honors in declamation in the Military Tract High School Association contest, held at Moline, Illinois, May 4, 1900. He was graduated at the Monmouth High School, June, 1900, and entered Monmouth College; left college in the spring of 1892, to take up school work.

He was principal of the Little York, Warren County, Illinois, High School for three years, and is now (1906) principal of the Kilbourne, Mason County, Illinois High School.

Frank Max Winbigler and Lucille Watt were married October 17, 1906, at Alexis, Illinois.

Lucille Watt, daughter of John G. and Anna (Porter) Watt, and granddaughter of the late Wray Porter, was born September 4, 1883, at Alexis, Illinois.

(H) Jessie Winbigler, only daughter of John Sutherland and Mary Louise (Small) Winbigler, was born April 22, 1883, at Gerlaw, Warren County, Illinois. She was graduated at the Monmouth High School, June 12, 1903, and is living at home with her mother.

(I) Harry Lloyd Winbigler, eighth son of John Sutherland and Mary Louise (Small) Winbigler, was born May 20, 1889, at Gerlaw, Warren County, Illinois. He is still in school.

(2) DR. ARCHIBALD ROBERTSON SMALL (author of this Genealogy) eldest son of George and Ann Eliza (Robertson) Small, was born January 11, 1850, at East Greenwich, Washington County, New York. He worked on his father's farm in the summers and attended the district schools in the winters until September, 1868, when he entered Monmouth College, at Monmouth, Illinois, which he attended until June, 1870. He taught school during the winter of 1870-1. In the spring of 1871 he commenced the study of medicine in the office of Drs. Webster & Crawford, at Monmouth, Illinois. During the winter of 1872-3 he attended his first course of lectures in the Medical Department of Michigan University, at Ann Arbor, Michigan. During the winter of 1873-4 he attended Rush Medical College,

Chicago, and was graduated at that institution February 17, 1874. He spent some months traveling during the following summer and visited his birthplace in Washington County, New York. In September of that year he commenced the practice of medicine in Little York, Warren County, Illinois, and remained there until April, 1876, when he removed to Decatur, Illinois, where he remained until April, 1885. His health being somewhat broken from hard work, he spent the summer in travel and in August, 1885, opened an office in Chicago, Illinois, where he remained in continuous practice until his death, June 21, 1907.

During his first three years in Chicago Dr. Small was on the staff of the South Side Free Dispensary. He was one of the founders of the Chicago Hospital and was a member of the first board of directors. For six years he was lecturer in the Post Graduate Medical School of Chicago on gynecology, and attending gynecologist to the Post Graduate Hospital. He enjoyed a large practice and devoted himself especially to gynecological surgery. He wrote many articles on gynecological and other medical subjects.

During his residence in Decatur he devoted considerable attention to Masonry, and was Master of Ionic Lodge, 312, A. F. & A. M.; High Priest of Macon Chapter, No. 21, R. A. M.; and Grand Lecturer, A. F. & A. M. of the State of Illinois.

Dr. Archibald Robertson Small and Minerva Rainey were married May 19, 1875, in Belleville, Illinois, by the Rev. Dr. Post.

Minerva Rainey, second daughter of State Senator Jefferson Rainey and wife, whose maiden name was Lyons, was born in 1852, at Marissa, Illinois. Jefferson Rainey was born in Tennessee; his wife was born in South Carolina. Mrs. Rainey's ancestors were Irish.

Minerva Rainey was graduated at Monmouth College in the class of 1872.

Dr. Archibald Robertson and Minerva (Rainey) Small had:

(A) Harold Rainey Small, born February 19, 1877.

Dr. Archibald Robertson Small was separated from Minerva (Rainey) Small October 14, 1889. The decree was entered in Judge Collin's Court, Chicago, Illinois.

(A) Harold Rainey Small, only son of Dr. Archibald Robertson and Minerva (Rainey) Small, was born February 19, 1877, in Decatur, Illinois. He was graduated at the Belleville,

Illinois, High School, in 1894; at Smith's Academy, St. Louis, Missouri, in 1896; at the Law Department of Michigan University, Ann Arbor, Michigan, in 1899. He opened a law office in St. Louis, Missouri, in January, 1900, and is doing well.

Dr. Archibald Robertson Small and Marie Genevieve Cahill were married May 26, 1892, in Quincy, Illinois.

Marie Genevieve Cahill, only daughter of Leo C. and Mary Ellen (Klosterman) Cahill, was born March 20, 1862, in Decatur, Illinois.

Leo C. Cahill was born May 24, 1834, in Cumberland, Maryland.

Mary Ellen (Klosterman) Cahill was born June 4, 1842, in Virginia. Her parents were born in Holland.

(3) Jessie Elizabeth Small, second daughter of George and Ann Eliza (Robertson) Small, was born August 11, 1852, at Naperville, Illinois. She was educated in the district schools and Monmouth College. She attended Monmouth College from September, 1868, until June, 1870. She is a talented writer and a brainy woman, whose influence has been felt wherever she has lived. She is a widow and lives in Lincoln, Nebraska.

Rev. John Abraham Pollock and Jessie Elizabeth Small were married November 12, 1878, at her father's home near Norwood, Mercer County, Illinois.

John Abraham Pollock, son of William and Jane (Elder) Pollock, was born October 6, 1850, at Huntsville, Ohio, and died September 21, 1899, at Colorado Springs, Colorado.

Rev. John Abraham Pollock was graduated at Monmouth College in 1876, with the degree of A. B. Afterward the same college conferred on him the degree of A. M. In 1877 he took a post-graduate course in the New College, Edinburgh, Scotland, and made a tour through Egypt and the Holy Land. February 12, 1878, he was licensed to preach by the United Presbyterian Presbytery of Sidney, at Kenton, Ohio. His first pastorate was at Burlington, Iowa, where he took charge July 1, 1878. In December of the same year he was ordained by the United Presbyterian Presbytery of Keokuk, at Columbus City, Iowa. He remained in Burlington until 1881, when he took charge of the Shiloh congregation in Rush County, Indiana, where he remained until 1886. He was then engaged in Evangelistic work in Indiana, New York, Ohio, Illinois and Iowa for two years.

He was presidential elector on the Prohibition ticket in Indiana in 1884, and a candidate for Congress on the Prohibition ticket of the Sixth Indiana district in 1885.

In September, 1888, he purchased the Indiana Phalanx, published in Indianapolis, which he published until 1891.

September 15, 1891, he transferred his membership to the Presbyterian Church, and was appointed Presbyterian missionary of the Indianapolis Presbytery, which position he held until November, 1893, when he removed to Lebanon, Indiana. In 1895 he removed to Tecumseh, Nebraska, where he remained until his death.

In May, 1899, he received the degree of Ph. D. from Franklin College, Athens, Ohio.

Rev. John Abraham Pollock was a man of firm convictions and an earnest, Christian man. He was a good husband and kind father.

Rev. John Abraham and Jessie Elizabeth (Small) Pollock had:

(A) Ethel Small Pollock, born April 26, 1881, in Burlington, Iowa.

(B) Anna Jane Pollock, born August 14, 1883, in Spiceland, Indiana.

(C) John Donald Pollock, born September 28, 1885, in Spiceland, Ind.

All three children were graduated at the High School at Tecumseh, Nebraska.

John Donald Pollock is a graduate of the University of Nebraska, having taken the electrical engineering course, and is now located in Chicago.

(4) Edward Hamilton Small, second son of George and Ann Eliza (Robertson) Small, was born August 31, 1856, at Wheatland, Will County, Illinois. He was a farmer until a few years ago, having bought the farm that his father had owned since 1861. He sold his farm a few years ago and went into the grocery business in Alexis, Illinois, but finding that occupation too confining he sold out the business and took a position as general agent of the state of Illinois to handle a stock food, and is making a success of it. He lives in Galesburg, Illinois.

Edward Hamilton Small and Fannie R. Sharer were married June 12, 1884.

Fannie R. Sharer, daughter of George and Sarah (Morgan) Sharer, was born April 4, 1866, and died May 12, 1891, near Norwood, Illinois.

Edward Hamilton and Fannie R. (Sharer) Small had:
(A) Herbert Robertson Small, born July 23, 1885.
(B) Minnie Irene Small, born June 20, 1887.
(C) Frank Leland Small, born April 19, 1889.

(A) Herbert Robertson Small, eldest son of Edward Hamilton and Fannie (Sharer) Small, was born July 23, 1885, near Norwood, Mercer County, Illinois. He attended the district school and the school in Alexis, Illinois. He is employed in the C., B. & Q. freight office in Denver, Colorado.

Herbert Robertson Small and Lilia Evelyn Dabler were married July 26, 1906, in Princeton, Illinois.

Lilia Evelyn Dabler, daughter of James Edgar and Jane Clayton Dabler, was born October 21, 1886, in Princeton, Illinois.

Herbert Robertson and Lilia Evelyn (Dabler) Small had:
(a) Edgar Robertson Small, born June 27, 1907.

Edward Hamilton Small and Alice Jane McFarland were married April 5, 1892.

Alice Jane McFarland, daughter of James and Nancy (Humes) McFarland was born November 8, 1859, and died August 29, 1897.

Edward Hamilton and Alice Jane (McFarland) Small had:
(A) Mary Agnes Small, born January 30, 1893.
(B) Clara Belle Small, born August 5, 1894.
(C) Ella Louise Small, born October 15, 1895.
(D) Allie Small, born August 22, 1897; died October 22, 1897.

Edward Hamilton Small and Ethel May Perkins were married July 20, 1898.

Ethel May Perkins, daughter of James Gilmore and Margaret (Oswalt) Perkins, was born February 14, 1873.

Edward Hamilton and Ethel May (Perkins) Small had:
(A) Ethel Margaret Small, born May 21, 1902, in Alexis, Illinois.

(5) Ella Mattoon Small, third daughter of George and Ann Eliza (Robertson) Small, was born January 24, 1860, at North Henderson, Mercer County, Illinois, and died August 27, 1895, at her home in Alexis, Illinois. She attended the district schools and one year in the High School in Burlington, Iowa, and one year in Monmouth College. She was a sweet and lovable char-

acter, and was universally popular. The day of her funeral every business house in Alexis was closed as a token of respect to her memory.

John Bowen Porter and Ella Mattoon Small were married January 27, 1881, at her father's home near Norwood, Mercer County, Illinois.

John Bowen Porter, only son of James D. and Mary (Irvin) Porter, was born January 25, 1855, four and one-half miles west of Alexis, in Warren County, Illinois. He attended the district schools and Monmouth College, and was graduated at Monmouth College in 1875, and at the Poughkeepsie, New York, Business College, May, 1876. He first engaged in farming, but soon gave that up and went into the hardware and agricultural implement business in Alexis, Illinois. He has recently sold his business in Alexis and bought a large farm in Northern Missouri, where he is engaged in farming and stock raising. He is married again and has a son by his second wife.

John Bowen and Ella Mattoon (Small) Porter had:

(A) Irvin Lourie Porter, born November 18, 1881, four and one-half miles west of Alexis, in Mercer County, Illinois. He was educated in the schools of Alexis and some time in Knox College. He is a teller in the First National Bank of Chicago.

(6) Alice Livingston Small, fourth daughter of George and Ann Eliza (Robertson) Small, was born July 9, 1864, near Norwood, Mercer County, Illinois.

W. L. Lafferty and Alice Livingston Small were married February 1, 1883, at her father's home near Norwood, Mercer County, Illinois.

W. L. Lafferty was a son of William Lafferty, who was a large land-owner in Mercer County, Illinois.

W. L. and Alice Livingston (Small) Lafferty had:

(A) A daughter, born February 18, 1884; died March 6, 1884.

They were afterward divorced. She lives in Alexis, Illinois.

(III) JEANNETTE SMALL, eldest daughter of James and Ann (Beveridge) Small, was born June 20, 1784, and died March 4, 1848.

William McGeoch and Jeannette Small were married March 4, 1803.

William McGeoch was born in June, 1775, in Scotland, and died May 8, 1846.

William and Jeannette (Small) McGeoch had:

(I) James McGeoch, born July 23, 1805; died September 13, 1833.

(II) Alexander McGeoch, born August 13, 1807; died July 6, 1862.

(III) Edward McGeoch, born June 30, 1810; died September 9, 1830.

(IV) John McGeoch, born June 27, 1813; died October 15, 1819.

(V) George McGeoch, born September 12, 1815; died March 29, 1882.

(VI) Jane Ann McGeoch, born April 16, 1818; died February 15, 1852.

(I) James McGeoch, eldest son of William and Jeannette (Small) McGeoch, was born July 23, 1805, and died September 13, 1833. He married Ada George November 5, 1832.

(II) Alexander McGeoch, second son of William and Jeannette (Small) McGeoch, was born August 13, 1807, and died July 6, 1862. He enlisted November 6, 1861, in Company "G," Ninety-third New York Infantry. Left Albany April 1, 1862. In the Army of the Potomac under General McClellan. Took part in siege of Yorktown. Slightly engaged at Williamsburg. Four companies as headquarter guard in seven day battle before Richmond and at Harrison Landing, where he was killed July 6, 1862.

Alexander McGeoch and Lydia Warner were married January 14, 1833.

Lydia Warner, daughter of Sylvester Warner, was born April 23, 1813, and died June 23, 1890.

Alexander and Lydia (Warner) McGeoch had:

(1) William McGeoch, born July 16, 1837; died June 21, 1870.

(2) James McGeoch, born December 22, 1839; died March 10, 1903.

(3) Mary McGeoch, born June 30, 1845.

(4) Jeannette McGeoch, born October 9, 1848.

(1) William McGeoch, eldest son of Alexander and Lydia (Warner) McGeoch, was born July 16, 1837, and died June 21, 1870.

William McGeoch and Mary Hunt were married January 1, 1868.

Mary Hunt, daughter of Norman and Celia (Neil) Hunt, was born May 13, 1846.

William and Mary (Hunt) McGeoch had:

(A) Ella McGeoch, born April 7, 1869; died November 1, 1890.

(B) William McGeoch, born October 26, 1870.

(B) William McGeoch, son of William and Mary (Hunt) McGeoch, was born October 26, 1870, and lives at Shushan, New York.

William McGeoch and Jennie Edie were married March 15, 1894.

Jennie Edie, daughter of George H. and N. Isabella (Armstrong) Edie, was born February 18, 1873.

William and Jennie (Edie) McGeoch had:

(a) Eleanor Isadla McGeoch, born May 6, 1898; died September 18, 1898.

(b) Mary Elizabeth McGeoch, born August 2, 1904.

(2) James McGeoch, second son of Alexander and Lydia (Warner) McGeoch, was born December 22, 1839, and died March 10, 1903. He enlisted September 7, 1861, in Company "A," Seventh New York Cavalry. Discharged March 31, 1862. Never engaged in active service.

James McGeoch and Mary Sheridan were married February 6, 1864.

Mary Sheridan, daughter of Patrick Sheridan, was born January 3, 1847.

James and Mary (Sheridan) McGeoch had:

(A) Alexander McGeoch, born February 8, 1865; died March 4, 1866.

(B) John McGeoch, born May 19, 1867.

(C) William McGeoch, born October 1, 1873.

(D) Charles H. McGeoch, born January 3, 1876; died in infancy.

(E) Lydia McGeoch, born September 22, 1884.

(3) Mary McGeoch, eldest daughter of Alexander and Lydia (Warner) McGeoch, was born June 30, 1845.

Aaron J. Arnold and Mary McGeoch were married January 31, 1866.

Aaron J. Arnold, son of James Arnold, was born April 3, 1843.

Aaron J. and Mary (McGeoch) Arnold had:

(A) Jennie Arnold, born September 5, 1866.

(B) Abner Arnold, born April 14, 1868.

(C) Lewis Arnold, born November 12, 1871.

(4) Jeannette McGeoch, second daughter of Alexander and Lydia (Warner) McGeoch, was born October 9, 1848.

Chauncey H. Hart and Jeannette McGeoch were married October 30, 1872.

Chauncey H. Hart, son of Ansel Hart, was born April 12, 1842.

Chauncey H. and Jeannette (McGeoch) Hart had:

(A) Lydia M. Hart, born November 8, 1878.

(B) George H. Hart, born August 12, 1883; died August 9, 1901.

(C) Esther Hart, born April 22, 1885.

(D) Carrie W. Hart, born January 1, 1892; died January 22, 1893.

(V) George McGeoch, fifth son of William and Jeannette (Small) McGeoch, was born September 12, 1815, and died March 29, 1882.

George McGeoch and Agnes Telford were married November 17, 1840.

Agnes Telford, daughter of Stephen and Mary (Cree) Telford, was born April 13, 1819, and died May 10, 1888.

George and Agnes (Telford) McGeoch had:

(1) Jeannette McGeoch, born September 6, 1841.

(2) John McGeoch, born April 30, 1844, died January 28, 1905.

(3) Mary Agnes McGeoch, born August 3, 1847; died September 6, 1866.

(4) James Edward McGeoch, born September 20, 1850; died February 2, 1851.

(5) William J. McGeoch, born August 29, 1852.

(6) George Edward McGeoch, born November 2, 1854.

(1) Jeannette McGeoch, eldest daughter of George and Agnes (Telford) McGeoch, was born September 6, 1841.

Anderson Foster and Jeannette McGeoch were married December 18, 1862.

Anderson Foster, son of Robert L. and Margaret (Simpson) Foster, was born July 19, 1838.

Anderson and Jeannette (McGeoch) Foster had:

(A) George M. Foster, born July 31, 1864.

(B) Jennie F. Foster, born August 23, 1866; died April 8, 1870.

(C) Infant son, born April 21, 1868; died May 19, 1868.

(D) Agnes Foster, born September 19, 1871.

(E) Susie B. Foster, born July 2, 1874.

(F) William Foster, born December 10, 1879; died February 21, 1892.

(A) George M. Foster, eldest son of Anderson and Jeannette (McGeoch) Foster, was born July 31, 1864, and lives at Shushan, New York.

George M. Foster and Jennie Randles were married January 24, 1889.

Jennie Randles, daughter of Alexander and Sarah (White) Randles, was born October 4, 1864, and died April 28, 1898.

George M. and Jennie (Randles) Foster had:

(a) Edith J. Foster, born November 6, 1889; died July 1, 1897.

(b) Anderson Foster, born December 23, 1891.

(c) Robert Foster, born April 20, 1898.

George M. Foster and Jennie Miller were married October 11, 1900.

Jennie Miller, daughter of David Graham and Jane E. (Skinner) Miller, was born November 20, 1865.

George M. and Jennie (Miller) Foster had:

(a) Ruth E. Foster, born May 20, 1892.

(D) Agnes Foster, second daughter of Anderson and Jeannette (McGeoch) Foster, was born September 19, 1871.

Alexander McGeoch, son of John and Mary (Fullerton) McGeoch, and Agnes Foster were married December 28, 1892.

Alexander and Agnes (Foster) McGeoch had:

(a) John McGeoch, born October 9, 1897.

(E) Susie B. Foster, third daughter of Anderson and Jeannette (McGeoch) Foster, was born July 2, 1874.

Charles Hedges and Susie B. Foster were married February 17, 1897.

Charles Hedges, son of Benjamin C. and Mary A. (Collins) Hedges, was born January 22, 1876.

(2) John McGeoch, eldest son of George and Agnes (Telford) McGeoch, was born April 30, 1844, and died January 28, 1905.

John McGeoch and Susie Foster were married March 12, 1866.

Susie Foster, daughter of Robert L. and Margaret (Simpson) Foster of Shushan, New York, was born September 30, 1846.

John and Susie (Foster) McGeoch had:

(A) Ralph L. McGeoch, born December 1, 1867.

(B) Frank H. McGeoch, born September 3, 1878; died March 31, 1902.

(A) Dr. Ralph Lyman McGeoch, eldest, and only surviving, son of John and Susie (Foster) McGeoch, was born December 1, 1867. He entered the New York Homeopathic Medical College in the fall of 1891 and was graduated at that institution in 1894. Late that season he located in Goshen, New York, where he has since lived.

Dr. Ralph Lyman McGeoch and Sarah Coleman were married June 9, 1902.

Sarah Coleman, daughter of Roswell Carpenter and Sarah (Wilkin) Coleman, was born March 15, 1868.

(4) William J. McGeoch, third son of George and Agnes (Telford) McGeoch, was born August 29, 1852, and lives at Salem, New York.

William J. McGeoch and Alice Beattie were married December 11, 1895.

Alice Beattie, daughter of Robert and Elizabeth (Beattie) Beattie, was born March 13, 1869.

(6) George Edward McGeoch, fourth son of George and Agnes (Telford) McGeoch, was born November 2, 1854, and lives at Cambridge, New York, R. F. D. No. 1.

George Edward McGeoch and Elizabeth McMillan were married September 13, 1876.

Elizabeth McMillan, daughter of Morrison and Mary Ellis (Robertson) McMillan, was born November 9, 1855.

George Edward and Elizabeth (McMillan) McGeoch had:

(A) Bertha McGeoch, born October 24, 1877.

(B) Stanley McGeoch, born September 10, 1879.

(C) John Loudon McGeoch, born June 15, 1881.

(D) Morrison McGeoch, born January 15, 1883.
(E) George Edward McGeoch, born January 5, 1885.

(A) Bertha McGeoch, only daughter of George Edward and Elizabeth (McMillan) McGeoch, was born October 24, 1877.

Rea L. Beveridge and Bertha McGeoch were married August 30, 1900.

Rea L. Beveridge, son of J. C. Beveridge, was born October 30, 1876, and lives at Cambridge, New York.

Rea L. and Bertha (McGeoch) Beveridge had:
(a) Mary Evalyn Beveridge, born July 8, 1902.
(b) Willard Albert Beveridge, born November 21, 1903.

(B) Stanley McGeoch, eldest son of George Edward and Elizabeth (McMillan) McGeoch, was born September 10, 1879.

Stanley McGeoch and Vesta McEachron were married November 18, 1902.

Vesta McEachron, daughter of Frank McEachron, was born September 13, 1884.

Stanley and Vesta (McEachron) McGeoch had:
(a) Bertha Mae McGeoch, born November 8, 1904.

(C) John Loudon McGeoch, second son of George Edward and Elizabeth (McMillan) McGeoch, was born June 15, 1881. He is (1906) in the junior class in Monmouth College, Monmouth, Illinois.

(VI) Jane Ann McGeoch, only daughter of William and Jeannette (Small) McGeoch, was born April 16, 1818, and died February 15, 1852.

James Donaldson and Jane Ann McGeoch were married in 1851, and had:

(1) George Donaldson, born in February, 1852.

(IV) ANNA RECTOR SMALL, second daughter of James and Ann (Beveridge) Small, was born in 1786, and died November 7, 1845, aged fifty-nine years.

Robert I. Law and Anna Rector Small were married April 12, 1809.

Robert I. Law, son of John and Agnes (Herrin) Law, was born February 23, 1776, in Salem, New York.

Robert I. and Anna Rector (Small) Law had:
(I) James Law, born April 11, 1810; died in Minnesota.

(II) Isaac Law, born September 5, 1815; died January 28, 1861.

(III) David Law, born March 29, 1813; died

(IV) Edward Law, born September 15, 1817; died June 17, 1892.

(V) Agnes Law, born October 20, 1820; died October 14, 1884.

(VI) Jeannette Law, born April 15, 1821; died in 1858.

(I) James Law, eldest son of Robert I. and Anna Rector (Small) Law, was born April 11, 1810, in Shushan, New York, and died in Minnesota.

James Law and Mary Jane Rankin were married at Washington, Pennsylvania, and had,

(1) Anna Law.

James Law and Agnes B. Coon were married in the spring of 1844, and had:

(1) Samuel Robert Law.
(2) Joseph Ireneus Law.
(3) Narcissa Anna Law.
(4) James Edward Law.
(5) William Law.
(6) David Hervey Law.

(II) Isaac Law, second son of Robert I. and Anna Rector (Small) Law, was born September 5, 1815, in Shushan, New York, and died January 28, 1861.

Isaac Law and Martha Jane Hutchison were married November 7, 1845.

Martha Jane (Hutchison) Law died September 28, 1885.

Isaac and Martha Jane (Hutchison) Law had:

(1) Agnes E. Mc. B. Law, born October 30, 1850; died March 13, 1887.

(2) Andrew Law, born November 23, 1851.
(3) Nettie A. Law, born August 4, 1853.
(4) Robert I. Law, born May 28, 1856.
(5) Martha J. Law, born December 18, 1857.

(2) Andrew Law, eldest son of Isaac and Martha Jane (Hutchison) Law, was born November 23, 1851, and lives in Salem, New York.

Andrew Law and Sarah Russell were married and had,

(A) Robert Law.

After the death of Sarah (Russell) Law, Andrew Law married Nettie Ledgerwood.

(3) Nettie A. Law, second daughter of Isaac and Martha Jane (Hutchison) Law, was born August 4, 1853.

Edgar Ledgerwood and Nettie A. Law were married and had:

(A) Roy Ledgerwood, born August 12, 1881.

(B) Lulu Jean Ledgerwood, born June 9, 1883.

They live at Putnam, New York.

(4) Robert I. Law, second son of Isaac and Martha Jane (Hutchison) Law, was born May 28, 1856, and lives at Middletown, New York.

Robert I. Law married Marilla Wagoner of Albany, New York.

(5) Martha J. Law, third daughter of Isaac and Martha Jane (Hutchison) Law, was born December 18, 1857.

Frederick L. Comstock and Martha J. Law were married October 21, 1896, and had,

(A) Frederick Law Comstock, born May 15, 1899.

They live at Gloversville, New York.

(III) David Law, third son of Robert I. and Anna Rector (Small) Law, was born March 29, 1813, in Shushan, New York.

David Law and Annis Potter were married September 26, 1838.

Annis (Potter) Law died November 27, 1841.

David and Annis (Potter) Law had:

(1) Eliza Agnes Law, born July 31, 1839; died April 19, 1870.

(2) Annis Potter Law, born November 14, 1841; died May 5, 1842.

(1) Eliza Agnes Law, eldest daughter of David and Annis (Potter) Law, was married to William Law in 1869, and had one son, John Potter Law, who died April 22, 1870.

David Law and Margaret Ann Robertson were married February 7, 1843.

Margaret Ann Robertson, daughter of Gilbert and Elizabeth (Dow) Robertson, was born April 4, 1812, and died July 20, 1844.

David and Margaret Ann (Robertson) Law had,

(1) Anna Mary Law, born July 20, 1844; died September 9, 1866.

David Law and Cornelia Thompson were married September 16, 1845, and had:

(1) Jeannette Law, born March 1, 1847.

(2) Hannah Law, born August 30, 1848.

(3) Andrew Thompson Law, born April 28, 1851; died March 4, 1855.

(2) Hannah Law, second daughter of David and Cornelia (Thompson) Law, was born August 30, 1848.

George L. Marshall and Hannah Law were married March 6, 1872.

George L. Marshall, son of Robert and Margaret (Law) Marshall, died in May, 1904, and Mrs. George L. Marshall lives in Shushan, New York.

George L. and Hannah (Law) Marshall had,

(1) Andrew Thompson Marshall, died in infancy.

(IV) Edward Law, fourth son of Robert I. and Anna Rector (Small) Law, was born September 15, 1817, in the town of Salem, Washington County, New York, and died June 17, 1892, in Fountain Green, Hancock County, Illinois. He came west with his family in 1852 and settled at Wheatland, Will County, Illinois, where he remained until 1856 or 1857, when he removed to Keokuk, Iowa, and afterward to Hancock County, Illinois.

Edward Law and Jeannette Robertson were married September 12, 1843, in Argyle, Washington County, New York.

Jeannette Robertson, second daughter of Archibald and Anne (Robinson) Robertson, was born December 4, 1821, in Argyle, Washington County, New York, and is still living (1906) in Moberly, Missouri.

Edward and Jeannette (Robertson) Law had:

(1) Robert I. Law, born March 6, 1845.

(2) Archibald Robertson Law, born August 4, 1846.

(3) Anna Louise Law, born December 10, 1848; died August 11, 1885.

(4) John Hamilton Law, born June 6, 1851; died January 21, 1852.

(5) Cornelia Jeannette Law, born February 29, 1853; died August 9, 1856.

(6) Eliza Alice Law, born September 14, 1856; died February 9, 1861.

(7) Edward Duncan Law, born July 3, 1862; died March 15, 1864.

(8) Birdie Agnes Law, born August 4, 1865.

(1) Dr. Robert I. Law, eldest son of Edward and Jeannette (Robertson) Law, was born March 6, 1845, in Salem, New York, and now lives in Galesburg, Illinois.

Dr. Robert I. Law and Alice Walker were married September 1, 1874, in Fountain Green, Hancock County, Illinois.

Alice Walker was born January 9, 1844, and died September 28, 1885, in Fountain Green, Illinois.

Dr. Robert I. and Alice (Walker) Law had:

(A) Archibald Robertson Law, born June 30, 1875.

(B) Alexander W. Law, born October 28, 1876.

(C) George Law, born March 14, 1880; died April 30, 1880.

(D) Louis L. Law, born August 30, 1881.

(E) Frank F. Law, born September 12, 1883.

(F) Fred W. Law, born September 22, 1885.

(D) Louis L. Law, fourth son of Dr. Robert I. and Alice (Walker) Law, was born August 30, 1881, in Fountain Green, Hancock county, Illinois, and is living at 563 East 62d street, Chicago, Illinois.

Louis L. Law and Mary Helen Hayes were married June 3, 1903, in Chicago, Illinois.

Mary Helen Hayes, daughter of John R. and Jean (Graham) Hayes, was born January 20, 1880.

Louis L. and Mary Helen (Hayes) Law had,

(a) John Walker Law, born February 12, 1904.

(2) Archibald Robertson Law, second son of Edward and Jeannette (Robertson) Law, was born August 4, 1846, in Salem, Washington County, New York, and was in South America at last accounts.

Archibald Robertson Law and Maggie Waters were married September 18, 1877, in Abilene, Kansas.

Maggie Waters was born November 12, 1854, and died September 20, 1889, in Greenleaf, Kansas.

Archibald Robertson and Maggie (Waters) Law had,

(A) Edward Archibald Law, born July 2, 1878, in Abilene, Kansas.

(3) Anna Louise Law, eldest daughter of Edward and Jeannette (Robertson) Law, was born December 10, 1848, in Salem, Washington County, New York, and died August 11, 1885, in Moberly, Missouri.

Alexander McCandless and Anna Louise Law were married September 10, 1868, in Oakwood, Illinois.

Alexander and Anna Louise (Law) McCandless had:

(A) James Edward McCandless, born April 22, 1870, in Louisiana, Missouri.

(B) William Robertson McCandless, born March 7, 1873, in Moberly, Missouri.

(C) Frederick McCandless, born September 11, 1883, in Moberly, Missouri.

(8) Birdie Agnes Law, fourth daughter, and youngest child, of Edward and Jeannette (Robertson) Law, was born August 4, 1865, in Oakwood, Illinois.

Nelson Harry Connfort and Birdie Agnes Law were married September 1, 1901, in Moberly Missouri, where they now live.

(V) Agnes Law, eldest daughter of Robert I. and Anna Rector (Small) Law, was born October 20, 1820, and died October 14, 1884.

William Shields and Agnes Law were married February 4, 1844.

William Shields, son of William Hope Shields, was born November 11, 1818, and died May 25, 1869.

William and Agnes (Law) Shields had:

(1) William Alexander Shields, born October 12, 1845.

(2) Robert I. Shields, born March 29, 1848; died October 4, 1860.

(3) James Edward Shields, born April 10, 1850.

(4) Anna Margaret Shields, born November 14, 1852.

(5) George Shields, and

(6) Andrew Shields—twins, born March 12, 1855.
(The former died January 12, 1881.)

(7) Nettie D. Shields, and

(8) Isaac L. Shields—twins, born May 24, 1858.

(1) William Alexander Shields, eldest son of William and Agnes (Law) Shields, was born October 12, 1845.

William Alexander Shields and Mary Zipporah Rogers were married December 21, 1882.

Mary Zipporah Rogers was born January 10, 1855, and died September 7, 1892.

William Alexander Shields and Helen D. Stout were married March 11, 1897.

(4) Anna Margaret Shields, eldest daughter of William and Agnes (Law) Shields, was born November 14, 1852.

Anthony M. Perry and Margaret Shields were married September 1, 1874.

Anthony M. Perry was born September 30, 1852.

Anthony M. and Anna Margaret (Shields) Perry had:

(A) Martha Perry, born July 9, 1875.

(B) Nettie S. Perry, born October 16, 1877.

(C) Gertrude Perry, born July 5, 1889.

(6) Andrew Shields, fifth son of William and Agnes (Law) Shields, was born March 12, 1855, and lives at Cambridge, New York, R. F. D.

Andrew Shields and Carrie Maria Wells, daughter of Henry M. and Jane B. Wells, were married March 15, 1882.

Andrew and Carrie Maria (Wells) Shields had:

(A) Robert Leroy Shields, born January 27, 1885.

(B) Andrew Malcolm Shields, born April 29, 1895.

(7) Nettie D. Shields, second daughter of William and Agnes (Law) Shields, was born May 24, 1858.

Dr. Thomas Merwin Ledgerwood and Nettie D. Shields were married May 29, 1894.

Dr. Thomas Merwin Ledgerwood was born October 31, 1855.

(8) Isaac L. Shields, sixth son of William and Agnes (Law) Shields, was born May 24, 1858.

Isaae L. Shields and Susie Miller were married November 25, 1885.

Susie Miller was born November 28, 1859.

(VI) Jeannette Law, second daughter of Robert I. and Anna Rector (Small) Law, was born April 15, 1821, and died in 1858. She was married to James Donaldson, and both died soon after marriage.

LINEAGE OF ARCHIBALD ROBERTSON SMALL, M. D.

(1) Crinan, Lord of Athol, Abbot of Dunkeld and Abthane of Dull, married Beatrice, (or Bathoc) daughter of King Malcolm II., and from whom descended all the Kings of Scotland from Duncan I. to Alexander III., except Macbeth.

(II) Duncan I., King of Scotland, (1033-1040) son of Crinan and Beatrice.

(III) Malcolm III. and Donald Bane, sons of Duncan I.

(IV) Madach, son of King Donald Bane, first ancient Celtic Earl of Athol. (1115.)

(I) Malcolm III., (Malcolm Canmore) King of Scotland, (1057-1093) eldest son of Duncan I.

(II) Duncan II., King of Scotland, (1093-1095) eldest son of Malcolm III., by his first wife, Ingiborge, widow of Thorfinn, Earl of Orkney.

(III) Malcolm, son of King Duncan II., second ancient Celtic Earl of Athol.

(IV) Malcolm, son of Malcolm, son of Duncan II., third ancient Celtic Earl of Athol.

(V) Henry, son of the preceding, fourth and last ancient Celtic Earl of Athol. (In the beginning of the thirteenth century.)

(VI) Conan, second son of Henry. (1214-1249.)

(VII) Ewen Fiz Conan, son of Conan.

(VIII) Angus, eldest son of Ewen Fiz Conan.

(IX) Andrew de Atholia, son of Angus.

(X) Duncan de Atholia, son of Andrew de Atholia, who gave the clan their distinctive appellation of the clan Donachie, or children of Duncan.

(XI) Robert de Atholia, son of Duncan de Atholia.

(XII) Duncan de Atholia, Duncanus de Atholia, dominus de Ranagh, or Rannoch, son of Robert de Atholia. (1392.)

(XIII) Robert Riach, (grizzled) son of the preceding, from whom the clan derive the surname Robertson. (1451.)

(XIV) Alexander Robertson, son of Robert, Robert's son, who first bore the surname ROBERTSON. He was the fifth Baron of Strowan. (Died 1507.)

(XV) JOHN ROBERTSON, first Laird of Muirton, Elginshire, second son of Alexander Robertson, by his second wife, Lady Elizabeth, daughter of Sir John Stewart of Baloing, Earl of Athol, (a descendant of Edward I., King of England) by his wife, Lady Eleanor Sinclair, daughter of William, Earl of Orkney, and a descendant of James I., King of Scotland.

JOHN ROBERTSON married Lady Margaret Crighton, whose descent follows:

(1) James II., King of Scotland, married Lady Mary, daughter of Arnold, Duke of Guilders, of the House of Egmond, and had,

(2) Princess Margaret Stuart, who was married, first, to William, third Lord Crighton, and had,

(3) Sir James Crighton of Frendraught, eldest son, who married Lady Catherine, daughter of William Lord Bostwick, and had,

(4) Lady Margaret Crighton, who was married to JOHN ROBERTSON.

The above marriage must have occurred about 1500, so that there is a space here of more than two centuries, seven generations, which I have not as yet been able to trace fully, though I have reasons, which I cannot state here, for believing that our immediate ancestor, John Robertson of Peterhead, sprang from the above marriage of JOHN ROBERTSON and LADY MARGARET CRIGHTON.

(XXII) John Robertson of Peterhead, Aberdeenshire, Scotland, (died about 1762) descendant of the above, married Anne Hamilton, one of whose ancestors, the first Lord Hamilton, married Princess Mary, eldest daughter of James II., King of Scotland.

(XXIII) William Robertson of Argyle, New York, (1752-1825) son of John and Anne (Hamilton) Robertson, married Mary Livingston, (1757-1793) daughter of Archibald Livingston, (1730-1792) (a descendant of the seventh Lord Livingston, Earl of Linlithgow and Calendar) by his wife, Eleanor McNaughton, daughter of Alexander McNaughton, (whose ancestry runs back to the Pictish Kings, 455) by his wife, Mary MacDonald, granddaughter of Sir James McDonald, second Baronet of Slate, (whose ancestor, John MacDonald, Lord of the Isles, married Princess Margaret, daughter of King Robert II.) and, I believe, a daughter of Sir Donald MacDonald, third Baronet of Slate. (though she may have been a daughter of one of the other sons of Sir James MacDonald) by his wife, Lady Mary Douglas, daughter of Sir Robert Douglas, tenth Earl of Morton, who was the eldest son of Sir William Douglas, ninth Earl of Morton, Knight of the Garter and Lord High Steward of Scotland, who before the war broke out was one of the richest and greatest subjects in the kingdom, by his wife, Lady Anne Keith, daughter of George, fifth Earl Marischal of Scotland.

(XXIV) Archibald Robertson, (1780-1849) second son of William and Mary (Livingston) Robertson, married Anne Robinson, (1794-1849) daughter of Duncan and Jeannette (Robeson) Robinson. The Robinsons came from Edinburgh, Scotland, to America, in 1801.

(XXV) Ann Eliza Robertson (1823-1893), third daughter of Archibald and Anne (Robinson). Robertson, was married to George Small, September 23, 1846.

LINEAGE OF GEORGE SMALL.

WILLIAM SMALL of Kindrogan married ANNE STEWART about 1720.

Lineage of ANNE STEWART. This is a branch of the Royal House of Stewart.

(1) John Stewart, the first of Urrard, was lineally descended from John Stewart, progenitor of the Athol Stewarts, who was the fourth son of Alexander Lord Badenoch, Earl of Buchan, a younger son of King Robert II.

He married a daughter of M'Grigor, and was father of

(2) Robert Stewart of Urrard, who married a daughter of Robertson of Faskally, and had, with other issue, (Robertson of Faskally, was a descendant of Alexander Robertson, brother of John Robertson. (XV.))

(3) Alexander Stewart, his heir, and George Stewart of Baloan.

Alexander Stewart married Christian, daughter of Leslie of Renrory, (now called Urrard) governor of the Castle of Blair, and was succeeded by his son,

(4) Robert Stewart of Urrard, who married Margaret, daughter of the celebrated Charles Robertson of Aukleeks, commonly called Fearlach, n'n T'ed, and had two sons, (Charles Robertson was a descendent of James Robertson, fourth son of Alexander Robertson, (XIV) by his first wife, Lady Elizabeth, daughter of Patrick Lord Glammis, grandson of Lady Jane Stewart, daughter of Robert II.)

(5) John Stewart, his heir, and William Stewart.

John Stewart of Urrard, married, first, a daughter of Menzies of Rotmills, by whom he had five sons.

(6) James Stewart of Urrard, his heir, married, first, Anne, daughter of Cambell Balgershoe, and had by her two sons and six daughters.

(7) ANNE STEWART, fifth daughter, was married to WILLIAM SMALL of Kindrogan.

(8) JAMES SMALL of Cambridge, New York, believed to be a son of William and Anne (Stewart) Small, was born in Scotland in 1749; came from Glasgow to America in 1774; settled in Cambridge New York, and died August 13, 1827. He was a soldier in the Revolutionary war; enlisted in the Albany County Militia, 16th Regiment.

James Small and Ann Beveridge were married in Cambridge, New York.

Ann Beveridge, daughter of George and Janet (Lourie) Beveridge, was born in 1755, in Strathmiglo, Fifeshire, Scotland; came to America in 1774; and died June 10, 1830, in Cambridge, New York.

(10) George Small, (1782-1855) second son of James and Ann (Beveridge) Small married Jeannette Lourie, (1783-1865) daughter of Alexander Lourie, who was born in Scotland.

(11) George Small, (1822-1898) fourth son and youngest child of George and Jeannette (Lourie) Small, married Ann Eliza Robertson, (XXV) September 23, 1846, and had,

(XXVI) Archibald Robertson Small, eldest son of George and Ann Eliza (Robertson) Small, born January 11, 1850, in East Greenwich, Washington County, New York.

In this lineage on the Robertson side is:
One line running back to Duncan II., King of Scotland;
one line running back to Edward I., King of England;
one line running back to James I., King of Scotland;
two lines running back to James II., King of Scotland;
one line running back to Robert II., King of Scotland;
one line running back to the Pictish Kings, 455, viz.:

John Robertson, 1st Laird of Muirton, descended from Duncan II, on his father's side, and from Edward I, King of England, and James I, King of Scotland, on his mother's side	3
Lady Margaret Crighton, wife of John Robertson, descended from James II, King of Scotland	1
Anne Hamilton, wife of John Robertson of Peterhead, descended from James II, King of Scotland	1
Alexander McNaughton, descended from the Pictish kings, 455	1
Mary McDonald, wife of Alexander McNaughton, descended from Robert II, King of Scotland	1
	7

In this lineage on the Small side are:
Two lines running back to Duncan II., King of Scotland;
one line running back to Edward I., King of England;
one line running back to James I., King of Scotland;
two lines running back to Robert II., King of Scotland, viz.:

Anne Stewart, wife of William Small, descended from Robert II	1
And through Robertson of Faskally, from Duncan II, King of Scotland, Edward I, King of England, and James I, King of Scotland	3
And through Charles Robertson, from Duncan II, and Robert II	2
	6
	7
	13

This lineage applies, as far as the descent from kings is concerned, to all the descendants of William Robertson of Argyle, and James Small of Cambridge, New York.

Those who are descendants of William Robertson can trace their lineage through seven lines to kings, and those who are descendants of James Small can trace their lineage through six lines to kings. Those who are descendants of both William Robertson and James Small can trace their lineage through thirteen lines to kings.

In addition to the above is the Hamilton lineage, including:

Thirty Parthian Kings, from Arsaces I., B. C. 256, to Artabanus IV., 226 A. D.

Five Græco-Roman Emperors, including Constantine the Great (274-337); Basil I. (867); Leo VI.; Constantine VII.; and Romanus II. (959).

Five Russian Czars, viz., Ruric (862); Igor; Sviatoslav; Vladimir; and Yaroslav (1051).

Three French Kings, viz., Hugh Capet (987); Robert; and Henry I. (1031).

These forty-three rulers, together with Malcolm II.; Duncan I.; Malcolm III.; Duncan II.; Edward I., of England; James I., of Scotland; James II., of Scotland; Robert II., of Scotland; and three Pictish Kings, named Nectan, make a list of fifty-four individual rulers—kings, emperors and czars—claimed as ancestors in this lineage.

INDEX.

S

www.ingramcontent.com/pod-product-compliance
Ingram Content Group UK Ltd.
Pitfield, Milton Keynes, MK11 3LW, UK
UKHW041630190726
13854UKWH00006B/2415

9 789351 288787